Praise for

DEAD MOM WALKING

"One of the most powerful stories I've read in a long time—intimate, astonishing, harrowing, and redemptive. *Dead Mom Walking* is such an important book, with lessons for everybody. . . . I can't get it out of my head." —Plum Johnson, author of *They Left Us Everything*

"The characters are so charming you'll simultaneously want to read the whole thing in one sitting and slow down so you can spend more time with them. *Dead Mom Walking* will break your heart and then mend it. Read this book; call your mom."

—Scaachi Koul, author of *One Day We'll All Be Dead and None of This Will Matter*

"An exquisite paean to the mother-child bond. Rachel's love for their mother is beautifully expressed from the first page of the book to the last."

—Catherine Gildiner, author of *Good Morning, Monster*

"This brilliant memoir had me sobbing and in stitches in equal parts . . . *Dead Mom Walking* cuts right to the heart."

—Tegan Quin, co-author of *High School*

"*Dead Mom Walking*'s jaw-dropping trick is the magically unbiased way it tells the whole story of its subject's life. Matlow's kind, determined humour shows it's possible to endure the irreversible: the loss of the first love of so many lives—our mother. Intricately loving."

—Thea Lim, author of *An Ocean of Minutes*

"A comedy for catastrophic times. . . . Reading about death in the middle of a global pandemic hardly sounds comforting. But through Matlow's brilliant sense of humour and beautiful manner of expression, somehow that's exactly what it is. . . . Ultimately, *Dead Mom Walking* . . . is a stunningly intimate love letter to Elaine, as Matlow utilizes their mother's own journals and hours of conversations they had in her dying days to bring considerable authenticity to the page. It's also very, very funny. I mean, don't get me wrong: you're going to cry too. But often you'll be crying and laughing simultaneously, which is probably the best way to approach our lives in general these days."

—CBC

"Mother and [child] bonding over a shared sense of nonconforming humour is one of many finely honed entry points in this moving memoir. . . . A welcome invitation to focus on what's essential; to find in life those things worth fighting for."   —*Xtra*

"Matlow really plunges into the scary territory of vulnerability with stories of how they were parented, how they deal with romantic intimacy, and how easily they were manipulated into silence by former boss Jian Ghomeshi during his time as host of CBC's *Q*."

—*NOW Toronto*

DEAD MOM WALKING

A MEMOIR OF MIRACLE CURES AND OTHER DISASTERS

RACHEL MATLOW

PENGUIN

an imprint of Penguin Canada,
a division of Penguin Random House Canada Limited

First published in Viking Canada paperback, 2020

Published in this edition, 2022

2nd Printing

"The Summer Day" from House of Light by Mary Oliver, published by Beacon Press, Boston
Copyright © 1990 by Mary Oliver, used herewith by permission
of the Charlotte Sheedy Literary Agency, Inc.

LIBRARY AND ARCHIVES CANADA CATALOGUING IN PUBLICATION
Title: Dead mom walking / Rachel Matlow.
Names: Matlow, Rachel, author.
Description: Previously published: Toronto: Viking Canada, 2020.
Identifiers: Canadiana 20210292210 | ISBN 9780735244894 (softcover)
Subjects: LCSH: Matlow, Rachel. | LCSH: Matlow, Rachel—Family. | LCSH: Mitchell, Elaine,
1943-2015—Health. | LCSH: Children of cancer patients—Biography. | LCSH: Cancer—
Patients—Biography. | LCSH: Cancer—Alternative treatment. | LCSH: Mothers and daughters.
Classification: LCC RC265.6.M37 A3 2022 | DDC 362.19699/40092—dc23

Cover design: Terri Nimmo
Cover image courtesy of the author

Printed in the United States of America

www.penguinrandomhouse.ca

Penguin
Random House
PENGUIN CANADA

For Mom/Elaine

PROLOGUE

I was lying on a buffalo skin rug, high on ayahuasca. My thoughts were going deep: *Why can't she just get the damn surgery? How long will she keep this up for? What exactly did she mean by the "quantum plane"?* I waited expectantly for access to a higher realm—and maybe some insight into my mom's magical thinking. Suddenly my face felt wet. I opened my eyes. The shaman was standing over me, flicking Peruvian flower water on my head, chanting "Sha-na-na-na-na-na-na."

Doing drugs was not my idea. I prefer to keep my visions 20/20. But what do you say when your sixty-seven-year-old mother asks you to go to the woods with her to take hallucinogens? To be clear, Mom was never the acid-droppin' hippie type. She was more of a New Age junkie, always on the lookout for a new fix. And now the stakes had never been higher: she'd been diagnosed with cancer and was trying every potion under the sun—except for chemo.

As part of her alternative healing journey, Mom had decided to attend an overnight ayahuasca ceremony in the countryside an hour north of Toronto. The psychoactive plant remedy, used by Indigenous

1

peoples in the Amazon for centuries, had become all the rage among Western spiritual seekers. Made from the vine and leaves of two separate plants and consumed as a molasses-like tea, ayahuasca's effects are said to be cleansing and transformative. It's been used to help overcome depression, anxiety, addiction, and many other conditions. "People say it's like thirty years of psychotherapy in one night," Mom boasted. *That's supposed to sound appealing?*

Unsure of what to expect, Mom had asked me to come along. "It would be nice to have you there for support," she'd said. "And maybe you'll have your *own* spiritual awakening." *Spiritual awakening?* My spirit likes to hit the snooze button and hates leaving downtown. But I loved my mom, and if she was going to experiment with drugs I'd rather be there to keep an eye on her. At the very least it would be a mother-daughter trip to remember (if only in flashbacks).

We arrived at a log house, where the shaman greeted us with the kind of deep, meaningful hugs that last way too long. He was a very friendly white guy in his mid-fifties who introduced himself by his Peruvian medicine-man name (I imagine his real name was something like Jerry Goldstein). Mom and I said hello to the few other participants, who were already huddled around in the living room. We found some floor space on the rug and rolled out our sleeping bags so that our feet faced the fireplace-turned-altar, adorned with feathers, crystals, and antlers.

Then, to my horror, the shaman proceeded to hand out large empty yogurt containers because, as he explained, it's common to "purge" when you take the "medicine." Apparently I was the only one not aware of this fun fact. But it was too late—the psychedelic slumber party had begun. The shaman blessed the ayahuasca and, one by one, we were invited to sit at the altar and do a shot. When it was my turn I gulped back the bitter brew and headed back to my cocoon, where I chased it down with some orange Vitaminwater. With notes of rancid coffee, rusted metal, and jungle rot, it wasn't a mystery why they called ayahuasca "the vine of death."

Now, going into this, I'd thought the shaman would just be on hand, like if I had any questions or wasn't feeling well. But no, this ceremony was intimate and interactive. As we started our trips he began making his rounds, each time with a different act. First, he waved a fan made of feathers in my face. Next, he shook dried leaves around my body. Then he blew tobacco smoke into my sleeping bag. *Um, thanks?*

By the time I was being baptized with flower water, I figured things couldn't get any worse. Then my stomach began to rumble. I absolutely hate throwing up, so I was determined to keep the poison down, even as my tummy churned like a washing machine. However, I discovered that if there's one thing I hate more than throwing up, it's hearing a room full of people—including my own mother—violently puking their guts out into yogurt containers. It was a sober vision of pure hell.

By about 4:00 a.m., the hope of sleep putting me out of my misery was all but lost. "It's music time!" someone announced. I braced myself as a long-haired hippie dude picked up a guitar and began to serenade us. "Free, free, like a dolphin in the sea," he sang repeatedly. He obviously hadn't seen *The Cove.*

If ayahuasca was bringing any clarity to my life, it was that saving Mom would have to wait for another day (and that I should never leave home without earplugs). I glanced over at her. She was adorable, all strung out, swaddled in her sleeping bag. *Is this how she used to look at me when I was a baby?*

I was feeling restless. I wondered if it would be rude if I excused myself to go watch TV in the bedroom. Maybe I could play Scrabble on my phone? There was really no way out. So I went back to the altar and downed another shot.

STAGE 1

1

WHACKED

"I think I have cancer."

Mom blurted out the words over elderflower martinis. *No need to freak out.* She'd always been an anxious person with a storyteller's penchant for exaggeration.

It was a sunny June day in 2010, and we'd met up after work at our favourite patio: the rooftop of the Park Hyatt. The Roof Lounge always felt like a mini getaway—a vertical vacation from life on the ground. You could get a stunning view of the city and snack on complimentary spiced olives and smoked almonds (the martinis cost $18).

"I had a colonoscopy and they found a polyp that they think is cancerous. I'll have to get some more tests done and see a colorectal surgeon next week," Mom said all in one breath, the verbal equivalent of ripping off a Band-Aid.

My stomach dropped. *Oh shit.* She wasn't exaggerating. I could tell she was scared. Her large hazel eyes were betraying her nonchalant delivery. I tried to keep my game face on—I didn't want to amplify her fears, or my own. I'd always told myself not to worry until there was something to worry about.

"It's going to be all right," I reassured her. "We'll handle it. Even if it is cancer, you'll get through it. Cancer is *no match* for you!"

"Thanks, sweetie." Mom smiled and took a sip of her martini. "How was your day?"

IT WAS TRUE. Mom was the most vivacious person I knew. She had radiant energy, an infectious smile, and an explosive laugh. It was so loud and distinct that my brother and I could always tell where she was in a crowded room.

No matter what, Mom stood out from the pack. She had frizzy shoulder-length brown hair (with a few blond and silver strands) and a style all her own: a mix of Parisian silk scarves, colourful bohemian knits, asymmetrical designer jackets, and vintage Issey Miyake and Missoni. Her extensive jewellery collection was more like wearable art: handcrafted Mexican silver rings with moonstones and fire opals, dangly earrings that resembled Alexander Calder mobiles, an oversized modernist clear Lucite cuff, a red-caped Superwoman broach made of Fimo. Mom was a true original (although when pressed to play the game "Who would play you in the movie of your life?" she'd debate the merits of her top picks: Diane Keaton, Susan Sarandon, and Catherine Deneuve).

Mom was sixty-six, but in recent years she'd come to describe herself as "ageless." She believed she was in the prime of her life. After decades of working on personal growth, Mom felt she'd finally come into her own as a confident, self-realized woman. As a teacher and mentor, she'd always inspired others—students and fellow women—with her heartfelt wisdom, ardent feminism, and independent spirit. Her latest cause was helping other women resist negative messages about aging.

She was about to self-publish a book called *Silver Fox: A Dating Guide for Women Over 50*.

Propelled by an unabashed joie de vivre, Mom sought out little things that brought her great pleasure—French perfume, bunches of dried lavender, hand-milled soaps, fresh flowers, Belgian chocolate. Her fridge never had much food in it, but it was always lined with small jars of fancy mustards and preserves. "You don't need to be rich to be good at artful living," she'd say. Mom didn't believe in saving things for a special occasion; every day was a celebration. She used hand-painted Italian pottery and Georg Jensen cutlery as her everyday tableware. She'd pop a bottle of champagne for no reason on a random weeknight and we'd stay up late laughing and talking about our lives.

Mom mapped out the city by French patisseries. In general, she had a horrible sense of direction, but she had a GPS-like knowledge of her buttery safe houses. If she was on Queen West, she'd get fluffy croissants from Clafouti; if she was on St. Clair West, she'd pick up a fresh baguette from Pain Perdu; and if she was in the east end, she'd be compelled to stop at Daniel et Daniel for a large tarte citron. Mom had a taste for the finer things. She always knew where to get The Best everything.

When the "Who would play you?" question was turned on me, I'd shrug. *Michael Cera?* I was thirty, but people regularly mistook me for a twenty-two-year-old boy. I didn't mind. The truth was I actually felt more like a sixty-five-year-old Jewish zaide. I wore men's floral button-up short-sleeve shirts, loved Cobb salad and seltzer, and spent my weekends playing chess. I may have been assigned female at birth, but on the inside I felt like Larry David.

It made sense to me. I took after my father, and people actually thought he *was* Larry David (there was no doubt about who'd play him in a movie). Beyond the physical resemblance, Teddy was also a lovable kookster who was always fighting the good fight—constantly writing letters to various organizations, explaining how they could do better. Teddy was passionate about justice. When he wasn't righting the wrongs of the phone company, he was a Superior Court judge, still working part-time on the bench at age seventy.

Growing up, I used to think the family genes had been split in half. My older brother, Josh, had inherited Mom's looks (he resembled a young Al Pacino) and her romantic view of life, whereas I looked more like Teddy—albeit with more hair—and had gotten his super logical mind. In my mid-twenties I even enrolled in law school (my supposed destiny), but I couldn't pull the trigger on going. As I got older, I gravitated more toward the artsy, alternative crowd—people like Mom. I may have inherited Teddy's mathematical wiring, but I developed more of Mom's interests in storytelling, aesthetics, and raw Brie de Meaux. I was a producer for the CBC's flagship arts and culture radio show. Meanwhile, Josh had cultivated more of Teddy's interests—in politics, advocacy, and sliced Havarti. He was running for Toronto City Council, and his wife, Melissa, was an animal rights campaigner.

Mom and I also had a similar sense of humour: the darker, the better. In 2006 we got tickets to the opening night of the Jewish Film Festival. It wasn't normally our scene, but we were excited about seeing the more interesting choice of film that year, *Sarah Silverman: Jesus Is Magic*. Just minutes into her set, Sarah joked, "I was raped by a doctor . . . which is so bittersweet for a Jewish girl." Mom and I laughed louder than anyone else, and as Sarah took on more taboo topics—the Holocaust, 9/11, slavery—we kept busting up. The fact that we were surrounded by a crowd of uptight stiffs who couldn't bring themselves to crack a smile only made us laugh harder. We kept giggling and rolling our eyes at each other as people around us started to walk out. By the time Sarah cut to a video of her best Jewish-girl-does-porn impression—"Fuck my tuchus! Fuck my tuchus!"—there was a mass exodus of disgruntled Jews shaking their heads in disgust. Mom and I were *killing* ourselves.

After the film we spilled out onto Bloor Street, high and giddy from laughing so hard. Our smiles hurting, we walked down the street replaying our favourite jokes. "Oh God, please let them find semen in my dead grandmother's vagina!" I began. "SIXTY million Jews? Now THAT would be unforgivable!" Mom joked back. It was our bonding at its finest.

Within our family, Mom and I spent the most time with each other. We talked on the phone regularly, often went to restaurants and movies together, and even took trips together. She could drive me nuts, but there was pretty much no one in my life I'd rather spend time with. We weren't exactly the *Gilmore Girls*—it would have made me cringe to call her my "best friend"—but we were really good friends.

If anything, Mom and I might've been more like Eddy and Saffy from *Ab Fab*—I was the down-to-earth realist and she the fun-loving dreamer (who always kept a cold bottle of bubbly on hand). I may have been the straight man to her eccentricity, but I hardly kept my composure; Mom could crack me up like no one else. She was quick-witted in her own right, but she was also unintentionally hilarious. And she knew it. When I'd catch her in the act of talking to a plant or twirling around in the living room, she'd look at me and laugh. "Well, you can put THAT in your act!" she'd say. In her mind, I was a stand-up comedian and she was my muse. She wasn't that far off. I often entertained my friends with tales of her latest New Age antics. Making fun of Mom was one of my greatest joys in life.

It was hard to define our dynamic. We were technically mother and daughter, but we were more like mother and son or, at times, daughter and father (she being the unruly teenage girl). Whatever we were, we complemented each other. Mom once told me, "When I was younger, I dated men like my father. Now that I'm older I date men like my daughter."

Mom and Teddy had been divorced for nearly two decades, but in recent years they'd become best friends. They lived only a ten-minute walk from each other and would often talk on the phone and go on long bike rides. They giggled like teenagers, and people often assumed they were still a couple. They'd both had relationships since splitting up, but neither had remarried. Mom told me how Teddy had once unknowingly responded to a singles ad she'd placed in *The Globe and Mail*. She never replied to his message—or even told him about receiving it—but he'd told her that he thought they had "a lot in common." Mom laughed as she recalled the story. "If only he knew that included two children and a settlement agreement!"

We were a close modern family. We celebrated one another's birthdays and regularly gathered for meals. Mom was the family band leader, always steering the conversation. "Have you heard about furries?" she once asked us all at dinner. "They're people who like to dress up in animal costumes, and sometimes they have sex!" Teddy and I exchanged looks of amusement. "They even have conventions." Mom was curious about everyone and everything, and got a kick out of the more unusual aspects of humanity. "A man in a tiger suit might be attracted to a skunk," she went on to explain, "or a raccoon might want to get into a porcupine's pants." Josh smiled at Melissa as if to say "Welcome to the family." My sister-in-law was from a conservative small-town Catholic family, where I'm sure anthropomorphic love wasn't typical dinner conversation.

Simply put, Mom was a breath of fresh air. All my friends—and girlfriends—loved her. She always said what was on her mind. No filter, no topic off limits. Mom gave zero fucks about what was appropriate.

"*Appropriate* is a political term used to keep women in their place," she'd say. Dinner parties were always more fun when Elaine was there. She talked with her hands, spinning stories that had everyone rapt with attention.

Mom was officially retired, but she still did some supply teaching at the alternative high school she'd worked at for twenty-five years. She'd just gotten back from a week-long silent meditation retreat in Massachusetts after finishing up the school year when we met at the Hyatt. Mom was something of a JuBu (Jewish Buddhist) and was always going on spiritual retreats and all types of adventures. She had plans to hike Machu Picchu and boat down the Amazon with her boyfriend, David, in August. Her life, as always, was tremendously full.

THE WEEK AFTER our rooftop drinks, Mom had an appointment with Dr. Gryfe, reputed to be one of the best colorectal surgeons in the city. Since Josh and I were both working, Teddy agreed to take her to Mount Sinai Hospital and call us afterward. I'd been nervous all week, and at work I was on high alert. I'd just filed my script for the day when Teddy called. It was impossible to get any privacy in our open-plan office, so I took my phone around the corner into a small editing room.

"The doctor says it's cancer," Teddy said. "But the results were not conclusive. He's not sure what exact stage it is. Your mother needs to get more tests done."

What does that even mean? I felt like I was in free fall, plunging straight down on a roller coaster. My stomach floated into my chest. I'd been telling myself not to worry until there was something concrete to worry about. And now there was. Having not even allowed myself to consider anything worse than early-stage cancer, the thought that Mom's life could be in serious danger shook me to the core. I felt disoriented. I got off the phone, somehow made my way over to my senior producer's desk, and asked if I could talk to her privately. I trusted Lisa; she was the one I turned to whenever I was having an issue at work. She got up and followed me back into the editing room.

I took a deep breath and tried to summon the words. "My mom . . . has . . . cancer." I could barely get them out before my body began to tremble uncontrollably and I broke down. I was shocked by my own outpouring of emotion. I *never* cried—maybe a few rogue droplets once in a while ("jumpers," I called them), but I hadn't chest-heave sobbed like this since I was a child. It was embarrassing. Lisa, who was several years older than me and a mother herself, was kind. She told me to go home and take care of myself. I felt like a kid again, having to go home sick from school.

When Teddy pulled up outside the CBC to get me, he seemed his usual stoic, composed self, but I could tell how anxious he was. With his left hand holding the wheel, he was rapidly flicking his right thumbnail against his finger. I asked him to take me to Mom's. I was scared and wanted to be with her; she'd be scared too, I knew, and I wanted to be there for her.

Mom lived in a two-bedroom walk-up in an old ivy-covered building called "The Hemingway." Ernest had once lived there, a fact that very much appealed to Mom's romanticism. Her apartment was filled with antiques, offbeat art and pottery, and scores of books. A few small shrines made up of candles and crystals occupied feng shui–approved corners of the space. Really the whole place was a shrine—to Mom's personality.

Mom was already in her blue silk pyjamas when I arrived. She poured us a couple glasses of Côtes du Rhône and we headed to the sunroom—her favourite room to hang out in. Three of its walls had large windows through which you could look out onto the distant treetops of the Cedarvale Ravine. I took my usual spot on one of two facing white loveseats while Mom settled into her white armchair.

"I feel whacked," she declared. "On the day of my colonoscopy, I remember looking around at the patients in wheelchairs, schlepping their IVs, and thinking, 'These people have crossed into the Underworld. Thank goodness I'm just here for a routine test.'"

My eyes scanned the room. There was the winged papier-mâché woman that hung from the ceiling, the two abstract ceramic art plates on the wall, the Buddha bell on the windowsill. Everything was in its usual place, yet it all felt strange.

"Whenever I was going through a hard time in my life," Mom continued, "I would try to gain perspective by reminding myself, 'At least it isn't cancer.'" She was making a half-hearted attempt at a joke, but her throat had tightened and I could see the tears welling up in her eyes. Her worst fear had come true.

I tried to reassure her that everything would be okay. "We'll get more information, and once we know what we're dealing with, we'll make a game plan."

Mom nodded, but I could tell she wasn't convinced.

A FEW DAYS later I went with Mom and Teddy back to Dr. Gryfe's office. As a journalist, I wanted the facts. I brought a pen and a pad of paper to take detailed notes. We sat in a semicircle with Mom in the middle.

Dr. Gryfe was in his mid to late forties but had a very "President of the Math Club" look. He'd probably Doogie Howser'd his way through medical school and never had a puff of a cigarette. Even more comforting—his last name evoked fond memories of the small, unconventionally light poppyseed bagels I grew up eating from Gryfe's Bakery, a Toronto institution. I presumed he was related to the famous bagel makers. We were in good hands.

Dr. Gryfe took his time, carefully explaining Mom's situation to us. Based on her MRI, he believed she most likely had Stage 1 rectal cancer, meaning that it was contained. However, there was a suspicious-looking lymph node that could indicate a later stage. It could very well be incidental, but he wanted her to get a biopsy. He explained how he planned to surgically remove her polyp and the surrounding part of her rectum by going in through her abdomen. She would have a temporary colostomy bag for three to four months to allow everything to heal properly before being resectioned. He also recommended radiation, and possibly chemotherapy, but said it probably wouldn't be necessary if her cancer was indeed contained.

Dr. Gryfe slid his dark-rimmed glasses up the bridge of his nose and reassured us: "There's a seventy to ninety percent chance of survival if it's Stage 1. If it's Stage 3, there's still a fifty percent cure rate."

I felt incredibly relieved. We were so lucky—it looked like it was only Stage 1 and highly treatable.

"What are my other options?" Mom asked. My head swivelled to search her face. I wasn't sure what she was asking. "Is there anything else you can offer me that's less invasive?" she clarified.

Dr. Gryfe said he could do a more minor operation that would involve going through the rectum to remove just the polyp. "But I wouldn't be able to remove the surrounding margins. There would be a higher chance of recurrence," he warned.

Mom sat back in her chair and let out an audible sigh. "Okay, thank you. You've given me a lot to think about."

Dr. Gryfe stared at her. "I recommend you get surgery as soon as possible."

"But . . . I've already bought a ticket to Lima!" Mom protested. "Machu Picchu is on my bucket list."

Teddy and I looked at each other, aghast. *How about putting NOT DIE on your list of things to do before you die?*

TEDDY AND I were nervous about Mom stalling, but we understood that she was in shock and needed time to digest the information. Hopefully a few more weeks wouldn't make too much of a difference and the trip would help her absorb the impact of the news on her own terms. Mom never responded well to being told what to do. She needed to feel she was the author of her own decisions. It was best to let her get there herself.

In the days that followed, Mom and I went over her surgery options— the pros, the cons, her fears. She seemed more agreeable to getting the smaller operation, even though she was being told it was the poorer choice. The more extensive surgery clearly made the most sense for getting all the cancer out, but the colostomy bag was a sticking point.

"I don't want to wear a fecal sac and diapers for the rest of my life," she said.

I tried to reassure her with the doctor's information: "The colostomy bag is only temporary. Your bowel might not ever be the same, but you won't be left in diapers."

I was trying to stay positive without denying the reality of her situation. It was going to be a rough few months, but I was convinced she'd get through it. Her strength and resilience were on her side.

Mom wasn't nearly as hopeful. "I'm terrified," she confessed. "I wake up every hour at night, sweating and shaking."

In August, Mom packed her bags for Peru. When it came to fight or flight, she always chose the latter, preferably with a window seat, to somewhere with good food and hiking.

WHILE MOM WAS away I got a permanent staff position at the CBC. I'd worked hard to prove myself over two years of short-term contracts on a show called *Q*, and now I had job security. I was thrilled. I'd taken a gamble by giving up law school to pursue a career in arts journalism, and it had worked out. I'd scored my dream job. Every day I got to engage with provocative ideas and fascinating people. I was getting paid to watch TV and movies! I got free books, concert tickets, invites to comedy shows, and film festival passes! And I could read whatever I wanted at my desk—Jezebel, Autostraddle, Bitch—nothing was NSFW.

Q was a daily arts magazine radio show that had launched in 2007. Airing across Canada and syndicated in the U.S., it ranked as one of the CBC's highest-rated programs. And although it was an entertainment show on the surface, replete with celebrity interviews and performances by some of the biggest names in music, it was really a show that interrogated the deeper meaning of culture, from literature and dance to punk rock and film to sports and international affairs. Bold-faced names shared billing with discussions of socially and politically relevant topics, and both guests and listeners routinely gushed over how deep the conversations cut.

I loved the work. My job was mainly to come up with story ideas, book guests, and research and write interview scripts. I could follow my curiosity wherever it took me. I hadn't come from a journalism background. Having written my master's thesis in media studies on Gwen Stefani and her Harajuku Girls, I enjoyed finding the nuance and complexity in pop culture. Most importantly, I had a platform to tell stories that really mattered to me: queer stories, trans stories, stories about people of colour. The show reached hundreds of thousands of listeners daily. My not-so-hidden agenda was to put as many marginalized voices on air as I could.

I also loved my fellow producers. They were some of the funniest, smartest, most special individuals I'd ever met. Within the general corporate atmosphere of the CBC building, we were a ragtag group of intellectual misfits. We'd nerd out together about the latest TV shows, movies, and celebrity gossip. I considered my colleagues to be good friends. Most of them, anyway.

Jian was the host of Q. He first found fame in the 90s as the leader of a satirical folk band and had since reinvented himself as a rock star radio host. Being cool mattered to him. He was middle-aged, but he sported a uniform of distressed jeans, dark V-necks, and a black leather jacket. He had a sort of wannabe John Stamos look: deliberately tousled dark hair, seductive eyes, perfectly maintained stubble, and a big cheeky grin.

As the child of Iranian immigrant parents, Jian had grown up first in the U.K. and then in the mainly white suburbs of Toronto. He'd described himself as an awkward Persian kid who'd been called names like "Blackie" as a child in England and "theatre geek" as a David Bowie–idolizing teenager. In university he became an activist for lefty social and political causes and was elected president of the student government. Jian liked being seen as a poster boy for sensitivity. He often brought up how he'd minored in women's studies and that Pride Day was one of his "favourite days of the year." Jian appeared to embody all that was good about Canada—progressive, multicultural, enlightened. He was the CBC's golden boy. But as successful as he'd become, he never shed his outsider mentality. Jian was still that kid who didn't fit in. He desperately wanted to be liked.

And in the beginning, I did like him. He was charming and funny, and I admired his ambition to make the show exciting and relevant to a new generation of public radio listeners. He encouraged my queer and quirky feminist story pitches and always pulled off my scripts beautifully. He spoke to trans guests—many of whom were understandably guarded when talking to the media—with tremendous sensitivity and respect, often relating to his own experience of discrimination growing up as a person of colour. I felt like we were both outsiders on the inside trying to make a difference. There was a kinship. Right away we started calling each other "Brother" or "Bro." He even nicknamed me "Rachel 'Lil Bro' Matlow" when he read the show's credits on Fridays.

The first December after I began working at *Q*, Jian invited me to a holiday party at his house. "You're the only one I'm inviting from the team," he said with twinkling eyes. "More than anyone here, I consider you a friend, not just a colleague." I was flattered.

One day soon after that, my fellow producer Tori swivelled around in her chair toward me, looked me straight in the eyes, and said, "Remember, he's not your friend." She wore a dead serious expression. I was taken aback.

It didn't take long before the bromance was over and I began seeing the disconnect between the person Jian projected out into the world and who he was in the office. He could be charming one moment and hostile the next. It frustrated me, but I figured this was just what working in the radio big leagues was like. I'd faced three hiring boards before I got made staff, and each time I was asked about my strategy for managing hosts with "big egos." I was led to believe that navigating Jian's unpredictable moods and behaviour was just part of the gig.

A few weeks after learning of Mom's diagnosis, I was walking out of the office one day when Jian caught up with me. "Bro, I'm sorry to hear about your mom," he said, with gentle eyes. He shared how a close family member of his had gone through cancer. "She's just fine now," he told me. "It's not easy, but people survive it." I was touched. Jian could be really sweet sometimes. Such moments were few and far between, but they kept me going.

WHEN MOM RETURNED from drinking pisco sours in Peru, she began consuming dozens of books by so-called experts critiquing mainstream cancer treatments. I glanced at some of the new titles piling up on her night table: *Radical Remission, Rethinking Cancer, Questioning Chemotherapy, There's No Place Like Hope: A Guide to Beating Cancer in Mind-Sized Bites, The One Minute (or So) Healer, Detoxify or Die, Be Your Own Doctor, Outsmart Your Cancer, What If You Could Skip the Cancer?*, and last but not least, *Knockout* by Suzanne Somers.

Mom read one memoir after another by cancer survivors who claimed to have cured themselves with vegetable juices, vitamin injections, raw garlic, and the like. It looked as if she were cramming for her comps. She was taking studious notes on various non-invasive methods that supposedly cure cancer: Gerson therapy (coffee enemas and more than a gallon of juices a day), the Gonzalez method (vitamin and enzyme supplements), the Burzynski protocol (something called "antineoplastons"), macrobiotics (a balance of yin and yang foods), the Essiac herbal formula (a specially blended tea), Panchakarma cleansing (Ayurvedic detoxification), the Breuss juice regimen (a forty-two-day juice fast), sodium bicarbonate (baking soda), ozone therapy (oxygen), and the only-asparagus diet (*only* asparagus?) to name a few.

I was unsettled. I'd been waiting three weeks for her to fly home and land in surgery. But Mom insisted that she needed more time to explore her options. "I'm not just going to give in to warlike treatment!" she told me.

I was anxious about her putting off surgery, but honestly, I didn't give her new research project much thought. Mom had always been into alternative stuff—she'd been a self-described "self-help junkie" for twenty years. It was a given that she'd seek out her own remedies. Just, like, *in addition to* surgery.

2

MOMMY QUEEREST

"Don't bother me, I'm meditating!"

Growing up, I knew that if Mom was lying upside down, I was not to disturb her. She would strap her feet under a belt at the top of a black vinyl reclining board and lie back at a forty-five-degree slant. This was her version of meditating.

Mom first dipped her toes into spiritual waters in the early 80s, after I was born. While working on her master's of education, she signed up for a Transcendental Meditation class. Teddy remembers her leaving the house one day with fruit and flowers (offerings for some deity) and coming home with a secret mantra. "Ooomy, goomy, goomy," Teddy would tease. Mom said she became interested in meditation because her fight-or-flight signals were constantly spiking. "I was always on the defensive. I needed to slow down," she told me. But she was soon turned off by TM's hierarchical structure, so she moved on to Zen meditation—and then found it too restrictive. "They made me sit cross-legged on the floor!" she complained. Mom eventually settled on Vipassanā, which is all about seeing things as they really are: "I took to it like an anxious duck to clear water."

She was also into Iyengar yoga when I was little. Mom was always folding herself into various poses around the house—doing a more comfortable version of downward dog, for example, where she'd bend forward and rest her outstretched hands on the kitchen table. Or she'd drop down on the living room carpet and kick her legs up into a shoulder stand. There are baby pictures of me climbing up on her, mid-pose, as if she were a human jungle gym.

Mom's proclivity for meditation and yoga was considered odd back then. We lived in the mostly Jewish, upper-middle-class Cedarvale neighbourhood, where head-to-toe Lululemon and an over-the-shoulder yoga mat were still decades away from becoming *de rigueur*. Mom was a teacher; Teddy was a judge. We lived in a nice house with a pool. We certainly *passed* as normal. But I always had a feeling that Mom wasn't like other moms.

Case in point: I remember in senior kindergarten coming home and announcing that I needed a Halloween costume for school the next day. After a few minutes of scrounging, Mom's face lit up with an idea. "You'll be garbage!" she proclaimed. She got a black garbage bag from under the kitchen sink, threw it over my five-year-old body, and used her hands to tear holes for my arms and head. It was her next move that was really inspired, though. She started fishing through the *actual* garbage bin for dry pieces of authentic trash that we then threaded together with string before festooning me from top to bottom. As a Jewish kid, it was as close as I ever got to trimming a Christmas tree.

The next day, I couldn't have been more embarrassed, surrounded by My Little Ponies, He-Men, witches, and ghosts. *How on earth did Mom think this was a good idea?* There I was, with an empty box of our dog's Milk-Bones dangling around my neck. My teacher, Mrs. Winemaker, looked me up and down before making a concerted decision to declare—a little too enthusiastically—that next year *she* wanted to be garbage for Halloween. *Goddess bless.*

Mom was very caring and loving in her own inimitable way, but she wasn't much of a capital M Mommy. As a joke, she would sometimes refer to herself as "Mommy" when she'd catch herself performing something quintessentially motherly. But it was always said in self-reflexive jest. She didn't bake cookies. She didn't brush my hair. She didn't put sweet notes in my lunch box. In fact, Mom never even packed my lunches. I distinctly remember when she said to me, "You're in senior kindergarten now. It's time you made your own lunch." We were standing in front of the fridge. I looked up at the towering shelves of food with utter confusion.

"What should I bring?" I asked.

"Your cousin Sarah brings a yogurt," Mom replied.

For much of elementary school I'd pack a cappuccino yogurt and a box of Smarties; when lunchtime came I'd pour the latter into the former and stir until the dye bled into a colourful swirl. Sometimes I'd bring mini pitas stuffed with Nutella. I usually rounded things off with a Mini Babybel, a Coke, and a Caramilk bar (for dessert). I was *very* popular in the lunchroom.

But even more than I enjoyed my signature concoction, I loved going to my friend Alimah's for lunch. Her mom, Barbara, was a stay-at-home mother, so Alimah could go home every day for chicken noodle soup, tuna sandwiches, and sliced-up carrot and celery sticks. Seeing Barbara in action was fascinating. She was more like the moms on TV: aware of Alimah's school assignments, making sure she did her homework, limiting how much TV she could watch. Their home was an oasis of routine and predictability. Barbara even assigned meals to days of the week. Wednesday was spaghetti night. Friday was pizza.

There wasn't much cooking going on at our house. Much later Mom would insist she'd been "chained to a stove for eighteen years," but the rest of us remember differently. For dinner we'd usually go out to restaurants, order in, or Teddy or Mom would pick something up on their way home from work. Every so often Mom would courageously attempt to concoct something interesting, like Greek fish or chocolate pasta. But it would be more of a performance than a bona fide meal. "*Mommy* made supper!" she'd sing.

She certainly wasn't interested in being the type of mother—or wife—who put her own life on the back burner, but she'd also made a conscious decision to not be "too overinvolved." She'd felt smothered by her mother growing up and was afraid of even coming close with me. Literally. Sometimes she'd look over at me lovingly and pet the top of my head. "Pat, pat," she'd say, careful to never intrude on my physical space.

Mom had had a list of things she'd do differently when she had a daughter one day. She would never tell me what to do with my hair. She would never make me feel guilty for choosing to do my own thing. Above all, she would never lean on me. "I never want you to feel like you have to take care of *me*," she'd say.

Mom believed it was important to teach me things. She explained how her mother always wanted to do everything for her when she was little, which she interpreted as a power play to make her extra dependent. With me, the pendulum swung. Mom wanted me to be independent. Ultra independent. I was often left at home alone, and was the only seven-year-old allowed to walk up to Eglinton—one of Toronto's major arteries—on my own.

I routinely made that six-block trip to do my errands. I'd go to my favourite candy store, The Wiz, and fill up a large bowl with Pop Rocks, Fun Dip, and Bonkers, and then head across the street to Videoflicks to rent a comedy like *Heathers* or *Ruthless People*. On the way home I'd stop off at China House for a bowl of wonton soup. At first the waiters were a little weirded out by a child dining solo, but they soon came to recognize me as a regular—who paid in quarters and dimes from her piggy bank.

When I inquired about Mom's free-range approach to parenting years later, she happily defended herself. "I taught you how to look both ways and cross the street, and you were very good at it. So I let you go off on your own!"

Teddy was the one to wake me up in the mornings for school, take me to the doctor for checkups, and make sure I ate enough fruits and vegetables to survive. "You're going to get scurvy," he'd warn. But other than that, no one really monitored me. I was allowed to eat as much Häagen-Dazs, watch as much TV, and stay up as late as I liked (I even had a TV in my room). Mom treated me like a mini adult. When I wasn't in school, I could do whatever I wanted with my time.

I relished my freedom—I wouldn't have had it any other way—but there were times when I'd fantasize about having some authority at home. *Time to take your medicine*, I'd say to myself as I popped my daily Flintstone vitamin, imagining an adult was forcing me. To fit in with the other kids at school, when I'd get grass stains or rips in my pants I'd pretend to be afraid of Mom's wrath. "*Man*, my mom's going to *kill* me!" I'd say, mimicking what I'd heard on the field. I knew Mom couldn't care less. (If anything she was proud of me getting rough and dirty.)

I loved Mom so much, but I'd sometimes wish she was more like Barbara. Once when I was sick and she didn't offer to bring me anything, I admonished her: "When other kids are sick, *their moms* bring them orange juice!" ("You don't want one of those *other moms*," she'd snap back. "*I'm* more fun!")

MOM MAY NOT have been like other moms, but the truth was I wasn't like other daughters. In the first seconds after I was born, Teddy was even convinced I was a boy. He says that when he took in all ten pounds of me, he immediately thought *Our little football player!* And cried out "It's a boy!" After giving me a once-over, the doctor quickly interjected: "Actually, it's a girl." "*That's* a girl?" Teddy asked in disbelief. Mom was beyond thrilled. She hadn't allowed herself to want a girl, but deep down she'd really hoped for one this time.

As I grew up, people continued to mistake me for a boy. I was often called "Josh's little brother." I was a tomboy—or what Larry David would later call "pre-gay." I had short moppy hair, wore only jeans and T-shirts, and felt a profound sense of disappointment with the girls' shoe section. I was pretty happy in general—I had friends and did well at school—but I always had a feeling of being on the outside. I didn't feel like one of the girls, and I knew I wasn't really one of the boys. The only other kid who reflected my gender was Casey from *Mr. Dressup*. And Casey was a puppet.

Once, when I was six, Mom attempted to put me in a dress for shul. I resisted. We struggled. She even tried to sit on me. "Please, Rachel! It's the High Holidays!" she begged. "I don't want to!" I yelled back, squirming my way out from beneath her. Back then Mom still cared a little about what people thought and didn't get that it was actually humiliating for me to wear feminine clothes. Thankfully, she quickly gave up, and I emerged triumphant in ripped jeans and high-tops as we left the house. Staying true to the list of things she would do differently from her mother, it was the last time Mom ever tried to dictate my sartorial choices (or any of my choices for that matter).

When I was seven, I told my parents that I wanted to join the local Forest Hill hockey league. I'd watched Josh on Saturday mornings and couldn't wait until I was old enough to play. What I actually thought was *I can do better than that.* (Josh, almost five years older than me, was by no means a jock.) Back then there were only boys in the league, so the organizers were apprehensive. But no one said no. When Teddy took me shopping for equipment he kept asking, "You're sure you're going to play?" as we approached the cash register. I was sure.

Even when I got two penalties in one game, Mom was so proud of me for being the only girl in the league. She admitted that if it had been Josh knocking over other boys, she would've been horrified. But her little girl being called a "goon"? She couldn't have been more pleased. She loved it when the other mothers would tell her that their sons were intimidated by me. "Way to knock 'em dead, sweetie!" she'd cheer.

Mom was an out and proud feminist, and she wanted me to be one too. She'd order children's books from the Toronto Women's Bookstore featuring strong female characters. (There were only a handful at the time; my favourite was *Molly Whuppie*, about a clever girl who fearlessly outwits a giant.) I was fully on board with being a baby feminist. I remember Mom teaching me the word "assertive," although I didn't need lessons in how to embody it. Mom recalled how, when I was three years old, she tried to scare me into submission. "I'm counting to three!" she warned. "One . . . two . . . three . . ." Apparently I just stood there, unimpressed. "What are you going to do?" I asked. Mom laughed and gave up after that. "I learned I had to go at things slant with you," she explained years later. "I couldn't go head to head. You'd win."

When I was eight, I decided to switch schools. I was bored at my neighbourhood elementary school. I was already able to multiply in parts and do long division, so grade two math just wasn't doing it for me. "I'm sick of counting animals!" I complained. One day I went to check out an alternative school called Cherrywood with Barbara and Alimah, who was considering transferring there. What I saw amazed me. There were no walls, teachers were called by their first names, and students could work at their own grade level. Their system made perfect sense to me. That day I came home having made my decision: "I've found a better school and I'm going there," I declared. Mom was totally supportive. She didn't want me to feel held back, and besides, she was an alternative school teacher herself.

On PD days Mom would bring me along to City School, where she taught English and drama. There were posters on the walls with slogans like STOP RACISM and BEING GAY IS NOT A CRIME, BASHING IS. I'd stare wide-eyed at the older students with their rainbow mohawks, lip piercings, and knee-high Doc Martens. Teenagers didn't look like that in Cedarvale. They fascinated me. And they all loved my mom, their rebellious role model.

Elaine was an unconventional teacher, even by alternative school standards. She taught a course called "Nature Writing as a Spiritual Path" and got her students to meditate and hug trees. She'd take her writer's craft class out to cafés to work and encourage them to write freely about whatever was going on in their lives, pushing them to go further than they thought they could go as writers. Mom thought it was important for students to own their education, to be involved, and to have a lot demanded of them. She was incredibly supportive of her students and treated them with more respect than adults usually did. "I wish your mom was *my* mom," they'd say to me. I'd roll my eyes, even though deep down I knew how lucky I was.

To Mom's credit, whenever Josh or I seriously asked her to change her behaviour, she listened. Unlike her mother, she wanted to be able to hear us. She stopped reading books during my hockey games after I told her I wanted her to watch; she refrained from gossiping about me and Josh to her friends when we asked her not to; and she even started bringing me juice when I got sick. "Mommy brought you *orange juice!*" she'd sing.

But the learning curve sometimes seemed like a gentle slope. I didn't always feel heard. When I was *really* upset with Mom or Teddy, I had to find creative ways of getting their attention. On one occasion when I was about seven, angry about who knows what, I took a pad of paper and wrote "Fuck" on every single sheet. Then, while Mom and Teddy were out, I went around the house taping up my expletive art—on the walls and furniture, inside drawers and cupboards. There must have been a hundred sheets. I didn't want to be cruel—I considerately used masking tape so as not to peel paint off the walls—but I did want to get my message across. *They'll see how mad I am*, I thought. They'd open the front door and be greeted with "Fuck." They'd walk into the hallway and see "Fuck." They'd open the fridge, "Fuck" again.

I didn't get the response I was imagining when they came home. I sat at the top of the stairs and watched as they stopped in their tracks, gazed around with wide eyes, and burst out laughing. "Get the camera!" Mom shouted to Teddy. I came downstairs and joined in the laughter, and then Teddy took pictures of me around the house cheekily posing next to my "Fucks." Neither of them inquired into *why* I was upset, but I was satisfied to at least get their attention. Like goys finding Easter eggs well into May, they continued to discover my four-letter treasures for weeks. "I found a 'Fuck'!" Mom yelled out as she opened the china cabinet to get the Shabbat candles.

MY PARENTS WEREN'T religious, but we still lit candles on Friday night and kept kosher in the house. That's how Teddy had grown up, and he hadn't thought to alter things (he was also a vegetarian, so it's not as if he had to sacrifice much). I resented not being allowed to have Lucky Charms—the marshmallows were considered *treif*. When Mom and Teddy actually *did* make rules, they seemed so arbitrary. *I can eat all the sugary cereals I want except the one that's magically delicious?*

By the same lazy logic, Josh and I were sent to Hebrew school every Sunday: apparently it was "what Jewish kids do." I hated it. The idea of God was preposterous to me, the stories were way too far-fetched, and I definitely wasn't into all the male pronouns. Mom would bribe us with a bacon-fuelled pit stop at McDonald's on the way (she wasn't one to care for Commandments of any kind).

Mom went along with Teddy's kosher thing at home. But when we were out of the house, it was a different story. She'd sometimes buy delicate slices of prosciutto before picking me up from one of my extracurriculars, and on the way home we'd park the car and dangle the mouth-watering strips of meat into our mouths, laughing like criminals.

Josh got to quit Hebrew school as soon as he had his Bar Mitzvah. In an effort to get my parents to allow me to quit too, I emerged from my bedroom one Sunday morning having taped crucifixes all over my clothes (I was crafty with the masking tape).

I walked up to Mom and said, "If you don't let me quit, I'll marry a Christian!"

"So what?" she said, unfazed.

"Okay, well then I'll marry a Nazi!" I shouted.

Mom burst out laughing. I'd won her over!

They eventually acquiesced, but not without warning me that I wouldn't be allowed to have a Bat Mitzvah. That was more than fine by me. I wasn't interested in selling out for some gold bling with my initials on it. And I certainly wasn't interested in becoming a woman.

Growing up, I spent the most time with Teddy. We liked the same things: Blue Jays and Maple Leafs games, mini golf, bowling, batting cages, catch in the park. He'd drive me to my hockey, soccer, and baseball games. There was no doubt I was his spawn, but I don't ever remember calling him "Dad." (If I had to take a wild guess, maybe it had something to do with my contempt for authority?) I was aware of his public stature—people literally called him "Your Honour"—and I was proud of him, but I mainly saw him as my playmate. Teddy may have passed as a distinguished authoritarian in society, but with me he was just a big kid. When he took me on a whirlwind tour of Florida's amusement parks, I had a hard time keeping up with *him*. "One more time," he begged as we completed our ninth lap around Space Mountain. "We can make it to ten!"

Mom, on the other hand, exposed me to more sophisticated culture: art galleries, museums, libraries, and culinary adventures. After our visits to the Art Gallery of Ontario, she'd always take me to Wah Sing on Baldwin Street for the best Chinese lobster in the city.

Mom didn't care much for kids' stuff, so on the rare occasion when we'd go to the movies, she'd pick the film. This often involved a battle at the ticket counter—but not with me. Like the time Mom had her heart set on seeing *Mo' Better Blues*, starring Denzel Washington as a jazz trumpeter juggling two women. I was ten. I braced myself as we approached the booth. *Here we go again.*

As expected, the teenage box-office attendant informed her that the film was Restricted.

"I'm her mother! She can handle it!" Mom declared, as if she were insulted he'd even *think* about refusing her child entry. He tried to reason with her. "But ma'am, there's sex and violence in it."

"Oh come on, she's already seen everything!"

This wasn't my first Spike Lee joint.

Even though I kind of hoped we'd get turned away and be forced to see a more age-appropriate movie, I admired the way Mom wouldn't accept things that didn't make sense to her. It didn't matter that she was married to a judge; she saw rules as an optional set of guidelines. And although her public pushback would sometimes embarrass me, it also seeded a sense of pride. I grew up knowing it was okay to challenge the status quo, to do things differently.

As usual, Mom wore the attendant down and we got into the movie. I recall it being a bit of a snooze. I guess an artful examination of jazz, sex, and salvation wasn't really my thing back then.

MY INTERESTS VEERED more toward puzzles. I loved riddles and logic games. My teachers thought I might even become a mathematician. But if there was one game that defined me, it was chess. (One of the best parts about going to Cherrywood was that playing chess counted as math.) I started competing in tournaments when I was ten, and would regularly spend my weekends in hotel conference rooms playing with nerdy boys. I was consistently ranked fourth in Ontario in my age group.

What I liked most about chess was that chance had nothing to do with it. No need for lucky cards or dice or troll dolls. It was up to me to use everything in my arsenal—logic, calculation, memory, even psychology. Mom would remark on how I never got flustered when I was down. "You don't give up. You become even *more* focused," she'd say with great admiration. I learned to rely on my strategic-thinking skills on and off the board, believing I could think my way out of any problem. In our family, if I argued my case well enough, I could get whatever I wanted. I remember saying to my parents, "If you guys can have coffee in the morning for your caffeine, I can have a Coke." For some reason, that one worked. "You're going to make a fine lawyer one day" was a familiar refrain.

When we were young, Josh and I had different interests and led pretty separate lives. It would be years before we started to connect as friends and not just siblings. Back then he spent most of his time in his room writing Leonard Cohen–esque songs. I may have *felt* like an outsider, but Josh truly was one. He wasn't into school or sports or anything else most boys his age were into. He was always working away on an intricate Plasticine city he'd created named Chronic. He spent years painstakingly constructing it, even using a pin to poke windows into the miniature skyscrapers and mapping out each distinct neighbourhood on graph paper.

Mom spent most of her time at home reading. I can still picture her sitting in the living room by the fireplace, a book in one hand and a pink Nat Sherman Fantasia in the other. She wouldn't even inhale—the thin, pastel-coloured cigarettes with gold filters were just props in her one-woman performance of "I am a Parisian." She'd put on one of her French records—Serge Gainsbourg or Edith Piaf—and escape into her French fantasy world. I can still hear Georges Moustaki singing "Ma Liberté." She played that one a lot.

At thirteen Josh moved into the basement and Mom moved into his bedroom. "A woman must have a room of her own," she explained, citing Virginia Woolf. She'd close the door and tap away on the keyboard of her hulking IBM computer. She became a member of a writers' organization called Sisters in Crime and even published a few short stories over the years—murder mysteries that usually involved the death of a lawyer or judge. I suppose she was letting off some steam.

I WAS TEN when Mom and Teddy split up, after years of bickering (mostly about who was "right"). They were caught in a power struggle. Mom would complain that Teddy didn't do enough housework. Teddy would complain that Mom woke him up in the middle of the night too many times, angrily reading him passages from *Ms.* magazine. I don't think either of them were remarkably mature, but I think the bigger truth was that Mom felt trapped, that she was losing herself in the marriage. She needed time and space to become the person she wanted to be. I know they felt guilty about getting a divorce. That year, I got a Game Boy for Hanukkah.

Mom moved into a bachelor pad she'd inherited from a fellow divorcé. It had one tiny spare room, which became my room, but I mostly chose to stay with Teddy and Josh. The house offered me stability and consistency that was hard to find elsewhere.

When I did stay with Mom, it was just us. She was now living on only her teacher's salary, but we'd still go out to restaurants in the neighbourhood. At home we did ear-candling treatments for each other and played a card game that featured feminist writers like Louisa May Alcott, Phillis Wheatley, and Emily Dickinson (Gertrude Stein was the wild card). While I'd be focused on collecting sets of four, Mom would tell me about her literary heroines: "*Little Women* is really the story of Louisa and her family. Louisa was Jo . . ." Often we'd just talk. More than anything else, talking was our thing. To this day there's no one in the world I've ever had an easier time talking to.

What I liked most about Mom's new place was that we didn't have to keep kosher. For breakfast I'd often heat up a can of Chunky clam chowder, although most mornings Mom would go out to the corner and bring me back McDonald's Hotcakes. She'd plop the golden Styrofoam container down on the kitchen table and sing "Mommy made breakfast!"

Meanwhile, back at the house, Teddy was struggling to get dinner on the table. Pizza Pizza was basically on speed dial; they even began sending us a present for every hundred pizzas we ordered. (Once we received two gifts in one year: a Pizza Pizza–branded telephone and, bizarrely, a pair of faux pearl earrings.)

Like Mom, Teddy had never had great role modelling for how to be an emotionally available parent. He was the youngest in his family—his brother and sister were ten and fifteen years older, respectively—and by the time he came along, his folks were done with parenting. When Teddy was four, his mother told him to run across the street to the neighbourhood school. "Tell them you're five," she instructed. He'd known neglect well.

To most people's surprise, the divorce wasn't initially that distressing for me. It only really started to hit me once my parents began dating. Just as I was entering adolescence, the two of them began behaving like full-blown teenagers. Mom fell madly in love with a man who was about to move to Albany to be the director of the New York State Museum. She took a sabbatical to study holistic ways of teaching and began a long-distance relationship with him, regularly leaving town for weeks at a time. Meanwhile Teddy began frequenting Jewish singles events, and suddenly there wasn't time for mini golf or bowling with me anymore. He'd leave me at home with Josh, who by then had become a bit of a wild sixteen-year-old.

When the opportunity presented itself, Josh would throw big parties; teenagers from different high schools across the city would turn up at our house. Josh would tell me I could come to his party as long as I didn't rat him out. He didn't have much of a choice—I lived there—but I agreed to his terms anyway. It was an opportunity to make a few bucks. While the Cure and R.E.M. blasted from the stereo, I'd covertly move around the house siphoning bottles of booze and pinching half-smoked cigarettes from unsuspecting teenagers, selling them on the sly to partygoers in other rooms. "Watch out for Josh's little sister!" they'd warn one another (by then I'd let my hair grow out so that people would stop calling me a boy). Teddy would inevitably come home to the debris and destruction left by a hundred teenagers, his bottles of Russian vodka refilled with water.

Teddy felt as though he was losing control and decided to start implementing rules. He tried to make Josh adhere to a curfew. He attempted to get me to call him "Dad." He tried his hardest to domesticate us, but it was too late—we'd already been raised by wolves.

I missed Mom like crazy when she was out of town. It was hard being without her at the house. Teddy, Josh, and I were fighting all the time. I would often call her crying, pleading with her to come home. She'd listen to me and lovingly calm me down, but she wasn't about to get in the car and drive back. She explained to me how important it was for her to have a full life of her own. "I'm not *just* a mother," she would tell me. "I need passionate love too."

As gross as it was to hear her say that, I understood that Mom had her own needs. I tried my best to respect her wishes, but there were times when I needed her to be there for me and she wasn't. It was Teddy who had to get me kitted out when I got my first period. He ran out to the drugstore and then presented me with a basket of Love's Baby Soft products and a box of inch-thick pads. I was horrified. It would've been embarrassing enough for any thirteen-year-old girl to have to deal with this kind of thing with her dad, but it was particularly uncomfortable for me, considering I felt like a boy and didn't even want to acknowledge my bodily changes in the first place. It was also Teddy who had to take me bra shopping for the first time. The two of us couldn't have been a more reluctant duo as we set out for the mall together in search of the undergarment that would not be named. When the saleswoman asked me what I was looking for, I couldn't even say the word. "I need something to wear under my baseball jersey," I mumbled.

IT WAS DURING those three and a half years while Mom lived part-time in Albany that her journey of self-discovery really took off. The northeastern United States is a hotbed of spiritual retreat centres. Mom began frequenting New Age havens like Kripalu, Omega Center, Zen Mountain Monastery, Insight Meditation Society, and Elat Chayyim, a Jewish renewal retreat in the Catskills. (There, she told me, they'd sit in a circle, with their index fingers touching their thumbs, and chant "Shal-Ommm, Shal-Ommm.") She often slept in dorm rooms and chopped vegetables alongside college students in exchange for what would otherwise be a thousand-dollar yoga vacation. Mom didn't need a large income in order to have a large life.

Her retreats gave her time and space to work out her issues. She still had a lot of childhood resentment, even though by then she was getting along well enough with her mother. She was proud that she'd taught her mother to treat her more respectfully. "It's important to set *boundaries*," Mom told me. Before her father died, he'd apologized to her in his Polish-Jewish accent for having not acknowledged her feelings enough. I know that meant a lot to her. But still, Mom was desperate to free herself from her family patterns. She would write unsent letters to her parents as well as responses from the perspective of her ideal mother or father.

I was happy that Mom was working out her shit, but sometimes I felt like I had to compete with her inner child. My heart would break every time she drove off in her cappuccino-coloured Honda with its ONE NUCLEAR BOMB CAN RUIN YOUR WHOLE DAY bumper sticker. I spent a lot of time crying on my own, until one day I decided I wouldn't cry anymore. I'm not sure if it was due to my natural temperament, my gender identity, or my parents not being fully attuned to my emotional world, but I resolved to toughen up and be a little man. Throughout junior high, I kept a busy schedule with sports and chess. I was on all my school's sports teams, including the boys' hockey team, and played competitive hockey, soccer, and softball on the side. I was the city's school chess champion two years running.

It was also in junior high that I experimented with being a girl, albeit only part-time. I was invited to friends' Bar and Bat Mitzvahs almost every weekend and could no longer get away with wearing pants to shul. When Saturday rolled around, I'd trade in my jeans and T-shirts for pantyhose and a dress. My friend Jane helped me pick out girl party attire at the mall and taught me about shaving my legs. My friend Sarah gave me a nudge when she'd catch me manspreading in a skirt in synagogue. Being a girl didn't come naturally to me, but I passed well enough. Boys liked me, and I even had crushes on them. Though, looking back, I think my attraction was probably more about me wanting to *be* one of them (or because at that age they looked like cute little baby dykes, with their short hair and smooth cheeks, like little Justin Biebers).

Meanwhile, Josh was deeply unhappy with his life. He was disinterested in school, and he and Teddy were at each other's throats. So one time when Mom was heading off to New York state, she brought Josh along and dropped him off at a Sufi commune near Albany. Josh stayed at the Abode of the Message for several months doing a work exchange. He couldn't have been happier to move out, to start a life of his own.

Mom brought me along with her to Albany a couple of times, too. On our last trip there she took me hiking in the Adirondacks. We climbed a steep, rocky trail up Crane Mountain, scrambling our way to the summit. We both felt a great sense of accomplishment as we looked out over the forest-covered mountains below. Mom was proud that she'd taken me, at thirteen, hiking up a three-thousand-plus-foot mountain. "When *I* was thirteen my mother took me *discount shopping* for our bonding time," she told me. On the way down we came to a large pristine pond where we decided to take a break, sitting next to each other on a giant boulder in the shade. Mom pulled out a watercolour set along with some paper. Together, both painting quietly, we stared out at the glistening water and tall beech trees in the distance. It was a serene moment we would often look back on fondly.

A couple of days later Mom broke up with her boyfriend. She'd felt increasingly torn between being with him and being with me in Toronto. I vividly remember seeing her break down in tears as we got in the car to drive home. She was always so conscious never to lean on me that she rarely showed any vulnerability around me at all. Years later, Mom would admit that although she'd wanted a great love, she was scared. "I had a strong feeling that if I married him, I would be happy for a year and miserable for the rest of my life."

When I was fourteen, I decided to live with Mom full-time. Teddy had sold the house, and I felt displaced. By then Mom had moved into the Hemingway. She made a concerted effort to make me feel welcome. This time, she gave me the bigger room.

It was during this period, in the mid-90s, that Mom's alternative lifestyle began to rub off on me. I went to yoga classes with her and wore a crystal aromatherapy necklace she'd given me as a gift. She took me on road trips to Buddhist monasteries and silent meditation retreats. In the car, we'd take turns listening to her folk music (Joni Mitchell, Phil Ochs, the Stone Poneys with Linda Ronstadt) and my Ani DiFranco, Tracy Chapman, and Indigo Girls tapes. We visited the Kushi Institute for Macrobiotics in Massachusetts, where we sipped twig tea and learned how to cut a carrot properly (from tip to stem) so as not to kill its life force. My teenage curiosity and idealism latched onto these alternative doctrines. I was drawn to the rules and guidance they provided.

But for Mom, soul searching was more than just a teenage phase. She was always trying out something new. Trance dancing, magnets, meridian tapping, past-life regression therapy, colour therapy, cranial sacral therapy, chakras, crystals, rolfing, reiki—she would embrace each fad with the same enthusiastic yet noncommittal curiosity every time. Her perspective was, Why not try everything? It doesn't hurt, and it might lead to unexpected wisdom. And hey, if they kept her looking younger, all the better! She regularly did these Tibetan exercises called "The Fountain of Youth," where she'd spin around with her arms outstretched. (Mom said that when she first saw "spinning" classes pop up in New York City, she mistakenly thought her exercises were taking off.) I saw the marvel in her New Age dalliances, but I definitely took them with a big grain of Himalayan salt.

For Mom, spirituality was like a buffet where she was free to pick and choose what she wanted—she could create her own narrative blend that suited her personality and her needs. It was all about knowing herself better, being able to laugh more about her frailties, and becoming as real as possible. As a feminist, she wanted to own her spirituality without giving herself over to dogmatic ideas or practices.

Mom was a badass Buddhist. Of course, she believed that rules were optional, even the ones the yogis wrote. Her Four Noble Truths were coffee, wine, reading, and talking, or what Buddha might call "contraband." When she was supposed to be staying silent on her meditation retreats, she'd leave me hushed, long-winded voicemail messages: "Hi darling, I'm not supposed to be talking, but I just wanted to let you know I'm okay. Um, it's so weird to be speaking . . ." She would smuggle in novels and escape to nearby villages to get *The New York Times* and a cappuccino. When she did a work exchange at Thich Nhat Hanh's monastery in the south of France, she led a group of fellow volunteers through the surrounding vineyards on a wine-tasting tour. "I was like the pied piper," she told me. "They all followed!"

ON MY SEVENTEENTH birthday I set out on my own journey of self-discovery. My best friend Syd had lent me her copy of *The Teenage Liberation Handbook: How to Quit School and Get a Real Life and Education.* Essentially a recipe for teenage anarchy, the book became our bible. The Good News? Rather than being confined to classroom walls, teens could reclaim their natural ability to teach themselves by following their own curiosity and having real-world experiences. I had seen the light! After reading a few more books on "unschooling," I knew what I had to do.

That January, I finished my last exam of the semester and flew to San Francisco. There, Syd and I hung out with an older anarchist couple we'd met who took us around to protests with their giant papier-mâché puppets. Like Mom, I learned to live large on not much. We couch-surfed at intentional communities in Santa Cruz and Palo Alto and travelled up the west coast of the U.S. on a backpacker bus called the Green Tortoise. We hitchhiked across B.C., working on organic farms in return for accommodation and three wholesome meals a day. As a city kid, it blew my mind to see what broccoli looked like in its natural habitat.

To say that I was self-righteous about my decision would be the understatement of the decade. If anyone ever said I was "dropping out of school," I'd diligently correct them. "I'm not *dropping* out," I'd say. "I'm *rising* out."

Mom and Teddy hadn't been surprised when Josh quit school, but they were a bit baffled when I did. I'd always gotten good grades. But like Josh, I didn't want to learn that way. I wanted to see the world and have adventures. Teddy was certain I was throwing away my future. Mom was a little anxious (being a teacher, she preferred not to have *both* her kids quit school), but she understood where I was coming from. She was ultimately very supportive, even seeing me off at the airport. "You have guts," she told me.

For the next two and a half years I travelled around the world to hippie hotspots with Syd and some of our other "unschooled" friends. I took silver jewellery-making lessons in Mexico, learned Spanish and taught English in Guatemala, trekked the twenty-day Annapurna

Circuit in Nepal, and attended talks by the Dalai Lama at his temple in Dharamsala, India. I was living the teenage dream. I would come home in between my long excursions and stay with Mom just long enough to make the money to go back out again. I worked at a bohemian gift store in Kensington Market that specialized in Ecuadorian sweaters and Circle of Friends pottery.

Eventually Mom and Teddy were cool with my new lifestyle. Sure, I'd quit school. But it wasn't like I was doing drugs—I was mainlining brown rice and Spirulina Sunrise bars. My form of teenage rebellion was being a hippie fundamentalist. I was a strict vegetarian. I used only "natural" body products. I refused to take any pharmaceuticals (not even Tylenol). I hung out at the health-food store as if it were the mall. My uniform consisted of second-hand jeans with colourful patches, striped Guatemalan shirts, and hiking books—even in the city. And, if that wasn't bad enough, the surest sign of my hippie cult status? *Dreadlocks.* It hurts to admit it, but I had 'em. In my meagre defence, it was the late 90s, when they were "in style" (and before I learned about cultural appropriation). I also theorize that my Manic Panic–dyed dreads were an expression of my dormant queerness—a gateway to the short dykey haircut I subconsciously knew I was moving toward.

ONE OF THE biggest perks to ditching high school was that I didn't have to deal with normal teenage things, like dating. I could totally avoid it. And I did, even if I couldn't avoid the subject altogether. The first spring after I quit school, Syd and I found ourselves pitching in at a women-only community near Nelson, B.C. This lesbian idyll was on a mountainside, up an old logging road, entirely off the grid. Even their bathtub was wood-fired.

One evening a bunch of short-haired wimmin arrived in their trucks, giddy with excitement. One of them had a VHS tape in her hands that she was cradling like some sort of Holy Grail. Our host let us in on the commotion: they were congregating to watch the "Coming Out" episode of *Ellen*. It was essentially the lesbian moon landing of 1997.

They all rushed into action. One of them peeled back a macramé tapestry to reveal a hidden TV in the corner of the living room. Another got the generator going. Everyone gathered around for the momentous—if pre-recorded—occasion. For one night only, we would plug back into civilization for the sake of Ellen DeGeneres.

I watched as Ellen finally got up the courage to say to Laura Dern's character "I'm gay," only to accidentally blurt the words into the airport P.A. system. I laughed out loud, but on the inside I was freaking out. It was the first time I remember seriously thinking, *I think that's what I am.* I was a vegetarian who played competitive hockey and softball, who in that moment "happened" to find herself in a room full of lesbian separatists. How many more hints did I need?

AFTER MANY MONTHS on the road, bouncing from place to place, the idea of staying put and going to university started to seem appealing— an exciting new adventure in itself. I had some older hippie friends who went to Trent, a lefty liberal arts university just over an hour's drive from Toronto, and would sometimes visit them there. Their courses in feminist philosophy and alternative media sounded way more interesting than high school.

Emboldened by my "bible," I booked a meeting with the dean and presented my case for why my *self*-education was just as valuable, if not more, than a high school diploma. He listened to my arguments and asked, "What if we said that if you go back to high school and get your English OAC [grade 13], we will *then* consider your application?"

I shook my head. "I'm not going back," I said. "It would be compromising my beliefs."

I was cocky, stubborn, and defiant. I told him that if he wanted to know whether I could read and write I'd be happy to provide some samples of my work. He agreed, and a couple of months later, in the spring after my nineteenth birthday, I received a letter of acceptance.

Teddy was more than happy to eat his words. Mom was impressed with how I'd subverted the system, but she was even more in awe of my steadfast—if not insufferable—confidence in myself. "You have a strong centre," she told me.

IN STEREOTYPICAL SAPPHIC fashion, I met my first girlfriend in my freshman women's studies class. Anya had short red hair and a wallet chain, and she rode a skateboard. I liked that she was five years older and didn't seem to give a shit what anyone thought of her. We flirted for several weeks before we finally kissed.

I was building up the nerve to tell Mom about Anya when I was home one weekend in December. I knew she'd be accepting, but I was still terrified to come out to her. I was only just starting to come to terms with my sexuality. Besides Ellen and k.d. lang, there weren't many celesbian role models back then. This was pre–L Word; it wasn't yet cool to be gay. Same-sex marriage hadn't been legalized. Matthew Shepard had just been beaten to death. As good as I had it, I was still scared. Mom and I talked about a lot of things, but we'd never spoken about my dating life, or lack thereof. Afraid of prying, she never asked me overtly personal questions, and I never offered up what was actually going on inside my head.

At one point that weekend, we were sitting in her sunroom when I finally blurted out, "I'm dating someone." Before I could even mention Anya's name, or her pronoun, Mom replied, "Wonderful! Invite her to Solstice!" She didn't even flinch. Sometimes Mom was too cool.

Mom had been planning an intergenerational women's winter solstice party, which that year happened to fall on a full moon. It would be the first time I'd be introducing my new girlfriend—essentially announcing "Yep, I'm gay!"—to twenty of our closest friends. I didn't think it would come as a big surprise to anyone, but I still felt nervous and self-conscious. In any case, it soon became clear that I needn't have worried about being the odd one.

When our guests arrived, Mom led everyone through a series of activities. First she got us each to light a candle and share our intentions for the next year. Then she got us all to hold hands, walk around in a circle, and chant, over and over, "Freedom comes from not hanging on, you gotta let go, let go-oh-oh!" (She explained that a witch named Sophia had taught her the chant.) Next she got us all to stand in a circle and make a human web by tossing balls of yarn to one another. We ended up tangled in a big stringy mess. Anya couldn't stop giggling. Mom thought she was high. I imagine Anya thought the same about Mom.

For the pièce de résistance, Mom ushered us all outside into the back parking lot. "It's time to howl at the full moon," she announced. We huddled around in our parkas and stared up at the night sky. "Aaah-woooooh, aah-woooooh!" Mom led the group in a series of loud howls.

A neighbour soon yelled down: "Shut the fuck up!"

"It's just me! Elaine!" Mom reassured him cheerfully.

Anya and I stood on the sidelines howling with laughter. I could see, from Anya's point of view, how this party, and my mom, might seem a little bizarre. I'd always written Mom off as quirky or eccentric—until I came to realize that she was just as queer as me, if not more. Considering the word's traditional meaning—"strange, peculiar, off-centre"—I'd say Mom managed to outqueer me at what was ostensibly my own coming-out party.

When I look back on everything now, as someone who's more comfortable in their genderqueer skin, I remember feeling confident and self-assured about so many things and yet totally strange and unknown to myself. I didn't quite fit in with either gender or in a world where people just followed the script handed down to them. But Mom's out-there-ness made it okay for me to be myself and to live life on my own terms, just as she did. I'm immensely grateful to her for that. But in the end, the pendulum may have swung too far—in her approach to me, and more consequentially, to herself.

3

QUICKSAND OF HER FEARS

While Mom had been communing with ancient Incan spirits, Dr. Gryfe had brought her case to the Mount Sinai tumour board, a panel of doctors at the hospital who help one another out with less than straightforward cases. When Mom and I returned to his office in September, he told us that they had all concluded the same thing: the polyp in her rectum was most likely first-stage cancer, but the suspicious lymph node was cause for concern.

The board's verdict did nothing to assuage her or bring her around. In fact, Mom only became more defiant. She outright refused to get the lymph node biopsy. "I read that the needle they insert could spread cancer through my body," she said.

"If you don't have surgery, you will die," Dr. Gryfe countered, his frustration apparent. "Your cancer could spread into your bones. It would be a very painful death."

Mom was not budging. "I need more time to think about it."

"Do you like to play Russian roulette?" he asked her.

I could tell that Mom was put off by his authoritarian tone. I was already anticipating the monologue to come: his patriarchal condescension, how he symbolized everything that was wrong with the medical system.

"I don't want to be rushed into treatment," she protested.

Dr. Gryfe was really exasperated now. "You are the most non-compliant patient I've ever had." He didn't realize he was adding fuel to the fire; declarations like this only made Mom feel more righteous.

"There are so many studies that show that patients labelled 'difficult' live longer than obedient ones," she told me as we walked out of the hospital. "I think I'm being overdiagnosed. I don't want to fall into the clutches of the system."

For Mom, "non-compliant" was a compliment. She felt she'd been compliant for too much of her life—as a daughter, as a wife, as a woman in general. She was done with being nice and agreeable. ("*Nice* is just another word for victim," she'd say.)

As we pulled out of the parking lot, Mom turned to look at me. "It's really good not to be passive," she said, both hands firmly gripping the wheel. "I'm proud of resisting Dr. Gryfe's bullying and fear-mongering."

CANCER WASN'T MOM'S enemy; the "system" was. Instead of acknowledging and treating her cancer head on, she focused her energy on a takedown of Western medicine. She was like a fanatical graduate student who'd just discovered Foucault. She'd been doing her homework and brought her *own* stats to the table.

"The cancer medical apparatus is the third-largest killer in North America!"

"Two out of three cancer patients die within the first five years!"

And then there was her *extremely creative* interpretation of Dr. Gryfe's charge: "Even Russian roulette would give me five chances out of six to live. Better than *his* stats!"

Mom's fears were getting the better of her. She was amping herself up. "Who can assure me that if I volunteer to get cut up, and then spend a year getting radiated and poisoned by chemo and likely infected, I'll live longer?"

Again, I tried to reassure her with the doctor's info: "It's only six weeks of recovery and three to four months of healing. Chemo isn't even on the table right now. And anyway, he explicitly said that he wouldn't force you to do chemo *or* radiation if you don't want it. If you do the surgery he's recommending, odds are you'll live for a long time."

I knew the lack of a definitive diagnosis was making Mom even more anxious. The doctors thought it was most likely Stage 1, but they couldn't say for certain. There was that suspicious lymph node, which probably meant nothing, but could also mean something. They certainly believed she had good chances of survival, but they couldn't *assure* her of anything. The doctors didn't have an airtight story, so Mom began filling in the gaps with her own.

"Is it Stage 1? Is it Stage 4? What do they even know?" Mom questioned, waving her hands around in the air like an orchestra conductor. "All my tests are clear except for a smudge and a dot on an MRI. They're often not read properly. My blood count isn't *that* far from normal. Maybe I don't even have cancer!"

I was annoyed, but I also felt bad for her. Mom told me she was still waking up in the middle of the night, trembling with fear. I wanted to help her get through the dread and angst. After all, in our dynamic, I was the cool-headed one. I knew she was prone to getting frazzled in stressful situations. Despite all her yoga and meditation, she still struggled with anxiety.

I remembered an incident from a few years back when I was staying with her. I'd gotten up in the middle of the night to get a glass of water, and on my way to the kitchen I found Mom in a state of panic, wearing rain boots and holding a garden spade.

"What's going on?" I inquired in my sleepy haze.

She let out a nervous laugh. "I'm burying my anxiety!"

"Oh yeah? How does that work?" I asked in my best trying-not-to-be-judgmental tone.

"I wrote down all my anxieties on a piece of paper," she explained. "Now I'm going to say goodbye to them forever!"

"All right, carry on," I said and headed back to bed.

The next day I'd forgotten about our late-night run-in until I noticed a fresh grave next to the Buddha in the garden.

EMBOLDENED BY HER new cause, Mom began assembling her own *Ocean's Eleven* militia of alternative healers. There was Michael, the "master herbalist" and Mom's right-hand man; Michael's girlfriend, Monika, who practised "plant spirit medicine" (and also did organic facials); and Pam, the reflexologist who'd somehow also become her therapist. Mom rounded out her roster with a cell energy doctor, homeopath, shaman, Chinese doctor, naturopath, reiki master, and acupuncturist. Mom was the ringleader. With their help, she'd pull a fast one on cancer.

That fall Mom began every meal by taking an herbal tincture that Michael had concocted for her: a special blend of plantain, lemon balm, New England aster, peppermint, marsh mallow, purple loosestrife, white pine, and cayenne. "They boost my immune system, target the cancer, and help calm me down," she said, as though she were auditioning for a late-night infomercial.

Mom bought a juicer and installed an alkaline water system (she'd read that cancer thrives in an acidic environment). She began eating more organic fruits and vegetables along with quinoa and brown rice, and stopped eating refined sugar. She even gave up her favourite French pastries. But she still allowed herself to drink three glasses of organic Pinot Noir per week. "Pinots have more resveratrol, a great anti-cancer substance, than any other grape," she explained. Every day she meditated and bounced on her mini trampoline (supposedly good for cleansing the lymphatic system). She also mentioned something about five angels who came to stay as house guests.

Although my own anxiety was mounting, I kept rationalizing that Mom just needed a little more time to come around. I would try to be patient and supportive. I didn't want to add to the pressure she was feeling from the doctors. I brought her a bunch of raw food and sent her articles about holistic cancer healing. I wasn't under any illusion that what she was doing could cure cancer, but I also didn't think it was all nonsense. I thought it was great she was eating healthier. I thought the meditation might help with her stress. I understood that doing things herself made her feel better.

And Mom's new regimen was making her feel more positive. She said she had no symptoms, good energy, and felt calmer being off sugar. "I feel wonderful," she told me, taking a pause before admitting, "well, most of the time. When I think of my life being hijacked by surgery, radiation, and chemo, I feel depressed, hopeless, and miserable. But when I think of doing things my way, I feel hopeful, even oddly happy."

I WAS CONCERNED about Mom, but my job still consumed most of my energy. Besides taking some mornings and afternoons off to go with her to appointments, I didn't have that much time to worry. Working on Q kept me in a relentless cycle: pitching stories, writing scripts, booking and pre-interviewing guests, editing tape. Jian had incredibly high standards, and he demanded nothing short of full loyalty and dedication from his producers. It was more than a nine to five job; I often attended events and read books for work in the evenings. Jian might call at any time. We were expected to sacrifice for the greater good of the show. (Or rather, because we loved what we did, we were told it was our "privilege.") There was hardly ever a moment to catch your breath. And Jian made it clear—you were only as good as your last story.

Josh, who was running for office, was preoccupied with the municipal election coming up that October. After returning from the Sufi commune and his subsequent travels around the Middle East, Josh had become an environmental activist. And attending theatre school in Paris in his early twenties—at Mom's encouragement—had prepared him well for a career in politics. I knew Mom's situation weighed on him, but this was the biggest moment of his career. And because he wasn't able to make it to her doctor's appointments, he was getting all his information from her. As far as he could see, Mom was continuing to live her life as usual. She was supply teaching and working toward her book launch. She even organized a fundraiser for Josh's campaign. It was weird that Mom hadn't started treatment yet, but there was no reason for anyone to freak out. She was telling everyone that she was "still collecting information."

However, it was apparent to me that the only information she sought was the kind that supported her new anti-medical-establishment beliefs. She certainly wasn't interested in reading any up-to-date medical literature from Wellspring or the Mayo Clinic. "*Up to date* in Western medicine means you're being fed info by Big Pharma," she told me. "Big Pharma owns the doctors. I'm sure they're well-meaning—they don't even know they're being bought—but it's corrupt."

It's not as though there wasn't some truth to what Mom was saying, but she came off as a conspiracy theorist. She wasn't aware of how paranoid and fanatical she seemed. Conspiracy theorists should at least know better than to *sound like* conspiracy theorists.

"People who've had success at curing cancer without it costing a lot have been jailed or run out of town," she proclaimed. "Big Pharma doesn't want us to know about these alternative cures because they can't patent herbs. No patent, no profits!" (I imagined that if she weren't so style-conscious she'd be wearing a hat with the slogan.)

I tried to reason with her. "I'm not denying that cancer is an industry. But can't *both* be true? Can't it also be true that Western medicine saves lives?"

"Yes," she admitted, a wry smile lighting up her face. "But there are theories that they save lives *in spite of* chemo and radiation."

According to Mom's research, the overwhelming consensus was that it was very possible to cure oneself. She really seemed to believe in the miracle cures she was reading about, despite the lack of scientific evidence to back up their claims. She was even considering going to one of the alternative cancer clinics—Gerson therapy in Mexico or Dr. Gonzalez in New York. She certainly wasn't interested in reading the articles Teddy was forwarding her from Quackwatch. She'd fire back with her own corroboration, making sure to CC me on the emails. "Watch This INCREDIBLE FILM on Successful Cancer Therapy" read one subject line. It was a link to a documentary about Dr. Burzynski, one of the cancer quacks she'd recently become so enamoured of. I watched the first few minutes of the video, which opened with a man in a white lab coat speaking to the camera. "I was astounded!" he exclaimed. "Dr. Burzynski had MRIs of brain tumours known to be universally fatal and they had simply disappeared. It was obvious to me that Dr. Burzynski had made the most important discovery in cancer treatment ever." Cue uplifting music.

I was shocked that Mom could be so naive. But I could also see how persuasive the video—and all her new miracle-cancer-cure books—could be, especially to someone who was extremely scared and vulnerable. I could see the allure of the promise, the possibility of control in the face of utter disorder. They offered an alternative reality, an escape hatch from the Underworld.

Even Oprah had a weakness for crackpots and junk science. In 2007, three years before Mom's diagnosis, she gave Jenny McCarthy a platform to spread false claims about vaccines causing autism. And even though the actress admitted she'd learned about autism from "the University of Google," plenty of viewers bought her messaging. Otherwise intelligent and reasonable parents were—and still are!—refraining from immunizing their children against measles. Oprah's protege Dr. Oz was also endorsing pseudo-scientific weight-loss treatments like "magic" green coffee beans and "miracle" raspberry ketone supplements. And Gwyneth Paltrow who, then in the early days of her lifestyle blog, was championing all sorts of bogus detox treatments (before going on to hawk vaginal steaming and jade yoni eggs). This is all to say that Mom may have been naive, but she wasn't the only one getting Gooped.

Maybe it would have set off more alarm bells if she'd come out as a religious fanatic who opposed medical intervention because "only God heals." But she had pockets of mainstream culture affirming her arguably just-as-fanatical and dangerous belief: that she had the power to heal herself.

As a recovering hippie fundamentalist, I understood Mom's mistrust of Big Pharma. But I also saw how the booming "wellness industry" exploits the anti-authoritarian part of us—the teenager in us all—that thinks we know better. And conveniently, its celebrity mouthpieces don't need to prove their magical remedies work; they just need to prove that conventional medicine makes mistakes. I mean, who wouldn't like to believe that we can escape our toxic world and heal ourselves with chaga mushrooms and superfood smoothies?

Still, I never seriously considered that Mom would reject conventional medicine altogether. She was eccentric, but not insane. In fact, I'd say that Mom was the most enlightened person I knew. She was intelligent in the traditional ways: she stood first in her class growing up, had read thousands of books, and could even recite poetry in Middle English. But beyond worldly knowledge, Mom was well-versed in matters of the heart. She had her own brand of wisdom based on personal experience, psychology, literature, and Buddhist philosophy. She had the air of a wise sage or crone, kind of like Yoda but with better skin and a more whimsical wardrobe.

Many of her friends and students thought of her as their unofficial life coach. She once jokingly described herself as a "baby shaman." Mom was open-minded, honest, and kind, and she always dispensed her guidance with compassion and a complete lack of judgment. She never spoke from a pedestal. She was aware of her own insecurities and less-enlightened qualities, yet she was able to put her ego aside to give others personalized and focused attention. She was as good a listener as she was a talker (and she was a pretty darn good talker).

Mom had such a warmth and interest in other people that strangers would open up within minutes of meeting her. I couldn't count the number of times I'd leave her to go to the bathroom and return to find her deeply engaged with a new friend. She struck up conversations wherever she went. She'd ask strangers what they were reading. She'd ask waiters and shop clerks about their lives. Mom didn't do small talk. She spoke to everyone—her hairdresser, the woman who did her nails, even border agents—about real things.

Mom was always my go-to person for advice whenever I had a dilemma or was feeling down. In my twenties I started opening up to her more, usually when I was heartbroken over a girl. She always knew what to say to make me feel better. I appreciated that she was never too

Pollyanna: "Sometimes you just have to put on your high rubber boots and walk through the shit," she'd say.

As New Agey as she could be, Mom was never flaky. She always maintained a clear and critical perspective. Even when it came to self-help she was discerning. She wasn't into trendy phenomena like *The Secret*, *Chicken Soup for the Soul*, and Eckhart Tolle. They were too cheesy and simplistic for her. Sure, she liked to spin around with her hands in the air, but she always kept one foot on the ground. MIT-trained mindfulness teacher Jon Kabat-Zinn and *Radical Acceptance* author Tara Brach, with a PhD in clinical psychology, were more her cup of twig tea. So I just assumed she'd come around to seeing how ridiculous—even fraudulent—so many of these purported miracle workers were, and that meditation and macrobiotics, however healthy, weren't powerful enough to heal her. But as the weeks went by she seemed only to sink deeper into the quicksand of her fears.

IN NOVEMBER I went with Mom to see Dr. Feinberg, another of the city's finest colorectal surgeons. The idea was to get a second opinion, but I think Mom was mainly hoping that a new doctor would tell her a new story—one she liked better.

Dr. Feinberg fit a familiar mould: Jewish, accomplished, self-assured. His assessment was pretty consistent with Dr. Gryfe's. As we sat in his office, he kept quoting a "ninety percent cure rate." "I'm optimistic that your cancer is highly curable," he told her. What was even more hopeful was his conviction that her suspicious lymph node was probably not malignant because it wasn't in the usual place for rectal cancer.

But Mom was still seeing the situation like some sort of truther. "Your cure rates refer to a patient's survival for only five years. Someone could die *the day after* and they would still be counted as being cured, isn't that right?"

"Yes, but most of my patients go on to live for a very long time," Dr. Feinberg reassured her. "We measure people for only five years because most recurrences happen within the first few years."

"It's not a conspiracy!" I barked.

"Things go wrong all the time," Mom said, looking at me. "Even if the operation goes perfectly, what's the chance of me getting an infection? *Pretty* high!"

I was flabbergasted. It was as if her house was on fire and she didn't want to put it out for fear of the fire extinguisher.

"There's only a two to five percent chance of you getting an infection," Dr. Feinberg clarified.

I chimed in again. "And would an infection even be *that bad* if it means getting the cancer out of you?"

"Yes, it *would* be that bad," she said. "People often die of the infection, not the cancer."

Dr. Feinberg was making a valiant effort to stay calm. "You really should have had this done two and a half months ago. You're young, healthy, and slim. I really don't think there would be complications," he added. Mom laughed and comically batted her lashes at the unintentional compliment.

Now Dr. Feinberg was really getting frustrated. He asked her point-blank: "At the end of the day, are you more concerned about the complications of surgery or the complications of inadequately treated cancer?"

Mom explained how she was taking some time to try out her alternative remedies.

"I'm not a fan of complementary medicine," Dr. Feinberg said coldly.

I could tell that Mom was put off by that, but I thought his use of the term "complementary" was quite generous—as if Mom's herbs could actually enrich the effectiveness of surgery and radiation, or balance it out like a fine wine pairing.

"I truly appreciate all the time you've given me, and I know you believe that your way is the only way, but there *are* about 350 different ways of curing people," she said with authority.

Dr. Feinberg couldn't hold himself back any longer. "You're misguided if you think alternative methods can help you. Those charlatans are just after your money."

The more anyone told Mom what to do, the more resolute she became. And I also don't think it helped that many of the doctors we were seeing were high-achieving, confident Jewish men—just her type. Mom had been butting up against them her entire life.

As we walked to the car, I tried to engage her in what I thought was relatively good news. Dr. Feinberg believed it was only first stage.

"Please, darling, I don't want to discuss it right now."

I backed off. I could see she was feeling overwhelmed. I recognized the same deer-in-headlights look on her face as she had when we'd left Dr. Gryfe's office.

Within a few hours her mood would swing like a weather vane and she'd be back to reading her new books, feeling hopeful and happy again. But in that moment she turned to me and said, in a tight, thin voice, "I'm more scared than I've ever been in my whole life."

4

BE TRUE TO SELF

"Unleash your Silver Fox!" In mid-November the evite to Mom's book launch arrived in my inbox. "If you are a woman over 50," the copy read, "*Silver Fox* is your portable guide to personal power, spiritual growth, and the best sexual love of your life." *Cringe.*

A couple of weeks later we gathered at Magpie, Mom's favourite Queen West boutique. She'd become friendly with its two owner-designers, whose experimental clothes were more like performance pieces: hand-dyed leather jackets with fringes, raw-edged jeans with antique zippers, dresses that looked as though they were made of crumpled newspaper. Their creations were radical, wild, and one-of-a-kind. Just like Mom.

When I arrived, the place was packed with attractive, stylish, sophisticated women of a certain age (Teddy, Josh, and Mom's boyfriend, David, might've been the only men in attendance). People were drinking wine and mingling among the shop's outlandishly dressed mannequins. Like a disco ball, Mom was the centre of attention, sparkling in her new silver sequinned motorcycle jacket. She dubbed it her "Silver Fox" jacket.

Mom was holding court, greeting friends and signing copies of her book. As soon as she saw me her face lit up. "Rachie!" she squealed, opening her arms. I gave her a big hug, and she inscribed a copy of her book for me (she always signed off *Love, E./Mom*—a subtle reminder that even though she was my mother, she was always Elaine first). I let her get back to her fans and looked down at the cover, which featured a photo of her sitting against a tree surrounded by tall grass, holding up a glass of white wine. It was so Mom.

I flipped to the table of contents. Chapters included "Your Life as Story," "Writing from a Dream," "Affordable Luxury," "New Aging," "Fear & Risk," "Getting Over a Broken Heart," "What I Call Spirituality," "Letting Go," and "Lovely Lust."

I braced myself as I continued to the preface.

"I want to share my transformation from 'ugly duckling' into Silver Fox," Mom began. "It took me from puberty to post-menopause to come into my own as a confident woman. Now, in my sixties, I find I am sought after.

"Even the term 'Silver Fox' is most often associated with men rather than women," she wrote. "Older men are still considered sexy, and are supported in their natural desire to find sexual partners. Older women are given different messages."

Mom was taking the label for herself! She was going to redefine it.

"Who is a female Silver Fox, you may ask? A Silver Fox has lived long enough to have ripened into her sleek and silver self. She is ready to live and love fiercely and fearlessly. She is in her prime because she knows who she is, knows what she has to give, and knows how to give it."

The book—filled with tips, writing exercises, and excerpts from her own journals—was all about teaching "women of a superior age" how to reclaim their strength and magnetism by journaling. "It's simply the best tool for learning the foxtrot of love," Mom wrote.

"I will guide you on an expedition that I have been on for much of my life—the search for the self through journaling. The more we become our true selves, the more we become irresistible. Putting down real thoughts and feelings, reading those thoughts and feelings, listening to our words, honouring the unvarnished truth—journaling in this way leads to love and compassion for self and other. Our words lay down a trail to success, in love and in life."

I never made it past the introduction. I was very proud of her, but I wasn't really her demographic. And honestly, I wasn't interested in reading about the details of my mom's love life.

SILVER FOX AROSE from Mom's experience as a lifelong journaler and teacher of journaling. For more than twenty years she'd been leading a women's writing group at a local community arts school. I wasn't exactly sure what went on in their weekly get-togethers ("Whatever happens in the circle stays in the circle"), but from what I'd gleaned, there was a lot of laughing and crying. Mom was known for her ability to create an environment where everyone felt safe to write down their deepest sorrows, regrets, anger, and fears, their most severe self-doubts and litanies of self-judgment. She empowered her fellow women to honour and accept their pain, not as a burden but rather as an important part of their personal history.

Mom's energy and enthusiasm for teaching was legendary. She lit a spark of creativity in people and made everyone feel as though their story was worth telling. When Mom shone her light on you, you felt lifted up and seen. It's no surprise that the women in her life held her in such high esteem. So many of them credited her with helping them truly accept themselves, warts and all. Mom was their role model for how to live life with integrity and courage. Even that night at the party one of Mom's friends cornered me to say, "I've learned so much from her as a teacher, and more importantly, as a human."

Mom didn't believe in enlightenment, at least not as an absolute. She didn't believe in reincarnation. She didn't believe there was a god who had her in mind. What Mom truly believed was that everyone has a story—a personal narrative that's constantly replayed and revised—and that awareness of it could lessen suffering.

"We write to uncover our truest selves, but in the telling, we are also able to create the person we want to be," she wrote. "As we write our journals, we revise our life scripts. We shape sentences to reshape ourselves."

Mom said she had a desperate need to journal to free herself from family conditioning—those limiting beliefs, protective habits, and defensive behaviours she developed early in life. And so she was constantly writing in her journals. They looked more like scrapbooks: a mix of classic diary entries, positive affirmations, inspirational quotes, stated intentions, letters to herself, unsent letters to others, and *New Yorker* cartoons.

MOM AND HER little sister, Barbara, grew up above their father's store, Mitchell's Menswear, in North Toronto. Their dad, Benny, was a Communist Jew who'd come from Poland as a teenager knowing only a few practical words in English ("Me shorten, me lengthen") and managed to become a successful fine tailor. Their mom, Frimmy, had grown up in a large Orthodox Jewish family in Winnipeg during the Great Depression. She was a devoted wife and stay-at-home mother.

For the most part, Mom adored her parents. They were responsible, kind, and generous. And they were nothing but incredibly loving grandparents. But as I got older, Mom filled me in on some of her lingering issues with them: Benny had been emotionally distant, and Frimmy had looked to Mom to mother *her*. She explained how she was named after both her parents' mothers (Eta and Ruchel became Elaine Ruth), whom they each cherished but never got enough from.

Mom told me that, growing up, she never felt cared for as a separate person. One of her earliest memories was dropping her mother's hand to explore a park when she was three, and her mother freaking out. "She'd been abandoned by the early death of her mother," Mom explained. "She continually let me know that I was a selfish 'cold potato' if I didn't attend to *her* needs."

Mom had always been a voracious reader, a fine means of escape from her voracious mother. Her nose perpetually in a book, even at the dinner table, she was the only kid given an adult membership to her local public library because she'd read all the books in the children's section. "When I wasn't reading I was writing novels, all imitations of *Anne of Green Gables*, all starring smart feisty orphan girls," Mom told me with a laugh.

She'd kept a journal since the age of nine, and she let me read her childhood diaries. Even back then she was working on personal development. She'd keep track of her positive and negative character traits ("courageous" and "lazy") and cut and paste articles from the newspaper, like one titled "Ten Teenager T's: Recipe for Personal Growth." She underlined "Be True To Self."

Mom claimed that before she got co-opted into being "nice," she wasn't afraid of anything. She climbed tall trees and scaled a seventy-foot bridge with her lunch bag in her teeth. When she was eleven she wrote a novel called *Prim and Unproper*. Mom identified with Jo March from *Little Women*; she, too, wanted to decide her own fate. Her mother had been a gifted dancer but was told by her older sister that she couldn't join a chorus line because "nice Jewish girls don't do that."

Mom would watch her mother ask her father for spending money, like a child asking for allowance, and think to herself that she'd never be dependent on a man.

At age twelve, Mom wrote a letter in her Nancy Drew diary to her future self.

Dear twenty-two,

Have you had a book published? Have you graduated from 'u'? Have you gone on a trip to Europe? Do you still climb, run, and get into mischief? Are you pretty? Are you happy, joyous, thrilled? Do you still steal in those wonderful minutes before you sleep for daydreams? I can hardly wait to be you, 22.

Your foolish,
Old self

P.S. Have you met Teddy?

I'd seen it with my own eyes: Mom's prophesy written in her twelve-year-old cursive. It was as though she had the magical power to manifest her own future husband.

Mom often fantasized about a "tall, dark, handsome hero" she called King Teddy (I believe she was inspired by Lucy Maud Montgomery's Emily trilogy, which featured a boy with that name). In her stories she mostly loved him but sometimes bitterly hated him. On occasion she'd replace him with a new version of Teddy. Her fantasies always ended with a kiss.

Mom said that self-esteem came slow and late to her life. She was confident until adolescence, and then she lost herself. "In high school I was a nerd who edited the yearbook and watched only depressing foreign films. I protected my weak inner self with intellectual pretensions." Friends remembered her as being beautiful and confident, but she recalls feeling so insecure. "I had no centre," she told me. It didn't help that her parents made her go to a different high school from her best friends because they wanted her to make friends with Jewish kids. Her parents weren't religious, but considering the times, I suppose they had an anxious sense of tribalism based on legitimate fear.

As a teenager, Mom called herself an anarchist, wore a peace button, and donned a red wool poncho she'd bought at the Village Weaver shop downtown. She told me how her father had remarked, "No nice Jewish boy will ever marry you if you wear that." But Mom had other priorities. Sure, she wanted to fall in love, but above all she wanted to have adventures. She vowed not to marry until at least twenty-five, believing that all adventures ended once you became a wife.

And adventures she did have. The first time she lived abroad it was to get away from her overprotective parents. After studying English and Russian literature at the University of Toronto, she sailed to London in 1966 to teach for a year. She'd always felt confident when it came to teaching. Her next departure, to Israel two years later, was to flee the looming inevitability of marriage. When she returned in her late twenties, she felt more grown up and was ready to settle down.

And that's when she actually met Teddy. A friend had set her up on a blind date with my dad, then a successful Jewish lawyer and activist. They fell in love, were engaged within a year, and after taking turns having cold feet, took the plunge in the summer of 1972. Mom said she was high on Valium and that Teddy was smashed on Harvey Wallbangers. I suppose they needed a little help getting down the aisle.

In one early diary entry Mom acknowledged how much her fantasy life meant to her as a child. At thirteen she wrote, "Mommy seems to think that my imagining sprees are silly and a waste of time. I most positively don't. It makes life so much more interesting and richer. And besides, I look forward to building castles in the air, so I go to bed at a reasonable time. Mommy should be glad of that." Seeing her at her book launch, I couldn't help thinking just how far those sprees had taken her. Fantasy wasn't only a means of escape from her overbearing mother; it was also a way of manifesting the reality she wanted. Journaling had turned her into the confident, self-possessed woman she was today. She had written herself into a Silver Fox.

BY EARLY DECEMBER Mom was still open to the smaller surgery, but she wasn't prepared to proceed until she had clear evidence that it was cancer. That may have been another stalling tactic, but Teddy called her bluff and arranged for his beloved gastroenterologist to perform a biopsy. He'd gone to Dr. Habal for several colonoscopies over the years. Unlike Mom, Teddy loved doctors—they made him feel safe and secure. He was always getting some part of his body scoped out.

Mom agreed to the minor procedure, and Dr. Habal was able to successfully remove a sample of her tumour. Teddy held her hand tightly as they awaited the results.

"Half the polyp has cancer cells," Dr. Habal informed her.

"Only fifty percent?" Mom replied.

"What does it matter? Fifty percent, twenty percent, ten percent . . . You need to get surgery to remove it," said Dr. Habal.

"But my blood count went down from 10 to 6.7," she said. "Doesn't that mean anything?"

"I'm sorry, but it actually doesn't. You could have a 2 and still have cancer."

Teddy and I weren't at all surprised by the results—if anything we were somewhat relieved. Mom could no longer question whether she really had cancer. There was irrefutable proof. Surely she'd quit stalling now.

A few days later I got a call from Teddy. "Your mother is as stubborn as a mule!" He said Mom told him she wasn't going to do surgery. Instead she wanted to continue with her own methods of healing indefinitely.

Oh, hell no. I went over to Mom's place to talk to her in person.

It was December, and her radiators were already on at full blast. Mom always liked to be cozy and toasty warm. We used to joke that she kept her place so overheated that the room-temperature water was boiling. We sat down in the sunroom.

"It's true. I have come to a decision," she said, sitting upright on her white armchair. "I'm not doing surgery or *anything* the doctors are offering me."

I stared at her in disbelief.

"I've had several months to read, talk to people, and think," she said slowly, as though presenting the closing arguments of a hard-fought court case. "I know I'm taking a risk in going off-road. But there's statistical evidence that I'll die if I go the conventional route."

"There's *statistical evidence* that you'll die if you don't get surgery," I shot back.

"I believe I have a better chance of a cure, and a better quality of life, if I do things *my way* than I would with the pseudo-certain offerings of Western medicine."

I looked at the white satin pillow she kept on the opposite couch. It had a silkscreen image of a woman riding a motorcycle and the words NOTHING COULD STOP HER. SHE WAS PASSIONATE. AND MADLY IN LOVE.

"I'm requesting that you all respect and support my decision," Mom said firmly.

It was one thing for her to stall, but now she was outright refusing treatment. Would she really continue to waste time experimenting with herbs, all the while letting her cancer grow?

"How do you think you'll cure yourself of cancer *without* surgery?" I asked.

"By building up my immune system and outsmarting it. I've read hundreds of personal stories by people who are alive twenty years after they were told to go home and die. People say it's a miracle when it happens. 'Wow, we can't find any!' This happens over and over again."

Facts were never Mom's strong suit. Part of what made her such a great storyteller was that she took a few liberties with the truth. She never made stuff up, at least not intentionally, but she'd embellish details for dramatic effect. "Josh liberated the bunny from the cage at preschool when he was only *three*," she'd say (when really he was five), or "Teddy was smashed on *fourteen* Harvey Wallbangers" (the number was never consistent). Although sometimes I had to wonder where her line between exaggeration and fantasy lay. She had this one story about how she would regularly bake us muffins when we were little. "They were chock full of healthy stuff, and then I'd throw in a ton of chocolate chips or blueberries," Mom would recall. "They were delicious!" But no one else had any memory of this. I remember her *talking about* these healthy muffins she wanted to make (and to be fair, I think she did make a batch or two when I was a teenager). Our lack of recall annoyed her deeply. From Mom's perspective, we had all ungratefully forgotten what an accomplished baker she was. "The muffins" became a loaded symbol of how our family memories differed. But this was no longer a matter of muffins. Mom's alternative facts now had dangerous consequences.

"But is there any *evidence*?" I challenged. I wasn't interested in Mom outsmarting her cancer with asparagus.

"Yeah! People have gotten better!"

"You think your cancer will just spontaneously disappear?"

"I don't think I'll have a spontaneous remission. Mine will be a long, hard-fought remission that I'll win for myself."

"Why can't you let the doctors help you?"

"I'm confident that I can pick and choose what's best for me." She huffed. "I've had enough of being held hostage by these doctors."

"The only thing you're being held hostage by is your beliefs!" I huffed back. My forehead was sweating. I wasn't sure if it was from my anger boiling over or the radiators being on full blast. "Why are you doing this?" I asked, my voice straining.

Mom paused before speaking. "I have to stay true to who I am."

Huh? I had hippie friends who were big believers in natural and holistic medicine and even they wouldn't reject conventional treatment if it were absolutely necessary.

Mom spoke again in a level tone, sad and serene. "I know I'll get well as long as I don't abandon myself."

"Please! Think about—"

"I've made my decision," she said, her demeanour quickly toughening up. "And I don't want to discuss it with you."

5

THE HABITAT OF POLLUTION

could see how this was going to play out. Chess is all about visualization and anticipation. Faced with an attack, you must evaluate the threat, sift through your available options, and find the best possible move to defend yourself. It all comes down to the decisions you make based on the number of moves you can see ahead. And if you forecast well, not only can you see the future, you can control it.

But it was as if Mom were looking at a completely different board—as if the doctors were telling her there wasn't much they could do to help her, as if she were bravely taking a chance to live the life she wanted instead of submitting to a hellish endgame. I totally would've accepted her choice to forgo medical intervention *if* she had late-stage cancer. I understand why people with a terminal diagnosis would choose to enjoy whatever time they have left rather than endure harsh treatments that may or may not extend their life. But that wasn't at all Mom's situation.

It's not like I even fundamentally disagreed with everything she was saying. I wouldn't be surprised if one day it were proven scientific knowledge that our own immune systems were the key to curing cancer. But the clock was ticking. Mom didn't have all the time in the world to experiment with herbs and health food. This wasn't *Lorenzo's Oil*.

Every time we got together I'd challenge her. "What about doing both?" I proposed over zucchini-noodle pad thai at Rawlicious in Yorkville. "Your way *and* surgery?" Mom and I were now meeting up at raw food restaurants instead of our usual French bistros.

"I'm *not* getting surgery," Mom said, opening her little suede pouch that held Michael's herbal tincture. "Outsmarting cancer is much better than hammering away at it with brutal, barbaric protocols," she insisted, bringing the glass dropper to her mouth.

"But is there any evidence that alternative treatments can cure rectal cancer specifically?"

Mom raised her finger as she held the tincture in her mouth. My frustration flared as I waited.

"It doesn't matter what kind of cancer it is. You treat the *whole* body," she explained after swallowing. "If you don't change the terrain, it can come back. My body, spirit, and mind were a host for cancer. Surgery would only remove the visible evidence of a diseased terrain. It's better for me to clear the habitat of pollution."

Mom was hardly touching her nut loaf wrapped in a collard leaf. I could tell that the foodie in her wasn't so pleased with her new pollution-clearing diet.

I challenged her further. "The doctor acknowledged that it's possible for certain brain cancer lymphoma to shrink, but he's certain that a rectal mass cannot regress."

"It doesn't have to regress the way *I* do things. It's not about it regressing." Just when I'd think I had her cornered, she'd slither out of my grasp.

"Then how does it go away?" I asked, barely containing my incredulity.

"It melts, kind of. It becomes regular cells, or it dies. It doesn't have to go backward, it can just get picked up by healthy cells. It just has to be cleaned up. Vacuumed or whatever."

Vacuumed or whatever?! I stabbed my chopsticks into my "noodles" and shot her a stern look.

"I'm not thinking I'm going to convince you," Mom said in a sing-song tone. "You just have to hang out with uncertainty, as I do, if you want to continue hanging out with me."

What did she mean, IF I want to keep hanging out with her?

AT WORK I was busy navigating another person's warped perspective. Jian had his own version of reality, and he expected everyone on the team to go along with it. He'd stick to our scripts almost verbatim—more than any other CBC host did—and yet he'd take public credit for introductions and questions he hadn't written. In the Q&As that followed our live audience shows, when fans would ask him how the show was made he'd say that producers merely helped him out with "research packs." (We secretly dubbed those sessions "Q&Ls": Questions and Lies.) He'd talk about how he was especially proud of "his" trademark opening monologues, except he didn't write those either (his contribution amounted to adding a cheesy rhyme at the end). He'd say on air that interviews and performances were "live in Studio Q" when often they'd been edited and pre-recorded days earlier. It was important to him that listeners thought the show was always live; he'd even pretend to say goodbye to guests who'd left the studio days earlier just to keep up the ruse, and would get angry if anyone tweeted about a guest or segment that wasn't in step with his manufactured timeline.

We had to play house, too. If a journalist was following him for a profile, he'd suddenly show up at our story meeting and act as though he regularly contributed ideas (when in actuality he'd go off to the gym while we were crafting the stories he'd later take credit for).

Jian would occasionally explode and berate us, but most of the time he worked in more covert ways to distort our reality and impose his own, wielding his cruelty in subtle, passive-aggressive ways that kept our minds constantly spinning. If he was upset with you because an interview didn't go well, he might give you the silent treatment for days or skip over your nickname in the show's credits (his way of signalling that you were in his bad books). He'd hold producers hostage at our desks for hours as we'd wait around at the end of the day until he was ready for our script consultations. If I dared to tell him I had to get going after working a full day, he'd question my dedication: "Other producers don't need to leave *early*."

He'd keep our guests waiting, too—a Bobby Fischer–like power play to get the upper hand (he'd make them sweat for a while before sauntering in like a movie star). When we had Gloria Steinem on the show, I had to keep her occupied for about twenty minutes while we waited for him to arrive. Although I was thrilled to be hanging out with one of my sheroes, I spent the whole conversation worrying that Jian wouldn't show up. After the interview, Jian asked me how I thought it went.

"She was great!" I replied.

"No, not *her*. How was I?"

Another time, a few minutes before a scheduled interview, he said he'd been in a car accident and wasn't going to make it on time. His prank calls always ended with him walking into the office, still on the phone, laughing at us. Always unpredictable, he kept us all off-balance and disoriented.

If one of us exhibited any excitement about a particular guest, he'd charm or flirt with them all the more, as if to win them away from us or make us jealous. Or later he'd brag about how he'd hung out with them. When he saw a toy we liked, he took it. *That's my truck!* After Woody Harrelson showed more interest in playing chess with me than in talking to him, Jian declared himself to be a chess player on the show (even though he barely knew how to move the pieces). For a second I wondered if he was stealing my identity to mess with me, but then I felt crazy for even considering such a possibility.

We were always walking on eggshells. As soon as we heard the jingle-jangle of the keychain on his hip as he strolled into the office mere minutes before showtime, we'd all tense up. "Good morning, Jian!" we'd say, like a bunch of animatronic Disney creatures who'd just had our power switch flipped on.

Jian boasted that he had "the best team in the business," but it felt like he resented our very existence. He needed us, yet I think we were a constant reminder that he didn't write his own words, that he wasn't who he purported to be. So he tried to render us invisible, excluding our names from the show's website or ignoring us at events. It was as if Jian needed to poach aspects of his producers' identities to create a hologram of a self. He would often take perspectives we'd shared in casual conversation and pass them off as his own during interviews. Our job was to write in "his voice." But we had created that voice. It was a blend of Sean's poignant and empathetic daily essays, Brian's impeccable taste in indie music, my ideas on feminist pop culture and queer identity. The show's many producers wrote in the voice of a fictional character, a composite of who *we* were.

Jian was a brilliant chameleon. The only difference between him and a professional actor was that he didn't draw a line between his on-air and off-air persona. He believed he was the entity we'd created. And he was so believable (the way he stuttered to make our words sound off the cuff, the way he mirrored guests' emotional states to foster a sense of intimacy) that listeners didn't understand it was a performance. The country loved him. People were always complimenting Jian to me. "He's so talented," they'd say. I'd clench my teeth and muster a smile. "He's very good at what he does," I'd reply. It was the truth. He was the best imposter in the business.

IT WAS BECOMING increasingly difficult to hang on to my sense of self. My voice was at once being stolen at work and actively rejected by Mom. Through Mom's lens, I was a one-sided, closed-minded disciple of Western medicine, just like Teddy.

"We have different belief systems. You *completely* subscribe to Western medicine," Mom said to me. "You have *complete* faith in it."

"No, I don't. I'm a hippie at heart!" I protested, reminding her, "I'm the one who took a homeopathic remedy instead of malaria pills when I went to India." In our days travelling around India and Nepal, Syd and I had swallowed little white pellets of something called China Rubra. Granted, I wouldn't do that *now*. My teenage anti-vaxxer days were well behind me. In my old age I'd come around to the realization that Tylenol works better for a headache than peppermint oil and that hair is not, in fact, "self-cleaning." Mom saying that I subscribed to any dominant system of power was laughable to me. Sure, maybe compared with her I was straight and narrow, but I was *actually* queer! I'd quit school! I'd even worked at a feminist sex-toy store in my twenties. Nobody in my life had *ever* accused me of being status quo. And now Mom was looking at me as if I were Alex P. Keaton just because I believed in science.

Mom wasn't listening. "We're butting faiths," she said, shaking her head.

"I don't have faith," I said. "I have evidence!" (In the words of Fran Lebowitz, "I don't believe in anything you have to believe in.")

"I believe that belief is hugely important," Mom said. "Many surgeons won't take patients who believe they'll die. They just won't take them into surgery."

"I'm sure the doctors can successfully remove your tumour whether you believe it or not," I snapped back.

"I don't believe in their way, so I'm not doing it. I have no faith that it will work out well for me. And I do believe that there are *lots* of other ways of doing things."

"What other ways? Herbs? Antioxidants?"

"I believe in my immune system the way other people believe in God."

"EXACTLY!"

Mom smirked, yielding a smile. "Listen, if I had faith in Western medicine I would endure its hazards. I wish I could believe in it. But I don't."

"But here's the thing," I said. "You don't *have to* believe in it. It's not Santa Claus!"

It was utterly baffling. The Mom I knew was never this irrational, fanatical, and closed-minded. Every argument came back to her belief in the power of belief. Mom's steel-barrier defence. The next time I was at her place I noticed she'd put up a shabby chic chalkboard in the kitchen and written on it in cursive *If you can change your beliefs, you can change your life.*

BY DECEMBER JOSH had been sworn in as a Toronto city councillor, and things were already intense. He was busy trying to get important work done in his community while mitigating the damage being caused by our new right-wing populist mayor, Rob Ford (later to become internationally known as Toronto's "crack mayor").

Josh and I hadn't had an opportunity to seriously talk about Mom's situation. "She's not seeing the situation clearly," I told him over the phone. "It's ridiculous the things she's saying. She doesn't want to get surgery to remove her cancer because she's afraid of getting an infection."

"But there's merit to many of the things she's saying," Josh said. "Chemo *is* poison."

"Sure, but she doesn't have to do it. Chemo isn't even being advised right now."

I asked him to tell Mom she needed to get surgery, but he was adamant: he wasn't going to argue with her. Josh tried to reassure me that he was doing his best to gently guide her toward other perspectives, though he admitted he hadn't had much luck.

"When we talk, I feel like I'm talking to someone who's been conditioned into a cult. Mom goes into these long monologues about how she's doing the right thing. It's not really a conversation," he said.

"Totally! I feel that way too. It's almost as if she's trying to convince *herself* more than others."

Josh was sympathetic to my fears and frustrations, but he didn't seem all that fussed. He just accepted that this was the way Mom was and that he wasn't going to be able to change her mind. He told me, calm and level, "Mom's on her own journey."

I wanted so badly for Josh to be just as distressed and outraged as I was. I knew it wasn't easy to go up against Mom, but I believed we had a responsibility to fight for her. That if you see a beloved family member hurting herself, it's your moral duty to intervene. This wasn't a time for calm diplomacy. I was sounding a call to arms; Josh was being Switzerland.

Teddy was my only ally. He was afraid of telling Mom what to do, but he'd since reached the verdict that enough was enough. He wrote her a letter.

Dear Elaine,

I am sending this message to you after much thought and hesitation. I know that you won't like it but I decided to send it anyway. It may be the most important message that I ever send, and the most important one that you ever receive.

As you know, I have felt very uneasy about your decision not to undergo radiation, surgery, and chemotherapy as Drs. Gryfe, Feinberg, and Habal have recommended to you. I listened to your reasons for wanting to choose alternative treatments instead, and I heard your appeal that we respect your decision and support you no matter what your decision may be.

I have, until now, tried to comply with your requests. I now have come to the conclusion that I cannot and should not, in good conscience, comply with them. I'll try to explain why.

I met with three doctor friends today and had private discussions with them. Each one is a leader in his field and highly respected. Their responses were almost identical. Without revealing your identity, I described what is going on "with my friend." They were in agreement that your decision was a bad one and, as Dr. Gryfe emphatically told you, would inevitably lead to a slow and painful death. They repeated what is obvious to most people, namely, that cancer has the potential to spread and destroy a person's body, and has to be removed as quickly as possible.

Although you are symptom-free now, the symptoms, and the horrible pain, will certainly soon begin and, when they do, your life will become awful. They agreed, acknowledging that they haven't examined you or seen your medical records, that if you undergo conventional treatment you have a high likelihood of obtaining an excellent outcome and being able to continue enjoying a pain-free, meaningful, and active life for a significant number of years.

Alternative treatments, no matter what you read or think, will not help you survive. They conjectured, I add, that you must be in a state of denial not to appreciate this and probably would benefit from psychiatric intervention.

I agree with these views and, because I do, I cannot stand by and watch you commit suicide in the most ghastly way possible. I recognize that you have the right to make the final decision, but I have a moral responsibility to you and our children to do what I can to save your life. If it were in my power to have the final decision taken away from you, I would willingly do so.

As difficult as it may be for you to understand why I have decided to send you this message, and thereby jeopardize our relationship, please try to understand why I am doing this. I love you as the mother of my children. I don't want you to needlessly die a slow and painful death, and I don't want anyone, especially our children, to witness what will inevitably happen to you and then lose you forever.

As well, I don't want you to regret your decision when the pain starts and when you may find that it is too late for the doctors to save your life. Please come to your senses and make the only decision that will allow you to avoid the horrors that you will otherwise face, and please do what you reasonably can to prolong your life. You mean a lot to many people who love you and would miss you.

I hope that you will not be angry with me for sending this to you. I considered that there was a risk and decided it is one that I had to take before it was too late.

Ted

Mom read his letter and promptly told him to butt out. But I know it hit a nerve. Later, whenever his letter came up in conversation, she'd scoff, roll her eyes, and mock him: "Am I going to commit suicide in the *most ghastly* way possible?"

Dumbfounded, Teddy and I regrouped. We talked on the phone a lot, desperately trying to make sense of why Mom was stalling.

"I think she's afraid of having a colostomy bag," Teddy said.

The chances of it becoming a permanent situation were low, and yet it was obviously her most articulated fear. Mom kept saying, "The operation will leave me with a colostomy bag for the rest of my life!"

I agreed with Teddy: "Yeah, I don't think a colostomy bag jives with her self-image. It's not her style." Mom prided herself on being a beautiful "ageless" woman. She'd just published her dating guide and was planning on teaching workshops based on it. I could see how her life might seem impossible if she didn't feel attractive. A fecal sac wouldn't go with her new custom-made Silver Fox jacket. Being a patient in general didn't align with her sense of self. She looked at other patients in the hospital as if they were passive casualties of "the system" who'd given up their rights and freedoms. "Once you give yourself over, it's difficult to remain a decision-making participant," Mom told me. "They go to work on you."

Mom obliged me by meeting up for coffee with a friend of a friend who'd survived colon cancer, and another time by checking out a colorectal cancer support group with me. Afterward she called them all "Kool-Aid drinkers."

"There is a cancer industry, and we've all bought into it," she said. "Most of us, anyhow."

I knew there had to be some deeper psychology beneath her resistance. Could this really come down her being afraid of a colostomy bag? Even if she were so unlucky, would she really choose death over having to live with one? What on earth would drive her to seize upon alternative cures—and by extension an alternative reality—to such an extreme extent? How does a person end up courting the very thing they fear most? As a producer at *Q*, my job was to figure out who people were behind their celebrity facade: what motivated them, what made them tick. But I couldn't figure out my own mother. She was proving to be the toughest nut to crack.

AT THE END OF December, six months after she'd been diagnosed, we were sitting in our usual spots in the sunroom when I started in yet again. "Cancer multiplies and multiplies. I don't understand how you think your methods can contain that."

"Let's leave it. I know it's not going to be a walk in the park. I know I'll have to be more disciplined than I've ever been in my life. I won't enjoy it. But I do think I have a better chance."

"You really believe you have a *better* chance?" I was straining to reach her. My whole body was convulsing with disbelief.

"Even if it were equal, even if it were fifty-fifty, why wouldn't I do it my way, which allows me to have the life I want?"

"*If* it were fifty-fifty," I scoffed.

"It's a big risk either way. I actually believe I have *more* than a fifty percent chance doing it my way," Mom said.

I couldn't let her believe her fiction. She could write herself into a Silver Fox; she could write her way to self-confidence and a life of adventure; she could even write her way to a man named Teddy. But she couldn't write herself out of cancer. Cancer doesn't give a shit what story you tell it.

"You have a ZERO percent chance doing it your way!" I shouted. "You won't have ANY life, never mind the one you want!"

"I've made my decision and I don't want to discuss it with you." *There it was.*

Mom got up from her chair and walked away. I followed her down the hallway into the dining room. "You can't keep shutting down the conversation," I hollered.

She turned around. "You're bullying me! I won't be able to be around you if you continue to push. It would hurt me terribly to stop seeing you. I really don't want that to happen. But I can't be around people who are fear-based. You are causing me harm."

"Who told you that? *Michael?*" I asked, treating his name like some supervillain's. The sheepish look on Mom's face told me I was correct.

"I love you, darling, but we can't be together if you continue to bring me down with your negativity. It would break my heart, and I *need* my heart in this challenge," Mom cried. Her eyes looked sadder than I'd ever seen them.

I was beyond frustrated that I couldn't reach her. I wanted her to come back. But above all, I was terrified that she was going to die. I couldn't bury *my* anxiety any longer. I clenched my fists and screamed at her: "YOU'RE TAKING AWAY MY MOTHER!"

Mom just stood there, stunned. I could tell that my words hit her hard; her eyes were glossy with tears. I knew she could see that I was suffering. She didn't want to hurt me, but she was still going to live her life the way she always had: on her own terms.

6

CHICKEN LITTLE

I was hurt that Mom would threaten to cut me out of her life, but more than that I was astonished. The Mom I knew would never have considered such a savage move. I tried not to take it personally. It was classic cult-like behaviour. I suppose in her eyes I was something of a Suppressive Person.

I resented that Mom was strong-arming me into submission, but I could also see that our constant fighting was destructive. It definitely wasn't helping the situation. It was a new year, and I would need a new strategy anyway. So I agreed to stop arguing with her.

In fairness, Mom said I could still talk to her about her cancer as it related to *my own* feelings and not what I thought she should do. She still wanted to be there for me as my mom—which I appreciated—but her caveat didn't work out so well in practice. I'd inevitably end up saying something like, "*I'm afraid* . . . that you're killing yourself." Then, as predictable as a pull-string doll, Mom would deliver her stock refrain: "I've made my decision and I don't want to talk about it."

For the most part I managed to keep my mouth shut. But I couldn't help speaking up once in a while when she'd say something egregiously untrue, like when I'd hear her insist that "rectal cancer is one of the worst types of cancer, even worse than pancreatic!" Her father had died of pancreatic cancer (as did Patrick Swayze, RIP) so I was aware that it was the deadliest of all. "That's not true," I'd say, and leave it there.

Teddy also agreed to stop telling Mom what to do. In early January, he wrote her a follow-up note.

Dear Elaine,

I am truly sorry for any grief that my earlier message caused. I sent it because I am very concerned about you and it was important to me to do whatever I could think of to "rescue" you. Once I sent it I was able to relax a bit, and I could actually feel some of the tension in my body dissipate.

I now promise you that I won't say another word to you about your options. I won't actively support what I think your present inclination is, but I will remain silent about it when I'm with you. I will, however, do whatever you permit me to do to help you get through this period and return to good health.

If you wish, I can begin by trying to connect your hard drive any morning next week but Monday.

Happy 2011.
Ted

I'D PROMISED TO stop fighting *with* Mom, but that didn't mean I'd stop fighting *for* her. My new plan was to get through to Mom's friends in the hope they could talk some sense into her. I wanted them to know the facts of the situation. I knew they'd been hearing only her side of the story. At every doctor's visit I'd diligently record all the precise statistics and time frames, but as soon as we'd leave Mom would reach for one of her trusted—and untrue—claims:

"The surgery is *incredibly dangerous* and there are no guarantees it will help me."

"I'll be left with a colostomy bag for *the rest of my life.*"

"I'll be subjected to chemotherapy *for sure* and there's a high probability the cancer will return anyway, and by then my immune system will be *shot.*"

I took the opportunity to suss out David's thoughts when Mom and I were over at his house for dinner one evening. David had the looks of Alan Alda and the pretenses of Indiana Jones. He worked in provincial politics and was always scheming up renegade power plays. "Authority is guilty until proven innocent," he once said. It was obvious that he adored my mom. They shared a love for fine wine, travel, and subverting the system.

David and I got along well, too. The three of us would sometimes hang out together, eating good food and trading tales of our respective adventures. I especially enjoyed going over to his house for red meat and red wine. David cooked up delicious steaks on the barbecue and had a cellar full of exquisite vintages. Like Mom, he was into affordable luxuries. He was very proud of the fact that he only ever bought used Jeeps but drank like a millionaire.

While Mom was setting the table, I approached David on the back porch. I was hoping he could be an ally, but it quickly became clear that he was choosing to support her. He seemed to have just as much contempt for the doctors as she did. "Feinberg's office is a crackpot operation!" he said, flipping a portobello mushroom on the grill for Mom. "You can't trust the medical system."

I was surprised he was being so one-sided. "But do you really think Mom's herbs are going to cure her?" I asked.

"The herbs act *just like* chemotherapy!" he said, his finger hitting the air like a drumstick on the words "just like."

"What do you mean?" I was trying hard to contain my disbelief.

"The compound Michael makes for your mom is made from the *exact same* herbs they make chemo from," he said, once again hitting the words "exact same" with his pointer finger.

I was shocked. *As if* chemo is made from lemon balm, peppermint, and marsh mallow.

I understood why David needed to stand by Mom—it wouldn't be easy to remain together if he didn't—but I was amazed by how much he really seemed to believe in what she was doing. He was drinking the herbal Kool-Aid too. (Literally! Apparently he'd started seeing Michael for his mild arthritis.)

I wrote an email to Lola and Arei, two of Mom's best friends and longtime members of her writing group. I explained that as much as I respected Mom's right to make her own decisions, I didn't think she was fully appreciating what the doctors were telling her. I shared detailed recaps of her appointments, including the exact stats quoted. "I would hate for her to die a painful early death when there's a confident doctor who's offering her a ninety percent chance of being cured," I wrote. "I'm really sorry if you think I'm crossing a line by sending you this note, but at this point, I really don't know what else to do."

Lola wrote me back:

> Your Mum has explained everything you've said to me. The only thing she doesn't seem to agree with is the percentages when it comes to a possible recovery rate. But she is very clear about how she wants

to proceed and ultimately she's the only one who can make the final decision about how to move forward and what the risks are. I can't imagine that she doesn't know the facts and is making the decision in a way that is not fully informed.

I know this isn't what you want to hear from me. But I can understand and appreciate her choice, so I can't lean on her to make a different one. I'm sorry to disappoint you in this way. You are the light of your Mum's life. You need to keep being that for her, even while disagreeing with the path she has chosen. And there is definitely a chance that she's right.

Arei took a similar stance:

I completely support your Mom's need to trust and believe in the method of treatment that she chooses. I also believe that she has tried and continues to try diligently to get the best information that she can about her condition and her options in order to make the most informed decision for herself that she can.

I also want you to know that I, too, am extremely cautious when it comes to conventional medicine, and from personal experiences my greater comfort and success in terms of my health has been with alternative approaches.

Your Mom has worked so hard in her life to be truthful with herself, conscious, and authentic. I have so much respect for what she has accomplished in that regard, and I believe she is bringing that same thoughtful, studied authenticity to her current situation.

If she has, and still chooses to continue on the alternative path she has chosen, I desperately hope that you will be able to respect and support her in it. I think you need one another's love and support more profoundly than I have words to express.

I believe, with all my heart, that you are trying to save your mother's life and I also know that she is trying very hard to do the same.

I loved my Mom's friends, but I was starting to think they were as far out as she was. I suppose alkaline water seeks its own level.

Next I called my aunt Barbara in Victoria, B.C. Her daughter Emily had had mouth cancer when she was just a teenager—it was scary, but she'd survived it after undergoing surgery and radiation. Emily had been in remission ever since, and had just gotten married. So I assumed that my aunt, more than most people, would have an appreciation for the benefits of modern medicine.

I assumed wrong. She sounded just as brainwashed as all of Mom's other Stepford Wives. "Belief is the *most* important thing," she told me in a trancelike voice.

Mom had everyone fooled. She had them convinced that she had carefully considered her options, had weighed the benefits and harms, and was making the best decision based on her so-called belief system. And that *I* was the one letting my fears get the better of *me*. I felt deflated, but I could understand why they'd be hesitant to challenge her: if Mom were willing to cut me off—her beloved child—there was no doubt she'd do it to them.

Reflecting back on their letters, I can also understand why Mom's friends didn't believe she was in denial. Mom was the queen of self-examination. She meditated. She looked at the dark corners of her life. She was aware of her control issues and insecurities, her chronic ambivalence in relationships. Always trying to uncover another layer of truth, she let her writing tell her what she didn't want to hear. She studied her dreams and even underwent cognitive therapy for her chocolate addiction. She'd led consciousness-raising groups for twenty-two years!

Mom had more self-knowledge than anyone we knew—and yet she was in denial. It *was* unbelievable.

They couldn't see—and for a long time, I even didn't see—how Mom coated her denial with a veneer of enlightened thinking. She used the language of patient empowerment to persuade others (and herself) that she was doing the right thing: that she was being an active patient who was staying true to herself and choosing quality of life. How could anyone possibly argue with that? Those were good ways of being! *Feminist* ways of being. What kind of horrible person wouldn't respect a woman's right to choose her own course of treatment? Me, that's who.

AND HER SO-CALLED healers? They were on the payroll. Yet I wondered just how supportive they'd be if they knew the full truth of her situation. With that in mind, I decided to write the most senior member of her militia: Michael.

"I have a great appreciation for alternative methods of healing," I began, "but it pains me to watch my mom totally ignore what modern medicine has to offer. Dr. Feinberg says he's optimistic that her cancer is 'highly curable' with surgery. I'm not sure how experienced you are with treating rectal cancer specifically, but do you really think she has a chance of being cured with herbs and healthy eating alone?"

"Your mother is an intelligent and aware person and perfectly capable of making whatever decisions are right for her," Michael wrote in his reply. "The best thing that you can do is give her your love and support. It's difficult enough for people who have this kind of illness to deal with their own fear and anxiety. The last thing they need is to have to deal with other people's, especially from those who are close to them. The worst prognosis is usually for those who succumb to fear; the best prognosis is for those who have absolute faith in the choices they make, whatever they are. If you really want to help your mother, try your best to keep your personal beliefs out of it."

As if SCIENCE was my PERSONAL BELIEF?

Livid, I googled Michael. He seemed to be big fish in Ontario's herbalism community. He ran his own herbalism school (based on his *own* "unique system"), where he offered a variety of workshops such as "The Spirit of Herbs," "Advanced Spirit of Herbs," and "Applied Spirit of Herbs." An image search revealed a middle-aged white man with silver wire-rimmed glasses and long, wild grey hair (in several photos protruding from a worn red baseball cap). I'd say the look on his face was a "special blend" of insecurity, blind devotion, and "distilled" self-importance.

I clicked on a couple of his YouTube videos. He talked a lot about "the modern medical reductionist paradigm," "the way we were meant to live," and how "healing is about learning to live in harmony with the natural world." But mostly he seemed to like hearing himself talk. I was not impressed. Perhaps he thought being dishevelled communicated his status as an elevated and powerful spiritual healer? I just thought he looked like unmowed grass.

IT WAS MADDENING. It felt like everyone thought *I* was the crazy one, like in an old horror movie when the wrong person gets dragged away to the insane asylum. With Teddy no longer putting up a fight, I was the only one freaking out. I knew in my gut that the situation wasn't good, but Josh still didn't seem bothered, which only added to my growing Chicken Little complex.

"You think it's just a snap reaction to this thing in her life, but she's been going to communes for years," he said. "She's always seen the world from a different place."

"Yes, but this is extremely strange behaviour, *even for her*. In general she's a fairly rational person. But what I'm hearing out of her mouth these days doesn't seem to make any sense."

"It makes sense to her—"

"I know it does. But the scientific facts say otherwise."

"But there are other facts. She sees the world differently."

As we spoke, I felt the maybes start to pile up in my head: *Maybe* Josh was right (Mom had always travelled to the beat of a different drum). *Maybe* I just hadn't perceived how fervent she was before now. *Maybe* I was being a bully. *Maybe* I just needed to trust her. After all, *she* was the parent.

I felt scared and alone. I didn't know what else to do, so I stuffed all my feelings into an internal compression sack and resolved to Move On. On the outside I appeared happy and high functioning—going to my cool job, playing hockey and chess on the weekends—but most days that winter I'd come straight home, plop myself in front of the TV, smoke a joint, and wash down potato chips with too much red wine.

7

A TOUCH OF CANCER

In the spring, I signed a lease on a new apartment. But before I could move in, I had to shack up with Mom for a few weeks. She was a bit apprehensive about the prospect (wanting to be able to do her healing practices in peace), but I promised I wouldn't be a nag. I was tired of sparring with her. For the sake of my sanity, and in order to remain on good terms, I had to chill out. And honestly, after months of feeling scared about her situation and overwhelmed by work, not to mention a recent breakup, I was just looking forward to being "home" for a little while.

The Hemingway had been my permanent address since I was fourteen. I'd continued to stay there off and on over the years—during breaks from university and grad school, and whenever I was between apartments in my twenties. Mom always took care of me there. She'd keep the fridge stocked with gourmet side dishes from Pusateri's Fine Foods—marinated calamari, heirloom bruschetta, tuna salad worth its weight in gold. She'd bring home my favourite caramel truffles from the Belgian Chocolate Shop. Whenever I stayed over, Mom would wake me up in the morning with fancy coffee. She'd add real Mexican vanilla, foam the milk, and shave dark chocolate on top. She may not have been much of a cook, but she was a damn fine barista.

Ironically, it was only as I got older that she became more of the nurturing "Mommy" I'd wanted when I was little. Maybe it was because I wasn't as needy as I was back then. Or perhaps with a decade of meditation workshops and Buddhist retreats under her belt she was able to be more attentive. (She even admitted to having been "asleep at the mommy wheel.") Either way, she made a conscious effort to be more present for me.

When I got a breast reduction in my final year of university, Mom stepped up and took care of me at her place during my recovery. I'd complained to my doctor about having back pain—which was true—but the bigger truth was that I wanted a slender, boyish chest. I'd already chopped off my dreadlocks (thank god), returning to my short-haired boy roots. I was becoming more myself.

For two weeks over my winter break Mom waited on me, bringing an array of artisanal fruit juices to my bedside table. I remember Syd being over one day and doing a double take when she saw Mom serving me a bowl of soup. Syd and I had been good friends since Cherrywood, and she'd never seen Mom perform such a maternal act. It felt really nice to be tended to by her. I appreciated her efforts, even if she was a little late to the party.

One day while I was recovering in bed Mom entered my room with a big smile on her face. "Look what I got you!" she sang, holding out a plush toy dog. I rolled my eyes. *Isn't twenty-two a bit old for stuffed animals?* But my icy heart melted once Mom placed him in my arms. He was pretty darn cute—a Cavalier King Charles Spaniel with white fur and floppy apricot ears. I named him Puppy.

Upon my return to the Hemingway, Puppy was still there on my bed, but the continuity pretty much ended there. My antique childhood desk had been moved into the living room, and in its place stood a large wooden structure that looked like an oversized telephone booth. "That's my new infrared sauna," Mom announced excitedly. "Infrared light is *great* for detoxification!" She explained that every morning she'd sit inside the sauna and read for thirty minutes. "I also drink green tea while I'm in it for greater effect," she said.

I made a concerted effort not to react. I was just there to hang out, watch reruns of *Sex and the City*, and enjoy my morning coffee service. No more fits of anger. My new approach was to simply observe and ask questions—without giving any DVD commentary. *You catch more flies with raw organic mānuka honey, right?* And a part of me thought that maybe if Mom described some of her pie-in-sky cures out loud, she'd hear just how ridiculous they sounded.

I looked around. The kitchen cupboard where Mom normally kept tea was now overflowing with bottles of supplements: IP6, vitamin C, vitamin D, selenium, vitamin E, papaya enzymes, castor oil, probiotics, colloidal silver, random gold-and-green capsules. On the fridge was a card with "Father Zago's secret recipe" for curing cancer: aloe juice, raw honey, and whisky. It sounded like something on the menu at a hipster cocktail bar.

She was now using only chemical-free makeup and household products. She'd bought a negative ion machine to purify the air. Mom was in Full Healer Mode. An extended game of alternative medicine bingo, my first week at the Hemingway played out something like this:

Monday morning
Mom was standing over the kitchen counter, mixing up a bowl of organic cottage cheese and flaxseed oil.

"What's that?" I asked, poking my head over her shoulder.

"It's the Budwig diet!" She continued to stir.

"The *whah*?"

"Johanna Budwig was a famous German scientist in the 1950s," Mom explained, carrying her breakfast over to the dining room table. "She was nominated for the Nobel Prize *seven times* for curing cancer, but Big Pharma shut her down because she refused to add chemo to her protocol."

I kept my mouth shut but couldn't hide my look of skepticism.

"Look her up if you want some reassurance," Mom said.

"Reassurance? Of *what*?"

"That things can work! She had a ninety percent cure rate with her diet."

I took my mug of coffee and sat down across from her at the table, watching as she took a spoonful in her mouth and wrinkled her nose. "It tastes awful," she said, grinning performatively. "It's a lot of flax-seed oil."

Tuesday evening

Mom's cell energy doctor, Dr. Beattie, lent her something called a Rife machine, an old-timey-looking device that would supposedly clear her cancer cells of negative energy. I thought it looked like a Scientology E-meter—and probably just as effective.

Mom held a cylinder grip in each hand and powered it up. "It was created by a man named Royal Rife in the 1920s," she said. "Of course, he was hounded because he was so successful."

"How does it work?" I asked.

"My cancer is sending out certain energy." She looked me straight in the eyes. "We're talking about the quantum world now. You *know* we're all made out of energy, right?"

I nodded tentatively.

"The Rife machine sends out charges that match the frequency of the cancer inside me. It destroys the cells in the same way an opera singer's voice can break a mirror."

I laughed out loud. I couldn't help it. Did she really think she could reverberate her cancer to smithereens? Mom shrugged and rolled her eyes at me. "I'm sure you'll want to leave Newton behind at some point in your life."

Thursday, after work

"I went to see my homeopath today!" Mom said. "I really trust her. And she's *completely* in my camp. She *completely* believes that I'm doing the right thing." Mom was particularly excited because her homeopath had given her some scorpion venom. "She bought it in Cuba for like $400, but she gave it to me for only $20," Mom explained.

"What does scorpion venom do?" I asked, barely stifling a giggle.

"I'm not exactly sure," Mom said. "But I've read about a lot of shamans having success with it."

Saturday morning, bright and early

"Would you like a mimosa, sweetie?" Mom called out.

I emerged from my bedroom and entered the kitchen, where Mom was opening a bottle of prosecco. She was her usual cheerful self. "The thing I like most about the Budwig diet," she remarked, "is that you're allowed to have a glass of champagne every day as long as you put freshly ground flaxseeds in it."

Saturday, an hour later

Mom did something called "oil pulling" while puttering around the apartment tidying up. She swished organic coconut oil around in her mouth for fifteen minutes—it was supposed to be good for removing toxins. "It also whitens your teeth!" she declared proudly.

Sunday afternoon

"I'm off to see my acupuncturist," Mom said on her way out. "You *do* believe in acupuncture, I assume?"

I looked up at her and smirked. "What exactly do I believe? That it can cure *cancer*?"

"Okay, never mind," she said, laughing.

Sunday evening

"What is this 'Guardian' thing you keep talking about?" I asked Mom, staring at the mysterious device on her night table. It looked like an aromatherapy lamp, but it didn't release any mist.

"It's another method of energy healing," Mom said. "I don't want to tell you more because, well, I don't really get it," she admitted, her voice trailing off. "But what the hell. I'll try anything that only takes five minutes."

Mom's game plan struck me as rather messy. She argued that it was of paramount importance to be a hundred percent focused on her course of action—that's how she justified closing herself off to anything or anyone who interfered—but it was impossible to tell exactly what that course of action was. What the heck was she even doing? She could barely explain half the stuff she was up to. Just as with her approach to spirituality, Mom seemed to be cherry-picking the parts of various protocols that appealed to her, skipping from one remedy to the next without ever fully committing or going deep.

"YOU'RE NOT GOING to live anyway if I die. There's nothing in this for you. You've gone rogue. I invite you to join the community of healthy cells, or I want you to recycle. That means *die*."

Mom was talking to her cancer cells. Out loud. Visualization was one of her everyday practices. "I imagine my good cells as little vacuum cleaners munching up the cancer cells," she said. "The way I see it, cancer isn't against you; it's part of your body. Cancer is a thug—there's no doubt about that, it kills you—but cancer is actually a last-ditch attempt to save you. Cancer cells are holding toxicity that would otherwise go into your bloodstream and cause a stroke or a heart attack. Cells only become cancerous because they don't know what else to do."

"So you don't see it as a battle?" I asked.

"No, I don't. The language of war is *so* patriarchal. I'm not fighting anything. I talk to my cancer cells with *respect*."

As far out as her theory was, I appreciated that Mom didn't see her relationship with the disease as a battle. I'd read a little Susan Sontag in university. In her 1978 essay "Illness as Metaphor," she challenged the victim-blaming language often used to talk about cancer, arguing that metaphors create moral judgments against patients and aren't helpful. Although I totally respected that many people with cancer feel empowered by verbs like "beat" and "conquer," I also understood Sontag's point that combat metaphors could make patients feel as though the onus was on them to "win the war on cancer." And what if they failed? Had they just not "fought" hard enough?

"The most truthful way of regarding illness—and the healthiest way of being ill," argued Sontag, "is one most purified of, most resistant to, metaphoric thinking." Mom may have been avoiding the patriarchal language of war, but she didn't seem any closer to the truth. She was trading in one rhetorical device for another, anthropomorphizing her cancer instead. It was a thug who could be rationalized with. Did she really think she could respectfully negotiate her way out, as if there were some sort of rhyme and reason to it?

As time went by it became clear that Mom really believed she could control her body with her mind. Week after week, new affirmations went up on her chalkboard:

I am willing to experience a miracle.

If you say it enough, you can convince your body.

My body knows how to heal itself.

Again, I didn't think it was all crazy. I mean, humans *are* made of energy, the quantum field *is* real, and flaxseed oil *is* cool. But I was worried that Mom was putting all her eggs in her belief basket.

Sontag was writing in response to popular theories arising at the time about there being a cancer personality type: that people with repressive personalities are more likely to develop the disease. She warned against such interpretations and instead argued that people should see illness as illness—not as some judgment on their character or a product of bad behaviour.

"Michael told me that, in his experience, the cancer patients who survive are usually the ones who use this challenge as a way to grow," Mom explained. And so she set about trying to heal old wounds, clearing her cells of negative memories. She told me that she and Dr. Beattie were working together to clear her energy fields of resentment, judgment, and criticism, and Mom's need to please.

"When Dr. Beattie first mentioned resentment, I told her I didn't have any," Mom recalled, laughing. "'Well, it's in your field!' she told me." Mom thought she'd already cleared up her resentment issues. She told me that part of why she was so surprised she got cancer was that she didn't think she had the "personality" for it. Whether or not this theory held any water, it was true that Mom didn't repress how she felt—she was constantly making her concerns clear. I'd never known her to hold back or bury her feelings (except for that one time she literally buried them).

According to Mom, her diagnosis was a sign that she had more work to do. Her cancer posed an opportunity to change. "I'm grateful to my polyp for signalling disorder," she told me. "Before the diagnosis, I was stuck in certain unhealthy relationships, indulging in pastries and wine, and struggling with anxiety and insomnia." She faulted herself for eating too much red meat—"I shouldn't have been eating all those steaks at David's!"—while ignoring stress and constipation for years. Mom was buying into the very theory of personal responsibility that Sontag had written against. (On the chalkboard: *I am willing to release the patterns that led to my cancer.*)

It was apparent that Mom was more focused on healing the person than on curing the disease. "I have to let go of who I thought I was," she explained. "No more working hard at appearing normal, whatever that is. I have to allow myself to be vulnerable, to be ever more real. No more convincing others and myself that I'm always 'just fine.' I want to be completely well. Not just cured of cancer."

A mind-body link made sense to me, but a direct connection between personality and cancer? I wasn't buying it. I appreciated that Mom was looking inward, but I was concerned that she was placing the burden—and the blame—fully on herself.

On the chalkboard:
My body is producing miracles.
I breathe in courage and breathe out fear.
I will bet on myself.

Why did Mom feel she needed to be the one to heal herself? Was it because she thought she'd caused her cancer in the first place?

Who knows why people get cancer. Genetics, cigarettes, living next to a toxic waste dump—sure, they're real factors. Erin Brockovich was right. But there was no reason to believe that eating steak had done this to her. The truth is that cancer is chaotic and confounding. It's not something that can be reasoned with. However, even if the doctors weren't ultimately in control either, I firmly believed Mom had a better chance of being cured with a surgeon's scalpel than with an imaginary vacuum cleaner.

But I didn't say that. I just listened.

MOM WAS UP to a lot of bizarre shenanigans, but I wasn't prepared for the arrival of the newest member of her healing militia: the ghost of my dead grandma. Her mother—who'd been the source of so much friction in her life—suddenly became her role model and spirit guide.

Grandma had been a health nut way before her time. She was an early devotee of food combining in the 1940s and didn't allow any sugar in the home when Mom was growing up. Mom told me how she'd have to hide in the closet to eat Aero bars so that her mother wouldn't yell at her (it wasn't a big mystery where her issues with chocolate came from). I remember how when Josh and I were little, Grandma would try to pass off carob bars on us. I'd fall for it every time, biting down on a waxy-brown square before spitting it out.

Mom began to channel Grandma. She told me how she'd woken up in the middle of the night from a torture nightmare. Shaken and scared, she asked her mother what she should do, and Grandma's ghost appeared. "'My darling Elaine, your body is capable of repairing itself,'" Mom recalled in Grandma's soft, sweet voice. "'Remember when I used herbs to reduce my arthritis so that I could dance at the Betel Centre? You just keep doing what you're doing.'"

This really made my eyes roll like Judge Judy. Grandma worshipped doctors! She may have made her own almond milk and squeezed too much lemon juice on everything, but she was way too nervous a person to have ever disobeyed doctors' orders. I was positive Grandma would go apeshit if she knew what her precious *Elainela* was doing.

Grandma had died five years earlier at the age of ninety-three. In her final years she suffered from dementia and had to move into a nursing home. As an adult, Mom had gotten along with her mother fairly well. But with dementia, Grandma would sometimes regress and freak out at Mom in exactly the same way she did when Mom was a child. "When I'm alone with her, she yells at me!" Mom told me. During that time, Mom played Pema Chödrön's *Don't Bite the Hook*—in which the American Buddhist nun explains how to stay centred and refrain from reacting to triggers—on a loop in her car. Although Mom had vowed never to abandon herself, she also didn't feel she could abandon her mother while she was ill. So she continued to look after her while also regularly taking off to Mexico to look after herself. She spent a few winters in San Miguel de Allende, a picturesque historic town in Mexico that's home to many artists and writers.

In my early twenties, before setting off for grad school in Montreal, I stayed with Mom and helped lessen the burden by visiting Grandma every week. Grandma was only ever her sweetest self with me. She showered me with love, but I also sensed her neediness under the surface. She'd always seemed more like a little girl than an old lady: she loved porcelain dolls, *The Little Mermaid*, the colour pink. Even as a kid I'd felt older, in a way, than Grandma. I could definitely see how Mom had been put in the position of having to parent her.

With the benefit of time and space (and plenty of fresh lime margaritas), Mom was able to gain a deeper appreciation for her mother. At age sixty, Mom came to the realization that her mother had given her far more than she'd been given by *her* mother—not an easy thing to accomplish. Mom knew her mother had always adored her, and she appreciated how supportive she'd always been. "She believed I could do anything—except give her enough love," Mom told me.

Mom said that ever since Grandma died, their relationship had only been getting better (so much better, I suppose, that they were now hanging out in the middle of the night). Yet despite this supernatural ventriloquism, which helped make her feel she was on the right track, Mom obviously still had doubts. Looking back, I can see how she was projecting her conflicted self onto the two of us: Grandma was the agreeable angel and I was the Western medicine–devoted devil.

As uncomfortable as it was to be confronted with Mom's wacky rituals and routines, when we weren't arguing, we still had a great time together. She still made fancy coffee in the morning, and we'd sit down in the sunroom for a few minutes to talk before I went off to work. Most evenings we just chatted and laughed over a glass of organic Pinot and vegetarian takeout. Mom even started making meals once in a while. She prepared lovely organic salads served in her Italian pottery bowls and set the dining room table artfully with brightly coloured Mexican placemats and cloth napkins. Sometimes we'd watch *The Sopranos* while Mom did her Rife machine. In those moments the ease between us returned and our differences melted away.

IN APRIL I moved into my new apartment and attempted to resume life as normal. By then I'd told several friends and close colleagues about Mom's cancer, and they would check in with me from time to time to see how she was doing.

"Has she started treatment yet?" they'd ask.

It was difficult for me to explain that she hadn't, and had no plans to. "Nope. She's trying to cure herself with herbs and healthy eating instead," I'd say, making a joke out of it, downplaying how scared I was.

Their responses ran the gamut from mild confusion ("Huh? Come again?") to abject horror ("Is she fucking crazy?!"). Often when I told people that Mom was refusing medical treatment, they'd assume she had late-stage cancer and that nothing much could be done to help her.

"No, it's treatable," I'd clarify. "She just believes she can cure herself naturally."

If they said "You must be *so* worried," I'd feel my panic and helplessness expand, and if they said "That's *so* selfish," I'd be compelled to defend her. Sometimes an awkward silence would ensue.

And so, after that first year, I stopped telling people that Mom had cancer.

IN THE SUMMER, one year after her diagnosis, Mom went to "shaman camp" in the Catskills.

"What did you do there?" I asked when she got back. I had a feeling there hadn't been much water-skiing and archery on the schedule.

"You're just going to make fun of me," Mom said. Her instincts were correct, but I promised I wouldn't. So she told me about the shaman from California (yet another Jew), who told corny jokes at every sacred fire and at one point jangled a leather-covered rattle over her head, sucked something in from her left shoulder, and then spit it out. "Find your own rhythm—don't move to another's beat," he told her. He instructed her to go down to the riverside and flip a log over thirteen times, each time letting out a deep, angry wail.

"I know it sounds woo-woo," Mom said. "But I believe I was receiving an advanced form of mind-body medicine, even if I can't explain it."

That fall Mom packed her supplements and Guardian gizmo and headed off on a six-week silent meditation retreat. She'd read about a man who supposedly cured himself of fourth-stage rectal cancer just by meditating. I think Mom was happy on her retreats. Sure, the legume-heavy monastery food upset her stomach—she'd often make trips to nearby villages to buy scones—but they served an important purpose: there, she was accountable to no one but herself.

I, on the other hand, continued to poke her from time to time—just never hard enough to get her mad at me. I'd occasionally suggest that she might want to get another scan to see if her cancer was progressing. Mom still hadn't even gotten the lymph node biopsy.

"I *know* it hasn't progressed," she insisted. "I feel wonderful!"

"Sure," I said, "but the doctors said that people often don't feel the symptoms until it's too late. And then it hits you like a ton of bricks. How would you feel if, say, in six months you were told that your cancer has spread?"

"You're not being supportive," she snapped. "That won't happen."

I told Mom how Steve Jobs died regretting his decision not to get surgery earlier (he'd had the rare form of pancreatic cancer that's treatable). Despite pleas from family and friends, the Apple CEO spent nine months trying to cure himself with juice fasts, organic herbs, acupuncture, bowel cleansing, hydrotherapy, and other treatments he found on the internet. He even consulted a psychic. When he was finally prepared to try surgery, it was too late. His cancer had spread too far.

But Mom had her own celebrity defence: "Rockin' Ronnie Hawkins cured himself of terminal pancreatic cancer!" she told me. (I *highly* doubted that.)

By the time Mom invited me to do ayahuasca, I was still hoping that if I tried my best to be supportive, she'd come around to getting surgery. (Perhaps ayahuasca would give her a vision of . . . reality?) But in the end it only reaffirmed her faith in the path she was taking. "I feel completely cleansed," Mom declared as we hit the road the next morning. After puking her guts up all night, I'm sure she was cleansed of something.

As the months passed, Mom became more convinced that her regimen was working. She forwarded me an article from a dubious-sounding organization called the Institute of Health Sciences; "The Surprising Benefits of Lemon!" claimed the citrus to be "10,000 times stronger than chemotherapy." In her message, Mom wrote: "Not a day goes by without validation! You'll be happy to know that I already take a fresh organic lemon drink every day."

I was still nervous, but I resigned myself to thinking that it would probably take evidence of her cancer growing for her to finally snap out of it. As unfortunate as it would be, that's what it would likely take to burst her bubble. It would be horrible if it came to that, but at least the doctors would still be able to help her. I was naive, but at the time, as far as I could see, a later-stage diagnosis was the worst-case scenario. It was the hope, or lie, that kept me going.

In the meantime, Mom continued to insist that she was feeling great. Her infrared sauna was supposedly helping, her energy was high, and she felt affirmed by her continued good health. She was now going around telling everyone that she had only "a touch of cancer."

MEANWHILE THE ATMOSPHERE at work was getting progressively worse. As the show grew, so did Jian's ego. He wanted more A-list celebrities, more live audience shows, more American stations, more publicity, more adulation. It was unsustainable. We didn't need a biopsy to know our workplace was pathological.

In the early years, when I'd felt Jian had gone too far in swearing or yelling at me, I stood up to him a few times. But he was incapable of apologizing and would twist things around to make it seem as if I wasn't dedicated enough, as if I was the problem. "You're the *only* producer who has an issue," he'd say. I'd leave our fights shaken, almost trembling, worried about what punishment awaited me. After finding myself removed from projects, I started to wonder whether standing up for myself was worth it.

At the start of the summer a few of us longtime producers began secretly meeting after work to discuss what to do. We chose the nearby Hooters for its sunny rooftop patio and yummy chicken wings, but mostly for the unlikelihood of running into our bosses there. Having learned early on that our individual complaints wouldn't be taken seriously, we decided to draft a document outlining our grievances as a group. We called the document Red Sky, a cheeky play on our annual Blue Sky show-planning sessions in which we were supposed to dream up where to take the show next. However we never felt we could speak freely or raise real issues with Jian in the room. The sky was definitely not blue.

A month later the six of us sat in a boardroom and presented our document to our boss and a middle manager. Fearful of how it would be received, we presented each section in pairs. We spoke of an "unsustainable" workplace driven by a "culture of fear," and how we were often held hostage to the whims of the host. "If we don't do what he says, we'll be punished in some way," we said. We asked that leadership hold Jian to account rather than operating out of fear of "stirring the beast."

Apparently Jian was spoken to, and a new part-time digital producer was hired to help us with the website. Oh, and we also got a pizza party. But nothing actually changed. It was clear that our bosses were unwilling to rein Jian in.

I didn't have the energy to keep fighting, nor did I feel I had many options. So I grew complacent. All I could do was try to minimize my exposure—to keep my relationship with Jian strictly professional, limiting our interactions and avoiding him in social situations. I would tune out his craziness and focus on my queer agenda. After all, I still loved the work itself. It was stimulating and intellectually fulfilling, and I felt it was important. Plus I loved my fellow producers. Ironically, I felt I could be myself at work. I was appreciated and loved just for being me: a quirky, irreverent boy-lady. As a queer person, it wasn't lost on me what a privilege it was to be so out in the workplace. I reminded myself that I had one of the most coveted jobs in arts journalism. Heck, I'd met everyone from the Indigo Girls to Oscar the Grouch. And on the rare occasion that Jian complimented my work and dedication, I felt amazing. Things could feel good for stretches at a time. But invariably, another land mine would be waiting down the road.

A FEW DAYS after our Red Sky presentation, Mom finally agreed to get a new MRI. I think she was hoping for validation that her methods were working. And so, two years after her diagnosis, Mom and I drove to North York General Hospital, this time to see Dr. Stotland, yet another of the city's finest colorectal surgeons (were we starting to run out?). It was the moment of truth. I was afraid of what we might find out, but I also felt reassured that if bad had indeed gone to worse, Mom would finally see the light and get on with surgery. I was really hoping the third time would be the charm.

That hope quickly evaporated. Dr. Stotland told us that he and his panel of doctors believed Mom now had Stage 2 cancer. He said it would be a waste of time to remove the tumour with the more minor surgery previously on offer, because it had grown into the muscle. He could do the more extensive surgery, he explained, citing a seventy to ninety percent cure rate if the lymph nodes weren't infected. And if it was Stage 3, Mom still had a forty to fifty percent chance of being cured.

Mom looked stunned. "But I feel so wonderful!" She'd been feeling so great that she really thought she might be in remission.

I asked Dr. Stotland if there was even a one percent chance that Mom didn't have cancer. I wanted Mom to hear his answer.

"No, she definitely has cancer," he said.

Dr. Stotland was direct and detached in typical doctor-like fashion, but there was a gentle kindness to him. He wasn't putting any pressure on her. He answered all her questions. Like the other doctors, he reassured her that she didn't have to undergo radiation or chemotherapy if she preferred not to. Mom seemed to be more open to him. I felt hopeful: maybe this time she'd finally come around. She had no more excuses.

As we walked to the parking lot, she once again had a frightened look on her face. The shock of being side-swiped by the truth. I could see the terror in her eyes.

"Mom, you tried doing things your way, and it hasn't worked."

"But it has been working! I should be dead by now, but I'm not!"

Mom had a way of spinning everything in her favour. Every time I tried to open a door, she'd shut it in my face.

"My new MRI looks almost the same as the last one. I just need to step up my—"

"It's not the same! Your cancer is growing. You need to get surgery *now*."

All my suppressed anxiety was bubbling up. The geyser was ready to blow.

"I believe there are other things out there. All the millions of things I've read say that—"

I stopped in my tracks, threw my hands in the air, and yelled at her: "YOU'RE IN DENIAL!" I'd reached my breaking point. I'd been doing my best to stay calm and supportive for so long, but I couldn't take it anymore. I collapsed onto a grassy slope next to the parking lot and buried my head in my arms. *I give up.*

Mom came over and sat down, putting her arm around me. She always came to me when we had a fight; it was one of the clear ways she was the parent in our dynamic. I was comforted by the feeling of her hand on my shoulder, even if I didn't trust that she was all there.

"You won't change my mind, darling," Mom began. "You can choose to love me just as I am or not. For both our sakes, I hope you're able to do that. You matter so much to me."

Mom mattered to me more than anyone. But to love her just as she was would be to lose her. It was an impossible bind: take a front row seat for her self-imposed execution, or leave altogether.

I lifted my head to look at her. I could see tears in her eyes. "I love you dearly, and I'm sorry you're suffering," she said in a slow, pained voice, pausing to take a deep breath. "I am *determined* to live."

STAGE 2

8

PERFECT GLOWING HEALTH

"Do you think we can have her committed?" I asked Teddy over the phone, half joking. As much as we wished we could force Mom to get surgery, we knew she was too lucid to ever be declared *legally* incompetent.

"If your mother dies it will be due to insanity," Teddy replied, without even an ounce of humour in his delivery.

I'd run out of ideas. Everyone was telling me there wasn't anything I could do to change her mind—especially Mom. I couldn't keep banging my head against a wall. It wasn't conscious, but I guess I slowly started putting my own blinders on. If Mom was going to act as if everything was fine I would do the same, even if I couldn't help interjecting with my stock rebuttal ("That's not true!") every once in a while.

I tried to convince myself that Mom's cancer wouldn't catch up with her for another fifteen or twenty years (it's not as if they kept stats on people with first-stage rectal cancer who just left it to grow). I tried to pretend we'd never discovered her polyp in the first place (if cancer falls in a forest and nobody hears, does it make a sound?). It's amazing the gymnastics our brains will do to help us cope.

Mom and David had broken up that summer. Mom told me she needed more space to take care of herself. "I've read that most spontaneous remissions happen when the patient says, 'Fuck it, I'm finally going to leave my marriage, or quit my job, or go live in a hut on Salt Spring Island and paint miniature landscapes,'" she explained. "I read about one guy whose doctor told him he would die in four months, so he took off travelling," she continued. "He stayed at a castle in Tuscany, rode the Orient Express, and went on a tour of three-star restaurants in France. Then his cancer disappeared, and he had no more money, so he sued his doctor." She flashed a self-satisfied smile. "This is my chance to do what I want in life, right now. This is my chance to live more consciously, to be more alive. My body has been out of harmony—physically, spiritually, and emotionally. I want to be vibrant again."

Mom called herself a "recovering people pleaser." It was her core belief that she'd always put other people's needs ahead of her own. Apparently Grandma's ghost was now corroborating it: "Just like me, you don't put yourself first, but everyone understands that a cancer patient must do that." It was true that Mom put a lot of energy into helping other people, but it's not as if she ignored her own needs. How much more permission did she need to live her Best Life?

OVER THE NEXT YEAR, life carried on as usual. Mom continued teaching at her alternative high school and leading her weekly women's writing group. She taught a workshop called "It's Never Too Late: Finding That Special Someone," based on her book. I kept busy at Q and continued my weekly hockey games, and every weekend my chess partner Joel and I would play for hours at our local café. Josh had his hands full at City Hall, trying to be reasonable at a time of unprecedented dishonesty and reckless behaviour from Rob Ford. Teddy started spending more time with Barbara, a woman he'd met at his Sunday morning film series. And then, in the early days of 2013, the newest member of the Matlow clan was born: Josh and Melissa's daughter, Molly. Mom had always said she didn't care if Josh or I had children, but when Molly came along she was over the moon.

It was a happy time, with many family get-togethers centred on baby Molly. We'd meet at the farmers' market on Saturday mornings and take turns carrying her around in her fleece teddy bear onesie. We rarely talked about Mom having cancer anymore. She believed she had it all under control, and had even stopped updating her affirmation chalkboard. Only one stayed up: *I am in perfect glowing health.*

But even if we weren't talking about it, I'd be reminded every time we sat down for a meal and Mom would take out her little amber bottle of Michael's herbs—the one remedy she consistently maintained. I *despised* that little amber bottle. That symbol of her denial. That distraction from getting the help she actually needed. She'd squeeze the dropper and hold the tincture in her mouth for thirty seconds while I fought the overwhelming urge to smack the bottle out of her hand. Instead I'd just sit there silently, swallowing my rage.

But my anger did seep out, just in less obvious ways. For example, when Mom and I drove anywhere, she always insisted on parking the car several blocks away. This made me absolutely nuts. As a driver, I always aimed to park right in front of wherever I was going. I would at least attempt to get the closest spot before circling around. But Mom never even tried. "There won't be any spots closer," she'd say. "Besides, I like to build in a walk."

"Why can't you at least *try?*" I'd plead with her. "Please! Fight for the spot!"

On the lengthy walk to our destination, I'd pettily point out every available spot along the way. "Oh, what's that big empty space over here?" I'd say, over and over again. Mom would just laugh it off. It was only a parking spot to her.

For the most part I was able to dissociate and live my life as if everything was okay. But just as in a game of chess, the brain is never hushed. On the surface it's a quiet game; all you hear is the ticking of the clock or the faint pushing of a wooden piece on the board. No one hears the battle in your mind, the ceaseless overanalyzing and second-guessing. The struggle may seem silent, but underneath, it can be deafening. So even while I tried my best not to think about Mom's situation, I always answered her calls. I never left town for too long. And I tried to be more appreciative of our time together, keenly aware that she might not be around for as long as she thought she would. When my anxiety did bubble up, Mom would try to reassure me. "I'm going to be living *well* into my nineties. You're going to *wish* I would die," she'd say, laughing. I desperately hoped she was right, but I wasn't holding my breath. As far as I was concerned, she was a dead mom walking.

IN THE SUMMER of 2013, three years after her diagnosis, Mom asked me to go to Spain with her to hike the Camino de Santiago. The 780-kilometre route across the northern countryside had been used for centuries by Catholic pilgrims making their way to the interred bones of Saint James. These days the month-long Camino was more of a non-denominational pilgrimage for people at a crossroads in their life and seeking some sort of transformation. Mom was hoping that by walking the seashell-marked trail, or at least nine days of it, she would receive a miracle.

I felt a bit sheepish about taking a trip with my mom. Several of my friends, particularly within the queer community, had strained relationships with their mothers and couldn't imagine doing such a thing. But Mom and I had a history of travelling together that dated back to my teenage years: to Upstate New York, to the Gaspé when I was thirteen, to Manhattan for my sixteenth birthday.

In my twenties we upped the ante. When I was twenty-one, Mom spent a year teaching at a Canadian high school in Switzerland. She called me at university one day and announced, "I've decided that I'd like to go on an *outer* journey with my *outer* child." Mom was taking me to Paris!

I took a few days off school and flew to meet her. We were giddy from the moment we met up in the lobby of Hôtel Jeanne d'Arc in the Marais. During the five days, we never made it to the Eiffel Tower, Champs-Élysées, or Arc de Triomphe. Instead, Mom led me on a tour of the city's Lost Generation of writers. We hit up haunts from Ernest Hemingway's *A Moveable Feast*, like Café de Flore, where Simone de Beauvoir and Jean-Paul Sartre wrote their books. "*She* was the better philosopher," Mom insisted. We walked through the Luxembourg Gardens, a favourite spot of Gertrude Stein and Alice B. Toklas. "Lesbian relationships are so much more civilized," she mused.

Mom was a great tour guide. She didn't speak much French, but she was fluent in fromage. Vieux Comté, Bleu d'Auvergne, Bouton de Culotte. Mom could carry on a whole conversation in cheese shops. It was impressive. Of course, she also knew her way around a patisserie. "That's a mille feuille," she told me, pointing to a rectangle of layered pastry sheets. "It means thousand leaves."

When she suggested we get macarons at Ladurée, at first I protested. "I don't like macaroons."

"Mac-ah-*ron*," Mom corrected. "They aren't those kosher-for-Passover turds you're thinking of." She was right; I was mesmerized by the bright colourful rows of delicate meringue cookies filled with cream. We bought a large box and sampled a bite from each one.

Mom taught me about Proust's madeleine as we dipped the little yellow sponge cakes into our tea at Mariage Frères. "He takes a bite, and then all of a sudden all these childhood memories start flooding back," Mom explained. I wondered what memories a cappuccino yogurt with Smarties might elicit.

Whenever we needed a bathroom break, Mom would lead me into the nearest luxury hotel, sauntering in as if she lived there. "I just *love* a nice hotel bathroom," she'd say, a little too loud.

I'd sit patiently in designer clothing boutiques while Mom tried on French fashions and asked me what I thought. And she'd go into menswear shops with me. Mom joked that I was "more like a gay son than a lesbian daughter." She once said, "We have a particularly special kind of relationship. I think it's partly because you're like a gay guy. Gay men seem to have less stress with their mothers than heterosexual daughters."

Throughout my twenties we continued to go on trips together. I visited her again that year in Switzerland, where we took an overnight train to Italy to see Venice and Florence. I joined her on one of her stays in San Miguel de Allende in Mexico, where we went to art openings, attended talks at the Biblioteca, and ate churros con chocolate at a café owned by a famous telenovela actress. Mom took me to the nearby Monarch Butterfly Biosphere Reserve, the winter home of the butterflies that fly down each year from Canada (or rather, their great-great-grandchildren that complete the journey). Mom and I rode into the pine forest on horseback toward the orange-winged colony high up in the middle of the mountains. I'm not sure whether it was the altitude or the tequila I'd drunk the night before, but as soon as we arrived I fainted. When I came to, I was lying on the forest floor with my head resting on Mom's lap, surrounded by thousands of butterflies swirling around me. I was in heaven.

But on the trip to Spain I started questioning my decision right from the minute we got on the plane. I watched as Mom teetered down the aisle in front of me, hitting the seated passengers on either side of her, one by one, with the dangling hip-straps of her backpack. "Mom, watch out for your bag!" I scolded. She'd always been a head-in-the-clouds sort of person, often unaware of her surroundings, but now I'd lost my patience for her daydreamer ways.

I wasn't allowed to get angry at her for what I was really angry about, so instead I got angry at her for everything else: the hotel she booked outside of town, her snoring, her slow walking, the way she took her sweet time to wrap her scarf just right. I felt like I was always on the verge of blowing up. It didn't take much to set me off. I was constantly criticizing her, and I know I hurt her feelings. But as much as I'd vowed to appreciate our time together, it was proving to be more of a challenge than I'd thought.

So, before we started out from Saint-Jean-Pied-de-Port in France, I told Mom that I preferred to walk at my own pace and that we could meet up in few days. Mom was totally fine with this plan; she didn't make me feel guilty. She was probably relieved to have a break from my constant chiding. We arranged to stay in touch and meet up in a few days in Pamplona.

When three days went by and I hadn't heard from her, I started to worry. I even called Teddy. I decided to wait one more day before calling the Spanish police. When I tried calling her again, Mom finally picked up. She explained that she'd been having such a fabulous time with her new Camino friends that she simply forgot. "I turned off my phone," she said, sounding like an oblivious teenager. I couldn't believe it—she had literally disconnected herself.

We ended up walking the nine days separately. We both preferred our own pace, our own paths. But when we finally reunited at Café

Colonny in the town of Logroño, we were genuinely excited to see each other again. I remember spotting her sitting on the patio with a glass of white wine, reading a book. "Mom!" I called out. "Rachie!" she called back. We gave each other a big hug.

Before flying home we spent a lovely last day at Frank Gehry's Guggenheim Museum in Bilbao. As we took in the spectacular metallic exterior from the riverside walkway, we came upon a massive thirty-foot steel spider sculpture by Louise Bourgeois. Mom immediately recognized it. "It's called *Maman!*" she announced. The towering spider was a tribute to Bourgeois's beloved mother, a tapestry maker, who died when she was just twenty-one. It was said to be an ode to her mother's strength, with its metaphors of weaving and nurturing, as well as the ambiguous nature of motherhood: the spider as both protector and predator.

As I walked underneath the creature's belly and looked up from below, Mom crept toward me with her hands formed into claws. "Maman! Maman!" she taunted playfully. I rolled my eyes, but I couldn't help smiling. Mom was a freak, but she was my freak. I loved her so much, but she also irritated me to no end. She was my mother and my tormentor—a powerful, larger-than-life presence spinning her own web of distortion. Was I trapped?

9

THE SKY HADN'T FALLEN

I could definitely see the upside of denial. Mom was cheerful and optimistic. She wondered whether the rolfing had freed frozen energy in her shoulders. Or if the reflexology, Japanese acupuncture, reiki, qigong, and yoga had released the lonely memories held in her cells. "Did the shaman spit out the resident evil spirit?" she asked (rhetorically, I hoped). "Whatever. I feel lighter. I'm walking through the world with more ease," she said.

I had to admit that being complacent was much more enjoyable than being freaked out all the time. And, honestly, as much as I desperately wanted Mom to get treatment, a part of me was relieved she wasn't going under the knife. Surgery scared me, too. Mom's way, we didn't have to deal with anything. Avoidance was pretty awesome.

Three years turned into four, and the sky still hadn't fallen. Mom and I were hanging out, going to restaurants and films as usual. She was back to eating biscotti every morning and drinking a variety of wine grapes. Now she was mostly focused on teaching, travelling, and finding true love.

The more that time trudged along without catastrophe, the more I began to doubt myself. Maybe things would be fine, just as they appeared to be. Maybe Mom was right. Maybe my calculations were off. It was difficult to maintain my view of reality, to anchor myself in what I knew. I was so inside Mom's labyrinth that I'd lost all perspective. Mom was more confident than I was. She was one hundred percent positive that she was making the best possible decision for herself, while I was only, say, ninety-seven percent sure she was making a fatal mistake.

Had Mom's magical thinking rubbed off on me? Or was it all just too bizarre to process? I mean, I may have been intellectually aware of the consequences, but I think the sheer implausibility of the situation had edged me into denial. "My mom's trying to cure herself with herbs!" was what I'd told my friends, as if it were just another of my funny Mom stories. The strange and terrifying reality—that Mom was letting her cancer run wild—was almost too crazy to comprehend. In the existential words of David After Dentist, *Is this real life?*

SINCE WALKING THE Camino with Mom (er, with*out* Mom), I'd become obsessed with long-distance hiking. I did a five-day trek to Machu Picchu that same summer. I was definitely going into the red with vacation days (and my bank account), but I felt I needed to get away for the sake of my mental health. I craved the simplicity of the hiking life. I didn't have to worry about saving Mom or navigating Jian's moods. My only job was to walk from Point A to Point B every day.

Mom and I had loved our respective Camino experiences so much that, a year later, we both set out to hike more of it—officially separately this time. I'd just completed the final twelve-day stretch and was heading home the next morning. Mom had just arrived with plans to hike for a week and then meet up with her sister to travel around more of Spain. We had one overlapping day together in Barcelona, and we were making the most of it. Mom and I spent the morning wandering the Gaudí pathways of Park Güell and the early afternoon ambling through the narrow cobblestone streets of the old Gothic quarter. We were getting along well. I'd made a conscious decision to not let myself get irritated, regretful of how critical I'd been the year before. Surely I could get through twenty-four hours without feeling annoyed.

Later that afternoon we drank cava in the sunshine at a little tapas restaurant outside the Boqueria Market. Our little bistro table was crowded with tiny plates of vinegared anchovies, artichokes, and green olives. We raised our flutes and toasted to the wonderful day we were having together. But as we caught up, it became apparent that Mom hadn't planned her hiking trip. She didn't know what route she was taking or even how she'd get to the trail from Barcelona. Back at our Airbnb I found her a cheap plane ticket online, but Mom had left her credit card at home. On purpose. She was afraid of losing it, so she'd brought only her bank card. I was concerned for her. *Who goes travelling without their credit card? Or a plan?* I insisted that we call Visa to retrieve her number in case of emergency.

I'd booked dinner for us that evening at a private supper club, hosted by a Michelin-trained chef—a belated seventieth birthday gift. Mom was jetlagged and wanted to have a nap beforehand, so I went to meet an old friend for a drink. A couple of hours later, as I turned the key to open the door, I could hear Mom cry out, "Oh good! You're back."

My eyes followed a trail of blood from the floor at my feet to the living area where Mom was lying on the couch, writhing in pain, holding her left elbow with her right hand. "I fell down the stairs. I think my arm is broken," she cried, trying to steady her rapid breathing. "I'm sorry about dinner."

I rushed over and sat by her side. "It's okay. Don't worry about it. Let's get you fixed up." It was shocking. I'd never seen Mom in such pain, so vulnerable, but I needed to remain cool and calm. She was shivering, so I covered her with a blanket. I fed her a couple of painkillers, cleaned the open gashes on her forehead and knee, and grabbed a silk scarf out of her bag to fashion a makeshift sling for her arm. Then I ran outside to hail a taxi.

It was a good thing we had Mom's credit card number.

The private hospital we were taken to was sleek and modern. I was surprised that no one on staff seemed to speak English fluently. I knew a little Spanish, but as proficient as I was at ordering jamón ibérico and pulpo gallego, I had no idea how to ask for an X-ray. "Fotografía?" I said to the nurse, pretending to snap a picture with my finger and pointing to Mom's arm.

"Ahh, una radiografía!" she finally guessed with all the glee of a charades enthusiast. "Sí!"

The doctor confirmed that Mom's elbow was broken. He wanted to book her in for surgery, but together we decided it would be best for her to return to Toronto with me. He'd stabilize her arm until she got to a hospital back home. Mom eyed him as he went about preparing plaster for her arm and butterfly bandages for her cuts.

"Did you wash your hands?" she asked.

"Not now!" I shushed her. The doctor continued shuffling around behind us. I was really hoping he hadn't heard her or understood enough English to be offended.

"What?" she sneered. "I read that a large percentage of doctors don't wash their hands."

"Zip it." I felt bad for her—I could see she was scared—but I was in no mood for any of her anti-medical drama. "You're going to have to be a *passive* patient," I hissed.

There was a lot going on. While I was on the phone with Visa trying to sort out Mom's insurance and flight home I was also trying to communicate with the hospital staff in my drunken-baby Spanish. So much for going twenty-four hours without her annoying me. *I tried.*

While the doctor wrapped up Mom's arm I went into the waiting room to call Teddy. Sometimes he felt like my co-parent. He would pick us both up at the airport the next day. The following morning I wrote to our Airbnb host to apologize for the bloody towels (I didn't want to tarnish my five-star rating) before heading to the airport. I dropped Mom off at her terminal and got her wheelchair assistance before dashing off to catch my own flight. As we said goodbye, my heart sank at the sight of her. There she was, arm in a cast, still wearing her blood-splattered T-shirt from the day before. I couldn't deny what I was seeing with my own eyes: Mom wasn't invincible. The cracks in her perfect glowing facade were beginning to appear.

BACK IN TORONTO, Mom delayed getting surgery for twelve days. "Elbow surgery is the *most* painful surgery there is," she was telling everyone. She didn't like her surgeon and didn't think he knew what he was doing. "He doesn't like me either," Mom admitted. *I can't imagine why.*

Finally Mom relented. "Michael says his herbs can't heal a broken elbow," she told me.

But he thinks they can cure rectal cancer?

That July I started dating Molly, a beautiful activist with dark wavy hair and big caring eyes. Molly worked in the labour movement, organizing union workers and writing equity policy, and was extremely strident in her beliefs. I'd playfully call her a "terrorist" and she'd not-so-playfully call me a "Liberal." (I wasn't, but to a lefty like her, there was no greater insult.) In my family she was known as "Big Molly" so as not to be confused with my niece.

I loved Molly's family. Her Jewish mom and Irish dad were revolutionary political types who subscribed to the *New Left Review*. Molly's parents still lived in the same old Edwardian house she'd grown up in, and she regularly went home for dinner. Her parents cooked delicious meals in their farmhouse-style kitchen, including homemade apple crumble served with a scoop of vanilla ice cream. Pictures of Molly and her older brother were displayed around the house. They even had one of those walls dedicated to measuring everyone's height. (On my first visit, Molly got out a pencil and put me up against the wall, marking the top of my head and adding my initials.) They were a perfect progressive TV family.

Molly was feminine, and a fighter. She liked that I was boyish—"masculine of centre," as the young queer folk would say—and even-keeled. We had shared values, but in many ways we were a case of opposites attract. I was irreverent and funny (at least to myself); she was earnest and sincere. She was a self-described "feminist killjoy" and appreciated how I brought her over to the lighter side. Molly wore her emotions on her sleeve—"I feel ALL THE FEELINGS," she told me—whereas I was only just learning how to express my emojis.

From our first date onward, we spent a lot of time together. I was happy and smitten. It was a welcome distraction from Mom and from work—especially in light of the distressing news I'd just gotten about Jian.

That spring, Jian's mood swings had gotten worse. A few of us had sensed he was more irritable, restless, and agitated than usual, and no one seemed to know why. By early July, when I got back from Spain, a trusted friend told me that Jian was being investigated by reporters over multiple allegations that he'd beaten women. I was shocked, but somehow not surprised.

Jian was in his late forties but dated women half his age. He'd often bring a young date to screenings and performances we'd attend together for work. A year earlier, a disturbing essay had been published on the website xoJane by a woman who'd accidentally found herself on a date with him in which he aggressively touched her body without invitation. Jian was a bully at work, so it wasn't a stretch to imagine that his cruel behaviour could carry over to his private life. Over the years he'd alluded to liking rough sex. I assumed it had something to do with that. But I didn't know what exactly was being alleged. I had little information to go on.

When I told my co-worker Brian what I'd heard, he revealed that he and Sean had already gone to management with the news a few days earlier. Apparently Jian had been questioned about the rumours, but he'd denied any wrongdoing. "They said they'll pull him off the air if they find any evidence he's lying to them," Brian told me. I was rattled, but I felt reassured that management was on it. I assumed they'd investigate the matter further and keep an eye on us to make sure we were okay. In the meantime I'd hang tight.

I didn't tell anyone else about this, not even Molly. Once again, I stuffed my feelings down into my emotional compression sack (you can fit a surprising amount in it). When Molly's parents asked me what it was like working with Jian, I recited my stock phrase: "He's good at what he does." Once we were alone, Molly asked me if I was okay— she'd noticed how pale and panic-stricken I'd looked at the mention of Jian's name. "Oh, I just don't like the guy," I said, waving it off.

That summer, my office felt more chilling than the HBO dramas I screened for work. Jian was covertly trying to put the kibosh on any stories having to do with sexual assault or violence against women. After another in-the-know producer suggested a segment about NFL player

Ray Rice, who'd been charged with aggravated assault for punching his fiancée, Jian yelled at him: "Are you trying to throw me under?!" His extra-erratic behaviour was confusing for the majority of producers who were still in the dark. When I finally filled a fellow producer in on why Jian was acting strangely, she was relieved to hear it wasn't all in her head. "I thought *I* was going crazy," she admitted.

A small group of us started going for coffee and informal group therapy every morning next door at the Ritz. We'd talk about Jian's latest power moves and try to calm one another down. His behaviour was making it extremely difficult for us to do our job. There was a lot of whispering about the elephant in the office. Brian took over directing after Sean left to work on another show—he could no longer in good conscience keep writing Jian's opening essays—but no one was told the real reason why.

By early August I was fed up with all the secrecy and confusion. My anxiety was at an all-time high. I walked into my boss's office. "You have to do something," I said.

"What do you think I should do?" he replied.

I resented him for turning the question on me. I didn't want to have to do his job for him. "I don't know, but things can't continue the way they are. He's driving us all crazy. You have to do *something*," I pleaded.

"Rachel, you have to remember that he's innocent until proven guilty," he said condescendingly, as if I'd never seen an episode of *Law & Order*. I could feel my veins pulsing. We weren't in a court of law; we were at work. As far as I could see he was using the presumption of innocence as an excuse to disregard the fact that Jian was already guilty—beyond a reasonable doubt—of making us all fucking miserable. It was a familiar feeling. There I was, sounding the alarm, but I was just seen as the kid who cried wolf. When really, there was a big bad fucking wolf.

LATER THAT MONTH I flew to Iceland for another escapist hiking adventure. I was sad to be leaving Molly so early in our relationship, but I'd booked the trip months earlier. Back in March I'd been conducting some fantasy research into hiking trails when I read about the Laugavegur Trail, a winding, fifty-five-kilometre route through Iceland's uninhabited southern highlands. It was described as one of the most remote trails in the world. The caramel-coloured mountains and black sands looked like another planet—exactly what I was craving. I took one look at the sparkling blue glaciers and majestic canyons and summoned my inner Liz Lemon: "I want to go to there." I booked my mountain huts that instant.

Having spent my first evening soaking in a natural hot spring at base camp, I set forth the next morning across neon green moss, snow patches, and rolling lava fields. I'd hiked about twenty kilometres when I came to the edge of a plateau. There I stopped to take in the breathtaking view: vibrant yellow rhyolite mountains in the distance and a pristine turquoise lake nestled in the valley below, where I'd be spending the night. They say that most accidents happen when you're close to home.

I very slowly began the steep descent down the mountain, pressing my hiking poles firmly on the ground and placing one foot gingerly in front of the other. I was carrying a heavier pack than usual—I had all five days' worth of food with me—as I zigzagged my way along the narrow, dusty trail. As I was nearing the bottom, my right foot slipped on some loose pebbles. It happened so quickly, but I remember it in slow motion: the tottering of my ankle as it struggled to keep me upright before finally giving way. I fell back into a seated position on the slope, dizzy, faint, and nauseated.

With whatever wits I had, I quickly detached myself from my backpack, afraid that if I passed out, my bag might roll over the drop to my left and take me with it. It took a few minutes of lying there in a blur for me to come back from the shock. I tried to stand up, but it was too painful to put any weight on my right foot. I sat back down. *Fuck, fuck, fuck.* I knew I'd really messed up. I was alone, in the middle of nowhere, on the ledge of a mountain, without a literal leg to stand on. "One of the most remote trails in the world" echoed in my mind. I was a city kid—what business did I have being out here on my own in the first place? I was officially a cautionary tale.

I stared at the crystal blue lake, only about five kilometres away. I was so close, but how I'd make it there was anyone's guess. Then, to my great relief, when I looked up behind me I spotted two figures heading down the mountain. A few minutes later, as they came around the bend, I greeted them casually so as to not cause alarm: "Hi! I twisted my ankle. Can you please help me carry my bag down?" They were a young couple, a woman and man, with indistinct European accents. Loaded up with camping gear, they were obviously much more prepared for the elements than me. For starters, they had a first-aid kit. The woman gave me a couple of painkillers and wrapped my ankle with a tensor bandage while her boyfriend went ahead with my bag down the mountain.

"Okay, walk," she instructed me.

I tried to stand up again and steady myself on the slope, but the pain was just too intense.

"I can't!" I cried.

"You have to!" she ordered.

Getting my navel and eyebrow piercings in the 90s had led me to believe I had a high pain threshold, but this was impossible to bear. So, instead of hiking down the slope, I ended up shimmying my way down on my butt. When I finally got to the bottom, the couple wished me well and handed me off to Oscar, an Icelandic tour guide who radioed ahead for help.

I joined up with his tour group of mostly Canadians, including a couple of doctors who handed me an assortment of pills for what we all assumed was my sprained ankle. Someone carried my bag. I figured out a way to walk by slanting my right leg outward and using only the inside of my foot. Luckily it was mostly flat the rest of the way, except for two rocky river crossings. Oscar, a Viking type, piggybacked me through the water.

I was high on adrenalin and the trail mix of painkillers I'd been throwing back, not to mention an immense feeling of gratitude toward my various saviours. About a kilometre away from the shelter, two very large men in red rescue patrol uniforms caught up with us and offered to carry me the rest of the way.

"It's okay. I'm fine!" I told them. *No need to be so dramatic.* (I'd sprained my ankle once as a child while playing at a friend's house. Mom brushed it off, but I couldn't walk—Josh had to come and wheel me home in his *Toronto Star* newspaper cart. I wonder where I learned to downplay my injuries.)

When I arrived at the shelter, I sat down by the edge of an icy stream and dipped my foot in. My ankle was the size of a grapefruit. But the swelling would go down by morning, I figured. That night I made rehydrated beef stroganoff in a bag, washed down some Tylenol with Jameson whisky, and somehow managed to climb up to my assigned top bunk.

In the morning, with my adrenalin down, I couldn't walk at all. I hopped on one foot over to the warden's hut, using my hiking poles for balance. Still hopeful, I wanted to inquire into the possibility of staying another night, thinking I'd need maybe one more day to recover. Elva, the hut warden's partner, was a trained first responder and insisted on examining my ankle.

As she gently rocked it up and down, there was an audible clicking sound. "I think it's broken," she said. "You have to go to the hospital." *Broken?*

Elva wrapped my ankle in a mouldable splint while her husband made some calls. Luckily a man named Siggi, the husband of another woman who worked on the trail, happened to be heading back to Reykjavik that day, and the surrounding rivers were low enough that he could come get me in his four-wheeler. I sat in the back seat with my leg propped up, bracing myself as we drove over rocky bumps and dips in the Mars-like surface of the highlands. At one point we passed by the notorious Eyjafjallajökull volcano that had erupted just a few years earlier, disrupting flights across Europe.

As we munched on the beef jerky and dried mango that I no longer had to ration for the trek, I took the opportunity to ask Siggi about Iceland's elves. I'd been fascinated by the country's relationship with the magical creatures ever since I did a story about it for work. Apparently more than half the population believes in elves or at least wouldn't rule out their existence. Roads are even diverted so as not to disturb their dwellings. (According to folklore, misfortune awaits those who build in elf territory.) Siggi told me there were even mediums who could communicate with them.

"What do people think of these . . . elf mediums?" I ventured. "Are they considered crazy?"

"Nah, just a little eccentric," he said, tilting his hand back and forth. Sounded like someone else I knew.

When we arrived in Reykjavik a few hours later, I thanked Siggi as he helped me into a wheelchair and rolled me into the ER. My doctor was a sweet woman with large red-rimmed glasses and a blond ponytail. "My name is Bjork," she said. *Of course it is.*

It turned out that my fibula—that is, my outer calf bone, not my ankle after all—was broken in two places. Bjork was amazed I'd been able to walk on it, adding that I was very lucky I didn't need surgery—it was a "clean break."

I called Teddy with the news. "I pulled a Mother," I told him. I was humbly reminded of one of her favourite sayings: "When you point your finger at someone else, there are three pointing back at you." Teddy booked me a new plane ticket home and was there to pick me up the next day. By now he was used to being the family airport–hospital express shuttle.

I'd rented out my apartment for the length of the trip, so I had to stay with Mom for a week. She took care of me as well as she could with her one working arm. Molly came over and slept in my bed next to Mom's infrared sauna, a hulking physical reminder that I hadn't yet told her about Mom's cancer. I was getting really good at this denial thing.

Mom and I laughed at what a sorry sight we were: she with her elbow in a purple cast, cradled in a sling; me with my leg in a blue cast, propped up on a chair. We looked like mirror images of each other, wartorn and broken. What had become of us?

The truth is that neither of us were getting out of this unscathed. I could no longer assume the role of the sturdy foil to Mom's fragility. I too was broken, crushed under the weight of a backpack filled with food, and what else? The cracks in my perfect durable facade were showing. And like her, I wasn't ready to acknowledge it.

I WENT RIGHT back to work. That September I was responsible for the show's Toronto International Film Festival coverage. I hopped up and down theatre steps, determined not to let a broken leg slow me down. I attended industry parties and went out to dinner with friends. I even went on a weekend camping trip with Molly and her family, canoeing and portaging on my crutches. "The only disability is a bad attitude," I'd say with a cheeky smile.

I didn't like accepting help from anyone—asserting my independence was another way to minimize my ailment. It was especially hard to let Molly help me. I liked being the steady, balanced one, but now I couldn't even carry a glass of water. It was hard to admit that I was both mentally and physically off-balance. I tried to stop her, but Molly insisted on doing my laundry and other chores. And, little by little, I let her. I don't know what was more challenging—allowing her to help me or admitting to myself that I wasn't as self-sufficient as I'd thought.

A couple of months into our relationship, Molly and I were hanging out on my couch one evening when she looked into my eyes and said "I love you."

I froze. I didn't know what to say. "Thank you," I replied. Molly gave me a tentative half-smile, searching my eyes. "I mean, I believe I feel that way too," I said. I didn't want to leave her hanging, but I also wasn't about to say something so meaningful on an emotional whim. "But falling in love is like being on drugs," I continued. "You're not thinking clearly. It's too early for me to say those words. I need more time to be sure."

"Okay," Molly said, rolling her eyes and then leaning back in to kiss me.

But it was the conversation we had a few weeks later that really made me squirm. We were lying in bed when Molly said she'd sensed some tension between Mom and me.

"Do you want to know the real reason I'm annoyed with her?" I asked.

"Uh, okay," she said, hesitant.

"Promise you won't feel sorry for me, all right? Don't say 'Aww' or anything, okay?" I was already anticipating the panicked feeling that other people's reactions used to bring out in me. Molly gave me that look of hers that lovingly said "You're a weirdo" and agreed to my terms.

I hid my face with my hands as I told her the whole story: how Mom had been diagnosed with cancer four years before, how against my wishes she'd been trying to cure herself, and how we mostly just pretended that she didn't have it anymore.

Molly was keeping a blank face as per my request. When I finally asked her what she thought, she told me things made more sense to her now. Apparently Mom had made a sly comment to her about me not agreeing with her "choices." I was relieved to have told Molly. I felt closer to her, even though I was still keeping to myself another distressing situation.

BY SEPTEMBER, it was getting harder for me to play-act as if everything was normal at work. I was sitting in the audience at the Sony Centre watching Jian interview Lena Dunham about her new book. "With more and more pop culture figures like Beyoncé and Taylor Swift embracing feminism, how do you see the movement evolving?" Jian asked. I knew the words before they faux-stumbled out of his mouth. I'd written them (he'd been bullying me into doing his homework outside of CBC as well). "It's all about equal rights for men and women," Lena replied. "I don't know why anyone wouldn't be on board for that—unless they're a monster," she said, half-joking. *Dun-dun-DUUUUN*. The audience chuckled, but I had a sick feeling in the pit of my stomach.

Given what I'd heard about him, I couldn't listen to Jian wax on about feminism anymore. I was used to being used by him, but now I felt gross about helping him masquerade as someone who genuinely cared about women. I knew I had to find a way out. But I was afraid of what he might do to sabotage my career if I tried to leave.

Jian liked to give random shoulder massages to a few of us producers in the office. Once in a while, without any warning, I'd feel his hands on my back. I'd instantly freeze up, but then I'd tell myself to relax, that he was just being nice. I didn't want to make him feel bad by shrugging him off. But I could never ever shake the feeling that in those instances he was sending me a direct message: *Don't forget, I'm in control.* He'd literally have his hands around my neck.

I didn't know exactly how I'd get away from him or where I'd go next. But sitting in the audience that evening, I knew I had to run. Just as soon as I got off my crutches.

10

BOILED FROGS

One Friday in late October I walked into work like any other morning—except I was limping. It was one of my first days off crutches. Q was already live when I arrived at my desk, turned on my computer, and put my headphones on to listen to the show's internal feed. I was surprised to hear the voice of one of our regular guest hosts instead of Jian. My heart began beating faster. *Could this be it?*

Although he cut it close every morning, Jian never actually missed a show without advance notice. My eyes widened and I slowly scanned the office. Everything appeared normal, but I had a strong sense that something was up. I walked over to the control room, where Brian was directing. As I opened the door our eyes met. In that split second I knew.

By that time I'd almost given up hope that the rumours about Jian would ever come to light, or that anyone would ever come to our rescue. I assumed he'd managed to sweep it under the rug like everything else. But that afternoon the team was summoned to the boardroom, where our boss and management informed us that Jian was taking an "indefinite" leave of absence. They wouldn't tell us why. People were confused, with some thinking Jian needed time off to grieve his father, who had recently died. Those of us in the know gave one another looks. Shit was going down.

Late Sunday morning, I got a text informing me of an emergency conference call. I dialed in just as the head of radio began reading a statement: "The CBC is saddened to announce its relationship with Jian has come to an end." My jaw dropped. I had a brief feeling of pure jubilation before the shit show started unravelling in real time.

Late Sunday afternoon, Jian posted a fifteen-hundred-word statement on his Facebook page in which he claimed that the CBC had fired him for his "private life." He compared his sex life to "a mild form of Fifty Shades of Grey" and dismissed the not-yet-made-public accusations as a "campaign of false allegations pursued by a jilted ex girl-friend and a freelance writer." *Fifty Shades of Grey? Jilted ex-girlfriend? Wow, this is what happens when he writes his own shit?*

By Sunday evening, my happiness about his being fired turned to heartbreak. The *Toronto Star* published allegations from three women who said Jian had physically attacked them on dates without consent. I felt nauseated and shaky as I read the details. "They allege he struck them with a closed fist or open hand; bit them; choked them until they almost passed out; covered their nose and mouth so that they had difficulty breathing; and that they were verbally abused during and after sex."

It's amazing, the difference between kind-of-knowing and *actually* knowing. It may not be much of a leap in terms of facts, but it's a giant plunge in terms of how it feels. It's like the lifting of a sheer veil. You saw the fuzzy outline of shapes, but now you clearly see the horror for what it is—you really *experience* it. Complete and utter dread. And, because you'd seen the clues, you get the bonus feelings of stupidity and regret.

When I arrived at work on Monday morning, it was obvious that maintenance had been working overtime. The twenty-foot poster of Jian that had been on the side of the building had been torn down, and the wall that bore his giant face outside our studio looked as though it had been scraped away by bears. They had loved him for so long, and now they couldn't get rid of him fast enough.

When I got to my desk, a pamphlet had been left on my chair. There was a black-and-white photo of a wilted flower on the cover under the heading "Experiencing a Traumatic Event: Recovery and Coping Strategies." It began: "You have been given this handout following the occurrence of an unexpected and potentially traumatic event . . ." *NO SHIT.* Colleagues were breaking down. Sean looked destroyed when I saw him in the hallway. He couldn't cope and was on his way home. We all looked like abused animals released from a cage after years of captivity. We were disoriented. The light hurt our eyes.

That afternoon I went to the studio to see Hozier perform his haunting song "Take Me to Church." I entered the control room where a few of my co-workers had already congregated. Someone handed me a glass of sympathy Scotch, sent to us from colleagues down the hall. We looked one another in the eyes, but no one said a word as we clinked our glasses. *Ding-dong, the witch is dead*—not a joyful cheers but a collective relief, a solemn acknowledgment. With the horrible allegations coming to light, there was nothing to celebrate. We sipped our single malt as Hozier's powerful voice rose to a crescendo. It was four minutes of solace before we got swept back into the tornado.

By the end of the week, eight women had accused Jian of assault. There was a sense that the country felt betrayed. Many people asked me, "How could such a sensitive, feminist guy assault women?" They'd drawn conclusions about him based on the show's progressive journalism. I hardly blamed them—Jian had never purported to be anything different from his on-air persona. He had people fooled.

The shock soon turned to rage. I was angry at Jian for what he'd done to those women, for the way he'd treated me and my colleagues, for everything I hadn't been allowed to be angry about before. After he was fired we could finally say all the things we'd been trained not to say. I could admit to other people—and myself—that he was horrible. It was liberating to be able to speak the truth, to have my reality validated. In the days and weeks that followed I spent a lot of time with my work friends. We helped one another make sense of Jian's distorted reality. And as we shared our individual stories, the fuller picture came into focus. We could see how he'd played us off each other. I learned the term "gaslighting"—how an abuser can sneakily get their victim to fundamentally doubt their reality. It dawned on me that we'd been psychologically abused. I'd been a victim too. I'd convinced myself that I was the puppetmaster (Jian read *my* words), but it had always been him. He ran the show, and I'd been forced to join his play.

I felt betrayed that he'd used *Q*—this thing we'd all built together—in the service of his dark private life. It was mortifying: I'd inadvertently helped Jian create a progressive feminist persona that he used to deceive and abuse women. I questioned what value my work now had. Had those six and a half years been for nothing?

I'd always believed that I possessed a strong sense of self. But then how had I allowed myself to stay in a toxic work environment—in an abusive work relationship—for so long? How had I let myself compromise my own values and beliefs? How had I become so disconnected from myself?

I remember how my colleague Debbie was furious and fuming one day. She looked at me: "When did it all become normal?" she asked. I paused to think about it. *Yeah, when did it?* I couldn't think of an exact moment or event. That's when it hit me: we were frogs who'd gotten boiled alive, one degree at a time. Over the years we'd slowly gotten used to the insidious warping of our reality, to the point where we no longer recognized our reality, or even ourselves.

I was having recurring nightmares about Jian, along three basic storylines. In the first, I'd be giving him hell. "How could you?" I'd scream, full of rage. In the second, he'd been given his job back and I had to work with him again. I was terrified and betrayed. Those dreams felt so scarily real that the next day I'd have to keep reassuring myself he wasn't coming back. The third storyline was the most disturbing. Jian would look at me with sad eyes and ask me why I had abandoned him. "Lil Bro, I didn't do it. You have to believe me. We're brothers." "I'm sorry, I can't," I'd say, anguished and crying.

The public could dismiss him as a one-dimensional monster, but my feelings were more complicated. This was a person who'd called me his brother for more than six years. ("You'll always be my true Lil Bro," he'd written to me on my thirtieth birthday.) As much as I'd hated him, there was part of me that still felt attached. Still cared. I'd wanted his approval until the very end, which made me feel guilty and confused. Had he ever really cared about me? Or were all the sweet moments just tactical ways of keeping me hooked so that he could use me?

I was walking through life like a zombie. For someone who always had their finger on the pulse, I barely had one. I was afraid of attending cultural events and of socializing in general. The whole country was talking about Jian. It was all anyone wanted to discuss with me. People were curious. "Did you know? Do you think he'll go to jail? Will he be able to revive his career?" They didn't understand that the situation was traumatizing for me. It was my life. Even people close to me didn't get it. And why would they? I'd always minimized the emotional toll of working with Jian. Friends knew I didn't like him, but I'd only ever really talked about the good parts of my job.

In the midst of this media circus, Josh invited me out for brunch. Although Mom and Teddy weren't tuned in to how devastating the fallout was for me, Josh at least had some idea of what I was going through. For the past year and a half he'd been embroiled in the Rob Ford crack-smoking scandal at City Hall after a video circulated on the internet showing the mayor puffing away on a glass crack pipe while spewing obscenities. The incident became comedic fodder for the likes of Jimmy Kimmel and *SNL*, but it caused Josh a lot of emotional turmoil. So he knew what it was like to have people constantly ask questions about a traumatic experience as though it were the plot of a TV show. We noted how "interesting" it was that we'd both found ourselves in the midst of two of the country's biggest scandals. "Yeah," I said, snickering, "I wonder what it is about *our* family . . ."

Molly felt like I was shutting her out. We'd been so close for the past four months, and now my anger and depression had come between us. She wanted to be there for me, to help me in ways I might accept. She sent me my union's harassment policies and grievance timelines. She wanted to get closer—to be on the inside of my grief and pain.

But my colleagues were the only ones I could really talk to—the only ones who truly understood what I was going through. We'd been work friends, but now we were war buddies. In between prepping our revolving door of guest hosts, we spent a lot of our days processing together, trying to help one another make sense of the past as we were being barrelled into the future. It's what kept me going back to work every day—along with the hope that we could finally have the show we'd always wanted. We'd made *Q*. We'd poured ourselves into it. I didn't want to leave it; I wanted to fight for it. I wanted to take it back.

Sometimes I wondered whether people thought we were overreacting—I even questioned it myself—because it was so difficult to articulate or pinpoint what exactly Jian had done to us. How do you explain the feeling of being on edge for years? Always trying not to rock the boat, assessing his energy and moods, anticipating his next blow-up or revenge plot, fearing what was coming next. The logic of language could not capture the experience.

At the time, #WhyIStayed was starting to trend in response to questions about why a woman would remain with an abusive man. Women were speaking out, sharing their stories. My situation wasn't the same, but I identified with the complexity of the relationships they described. I thought about why I'd stayed: I stayed because I thought the bigger picture of doing so many feminist, trans, and anti-racist stories was worth it. I stayed because I loved the work and many of the people I worked with. I stayed because it was my first big job in my field and people told me it was normal. I stayed because I mistakenly believed that it was a badge of honour to be able to "handle" Jian.

As I was opening my eyes to what had happened to me, it seemed as if the whole country was waking up from a sort of cultural denial. It was a watershed moment. The beginning of the #MeToo movement. Women were coming forward with their own wrenching stories of sexual assault and harassment and their own allegations against major public figures. There was a dramatic shift in the national conversation about sexual assault and consent. We were getting a better understanding of the nuances of sexual assault and the challenges facing women wanting to report it. It was a painful time for many, but it was also inspiring.

In November, Jian surrendered to police and was formally charged with four counts of sexual assault and one count of overcoming resistance by choking. We all stood around the TV in the office, as we'd done for milestone events like Oprah's last episode and Obama's inauguration, and took in the surreal sight: Jian arriving at a downtown courthouse in the back of a police car. My thoughts were with the women who'd come forward. The highest stakes in the aftermath of Jian's termination were about justice for them. I was tremendously grateful—they saved us.

THROUGHOUT THE ORDEAL, Mom's cancer took a back seat. As far as she was concerned, her elbow was her only health issue. After she got her cast off, she blamed the surgeon for the fact that she hadn't regained full mobility. She felt disfigured. Whereas I was hoping her elbow operation might inspire her to get the more pressing surgery, her self-proclaimed "botch job" only confirmed to her how evil Western medicine was.

Her cancer came up only when she talked about her writing. Mom was proud of being a medical system renegade, and was even considering a sequel to her dating book: *Silver Fox Says No to Chemo*. I think she was hoping to add her story to the miracle-cure-memoir genre. For now, though, she was working on a play about her cancer journey. She'd asked for my help editing it, but I'd been putting it off.

One day when I was at her place, Mom asked if she could read it to me. I figured I'd get it over with. So I took a seat at the dining room table as Mom stood at the head with her script.

"It's called *My Way*," she announced.

I smiled and took a deep breath. *Nothing veiled about that title.*

Mom began, "I want you to know that I did not start out as a medical rebel and I'm not in denial."

Oh dear. If you have to say it . . .

"I want you to know that I have always questioned authority. I have been complimented on my bravery in choosing to 'drive my own car,' to leave the freeway of conventional Western medicine and map an off-road course of treatment. I was able to resist the fear-mongering of the doctors, friends, and relatives."

I gave her a two-finger salute. Mom laughed and then quickly got back into character. She read out each scene with dramatic flair, playing various characters with different voices.

SURGEON: I'm offering you one more chance to do what you ought to do.

MOM: I know you believe that your way is the only way, but I'm going to continue to direct my own healing.

SURGEON: What are you talking about? No one takes charge of their own cancer treatment.

MOM: I really am grateful for all you've done for me. But given my particular situation, I've made my particular choice.

SURGEON: Do you have any idea what kind of death awaits you? I hope you're making arrangements for assisted suicide. I'm firing you.

It was obvious who the hero was going to be in this story. At one point, Mom got into a heated conversation with her cancer:

MOM: I don't want to fight you.

CANCER: Good call, babe. You wouldn't win.

MOM: But I don't want you anymore. I want you to leave.

CANCER: You want to dump me? Not so easy. We have a contract.

MOM: I know I married you. But you're a thug and you scare me. You're such a control freak, always needing to have your own way.

CANCER: Look who's talking. Yeah, I'm a thug, but you wanted protection and I rescued you from a heart attack or a stroke. Baby, you made your body into a toxic swamp, all that pastry, that marbled animal fat, those many many glasses of Chardonnay. Not to mention your clogged spirit, judgmental mind, overreactive emotions. Where do you think you're holding your resentments? Yup, right where the sun don't shine.

MOM: Okay, I once needed you and you came through for me. But now you want to devour me—just like my mother, just like my lovers, adore me and devour me.

CANCER: I do adore you. We're mated. We're like one person.

MOM: Listen, I'll make a deal with you. Join the community of the other cells—you'll be more fulfilled. Or recycle—die to be reborn as a cell with status. You could be a brain cell!

I didn't know whether it was the funniest thing I'd ever seen or the most disturbing. Was her cancer Teddy? David? Grandma? Mom was clearly working out some serious relationship issues.

The play ended with Mom turning to the audience (in this instance, me) and announcing, "I gotta dance. Will anyone join me?" I forced a smile. I was not into audience participation. Mom walked over to her CD player and pressed play. As Gloria Gaynor belted out the opening lines of "I Will Survive," Mom raised her hands in the air and began twirling around the living room.

I remained seated with my elbows on the table, propping up my face. I was stupefied.

"I don't think I can help you," I told her after the music wound down.

"Why not?"

"Because . . ." I paused to sum up my swirling thoughts. "You are the *epitome* of the unreliable narrator."

IN DECEMBER, Mom admitted to feeling some horrible symptoms: roiling stomach, nausea, low energy. She'd lost weight, too—she believed she had parasites from eating "bad sushi" several months earlier.

She decided to go see her new GP, Dr. Brunt. Mom's old GP had been bumming her out—"Every time I went in she was sure I was going to die. It was *so* depressing"—but she liked her new one. "She's totally not alternative, but she's totally great."

Dr. Brunt convinced Mom to get an MRI just before Christmas; we'd have to wait until after the holidays to get the results. On New Year's Eve Molly threw a big house party. I avoided everyone, and ended up watching horror movies in the attic. You know you're in a bad way when the Babadook is a welcome distraction.

The new year started off with a bang, or rather, a blow. Mom's MRI didn't detect any presence of parasites. It did, however, reveal the presence of third-stage rectal cancer—Mom's cancer had grown into the wall of her rectum.

The diagnosis had snuck up on me. How had I not seen that Mom's health was going downhill? It was so obvious in hindsight. She was always picking at her food, always sending it back at restaurants because it tasted off. She looked pale. She was tired all the time. I remembered Teddy saying, "Your mother doesn't look well. Her complexion is different." I'd agreed, and yet somehow it didn't register. Had I been so consumed with my broken leg, my new relationship, the Jian blowout and resulting depression that I'd dropped the ball altogether? Or had I become so complacent, so disconnected from reality, that I wouldn't have seen it anyway?

It certainly wasn't conscious, but maybe on some level I believed that Mom was so powerful, so untouchable, that she would find a way to manifest the reality she wanted. That despite not getting treatment she'd be able to stall her cancer with her sheer will. After all, Mom was magical.

STAGE 3

11

WHACK-A-MOLE

When we near the end of a match, my chess partner Joel knows he has to hold the metaphorical pillow tightly when trying to snuff me out. I always come back from the brink for one last fight. And in the early days of 2015, I was down. But Mom was right, I never give up easily—I become even *more* focused. Time was running out, and I had to muster whatever energy I had in order to fight for Mom once more. I begged and pleaded with her to see a surgeon. It was my sole wish.

I soon regretted not having been more specific. Mom bought a ticket to Brazil to see a "psychic surgeon," known as John of God, who performed invisible procedures with the help of spirit assistants. *Fuck my life.* He wasn't a licensed doctor, yet he claimed to channel the spirits of long-dead physicians and saints. I looked him up. To call him a charlatan would be putting it mildly. There was no credible medical or scientific evidence to support any of his miraculous claims, just several reliable investigative reports exposing him as a con artist. He brought in millions of dollars every year shilling his blessed products: herbs, water, crystals, and magic triangles he'd autograph upon request—two blessings for the price of one.

Mom was surprised to learn that her cancer had grown. Apparently Michael was, too. But instead of blaming him she blamed herself for straying from her protocols. "I went off my diet," she lamented. She wanted to refocus on her remedies, to return to her affirmations, to her cottage cheese and flaxseed oil. Back to her five daily drops of scorpion venom. She was off sugar again, and coffee too. Well, drinking it at least—she started going for organic coffee enemas. Mom was still confident that her body would not betray her.

Around this time I began having my own stomach issues. I felt intense cramping in my abdomen. Yet even as it grew more painful with each passing day, I didn't give it too much thought—I was too concerned about Mom.

Of all the surgeons we'd seen, Mom seemed most receptive to Dr. Stotland, so I continued to beg her to see him one more time. I fought with her over and over. She put up a good fight. She cried. She even hung up on me. But this was a battle I was not backing down from. This was my last chance. *Her* last chance. There was nothing left to lose— except her.

"If you don't do this for me I won't be your friend anymore!" I threatened, giving her a taste of her own poison. I didn't mean it. But I was beyond desperate.

In mid-January, Teddy got a stubborn headache that became so severe he took a taxi to the hospital, where a CT scan revealed that he'd suffered a minor stroke. Life was starting to feel like a haywire game of whack-a-mole. It was scary, but Teddy was lucky—there appeared to be no permanent damage. He was in good spirits when Mom and I visited him in the hospital—he loved the attention he got from doctors and nurses.

I sulked in the corner, angry that Mom still wouldn't agree to see a surgeon again. I looked at Teddy in his hospital bed and Mom beside him, pale and thin. The fragility of my parents' existence had never been more apparent. We all thought Teddy would be the first to go. Even he thought so. He'd already picked out and paid for his casket! For years he'd been emailing Josh and me regular updates to his end-of-life plans. Every few months we got a message out of the blue with the subject line "Kicking Off," detailing where to find his power of attorney (in the liquor cabinet) and often closing with the postscript "I'm not leaving yet."

MY STOMACH CRAMPS were worse now. I'd been in pain for nearly a week, and it was getting to the point where I could barely hold it together. I was hunched over at my desk at work one afternoon, my left hand holding my abdomen, my right hand on the mouse. I couldn't concentrate. My forehead was sweaty and I could hardly keep my eyes open. The computer screen went blurry. As if in slow motion, I tipped over, fell to the floor, and just lay there.

"You okay?" Brian asked.

"I think I need to go to the hospital."

As Teddy was being discharged upstairs, I was being admitted downstairs.

Molly met me in Emergency. I would never have asked her to come, but I was touched that she did. She lay down next to me in the hospital bed while a nurse hooked me up to a morphine drip. The pain was so intense I could barely talk.

Molly pulled out her iPad and cued up an episode of our favourite not-so-guilty pleasure, *The Fosters*—a cheesy yet addictive lesbian family drama. It wasn't a typical date night, but what was typical these days?

The doctor entered my curtained-off room, clipboard in hand, and peppered me with questions that all seemed to focus on whether I might be pregnant. "Are you sexually active?"

"Yes," I said, smiling at Molly. "But I assure you, our birth control method is foolproof." The doctor looked up from her clipboard and laughed. Then she apologized in advance for making me pee in a cup, saying it was a matter of protocol that I take a pregnancy test. They also had me do a blood test and an ultrasound.

Finally, after all the poking and prodding, appendicitis, ulcers, and pregnancy (phew!) were all ruled out. They gave me a prescription for inflammation. The cause of the pain remained a mystery, although the doctor did say that nearly half of stomach-pain cases go unsolved. I know it seems obvious now, but at the time it didn't occur to me that it might be from, I dunno, *stress?* That I was having my own mind-body breakdown? I just filed it away as a medical cold case.

"Can I have one more hit of morphine for the road?" I asked. They moved me to a row of vinyl reclining chairs in the hallway for my last morphine drip. Molly went for a walk while I kicked back and tried to relax.

"What do you do for a living?" asked the older man in the chair next to me.

"I work in radio," I said, being deliberately vague. I was no longer voluntarily telling people I worked on *Q*.

"I love the radio! What station?" *Talk about a buzzkill.*

"CBC," I said, keeping my eyes fixed on the ceiling. I hoped he'd get the hint.

"Ah, the CBC! Do you know that guy who punches women?"

There wasn't enough morphine in the world.

By the time we left the ER, the pain had finally subsided. Even better, I felt happy for the first time in ages. I hadn't realized how depressed I'd been, how much weight I'd been carrying around, until the heaviness lifted. I felt strangely like myself again, funny and light and energetic. Molly and I held hands and laughed as we threw open the hospital doors and skipped all the way home. For one night only, I didn't have a care in the world. *Thanks, opiates!*

Mom really must have felt sorry for me, because that evening she sent me a text: "OK I'm going to go to the surgeon with you because I love you so much and know you have my best interests at heart. I'm sorry you're so scared. I hope you sleep well and feel better tomorrow. As my mother used to say, roses in your pillow."

Mom and I made a deal. We'd go see Dr. Stotland together as a family, and then, for one hour, she'd listen to what we all had to say. I promised that if she complied, I would never hassle her again. Mom agreed but said she couldn't do it till late February. There was somewhere else she needed to go first.

IN MID-FEBRUARY MOM flew to Costa Rica for a week-long juice fast in the jungle. She was hoping to cure herself of parasites and candida (and hey, maybe cancer while she was at it). She still wasn't convinced that it was her cancer making her feel unwell.

For seven days Mom drank only fresh-pressed juices, superfood shakes, and vegetable broth. She had a great time doing shots of maca and moringa around the pool with her new fast friends. The others were there mainly hoping to shed a few pounds, but it was Mom who took the title of Biggest Loser. Before her flight home she emailed Teddy, Josh, and me, asking to be picked up from the airport: "I'm going to use a wheelchair because I do get tired standing for a long time, but don't be scared. I'm mobile, if skinny, and definitely feel better."

It was shocking how thin she looked. "I know, it's horrifying. I look like a concentration camp victim," Mom admitted. She insisted that her frailty was a result of the juice fasting and that she'd gain the weight back soon, but I could tell she was frightened. "My life is a clusterfuck these days," she said. She was rereading *Radical Remission*, her favourite book on spontaneous healing, to calm herself down.

I wrote to Dr. Stotland in advance of our visit to let him know what had happened since we'd seen him last, when Mom's cancer was Stage 2. I told him that I felt she was killing herself, and that there might be a way for him to validate her alternative ideas while still advocating for medical intervention: Mom not only needed to believe in treatment but also to feel it was her choice.

When the day finally rolled around, the four of us gathered in Dr. Stotland's office. He got straight to the point. "There's no question your tumour has progressed," he said. "You've gone from local to advanced cancer. It's gone deeper into the wall. Hopefully, not beyond."

"Is there anything Western medicine can offer me besides that operation?" Mom asked.

"We don't even know if we can offer that anymore," he said. "You might not be a candidate for surgery. We have to see if there's cancer elsewhere in your body." Dr. Stotland urged Mom to get a CT scan so that he could see whether her cancer had spread to her lungs or liver. If it was only Stage 3, Mom would still have a sixty percent survival rate if she did surgery, chemo, and radiation. "We hope you don't have Stage 4," he said. "That's much more complicated."

"It hasn't gone into the liver. I know it," said Mom.

I turned to her. "How do you know that?"

"I have no symptoms," she said.

"What are you talking about? Look how skinny you are!"

"That's because of my parasites and going on the cleanse."

"Most people don't have symptoms until they are where you are now," Dr. Stotland said. "People who don't get colonoscopies only find out they have cancer when it's advanced. Most people I see are starting off where you are now."

I looked at Dr. Stotland. "What is a death like from rectal cancer?" I knew it would be hard for Mom to hear it, but this was my version of tough love.

"I've heard it," Mom protested. "I don't need—"

"It's not fun. It's horrible," he answered before she could protest any further. "If it goes into the bones or nerves, it's misery." I was pleased he was taking my cues and was silently cheering him on. "If this thing doesn't spread, it will grow and block you off until you get an infection that will kill you. At that point, we would hope that your bowel would perforate because that would kill you quicker."

"Woo, not fun." Mom let out a deep exhalation. Dr. Stotland excused himself for a few minutes.

"It would be a big trauma to have surgery," Mom said. "What if I can live for another ten years without doing it?"

"That's not the direction you're going in," I said.

"But I went off course. Cancer comes back if you go off course."

"It didn't come back. It never went away!"

"I know it didn't go away, but I was going to live with it forever. A lot of people live with their polyps forever."

"That's not the reality. Cancer grows."

"Not necessarily, not if you do the right things it doesn't."

Josh interjected. "You've fallen back into a circular conversation."

"Rachel, your mother is entitled to do whatever she wants," Teddy said. We were all talking over one another.

"You know what this reminds me of?" Mom said, sitting back and smiling. "When we all went to see that psychiatrist we took Josh to because he was nuts and acting out."

"I think I was just responding to my parents' behaviour," Josh said, laughing.

"Which shrink was this?" Teddy asked. We were all talking over one another again.

"Hey, stop it!" Mom said. "It's my job to be the interrupter in the family." She went on: "At the end of the session the shrink declared, 'Josh is the sanest person in this family.'" Mom looked over at me. "And then you said in your high squeaky voice, 'No, *I'm* the sanest!' And then on the car ride home, Teddy, you said, 'I really think *I'm* the sanest.' And then I quietly thought to myself, 'It's actually *me*.'"

Dr. Stotland came back into the room. "You've got to figure out what you want to do," he said.

"I want to think it over. I'm very scared," Mom said.

"What are you scared of?" he asked.

"I'm afraid of the treatment. It's true," Mom admitted.

"I don't like doctors myself," Dr. Stotland said. "I'm a basket case when I have to go. We all have our things. But if you take a step back and see what medicine can do, there are benefits. It's the fight of your life. It's no joke. But it's effective. And it's the best we have."

I was giving him a standing ovation in my head.

"The next step is getting a CT scan," he said, getting up to hold the door open for us.

As we all got up to leave, Mom turned to him. "If I'm lucky and I cure myself, would you be interested or offended if I came back to tell you about it?"

Teddy, Josh, and I exchanged a glance.

"I'd be more than interested," Dr. Stotland said, smiling kindly.

"Of course he'd be interested," I joked. "It would be like the Immaculate Conception of oncology!"

As I walked past him he whispered, "I'll be in touch."

We shuffled down the hallway and confirmed our plan to meet up on Sunday at Teddy's to discuss the matter. As painful as it was to see Mom so terrified, a part of me was glad to see her in touch with her fear.

That evening, Dr. Stotland called me from his car on his way home from the hospital. "Has your mother always been like this?" he asked. I didn't even know where to begin. "My secretary is also into alternative stuff," he continued, "but when she got breast cancer she decided to take advantage of both worlds."

"I think that would be my approach, too."

"Has she ever seen a psychiatrist?"

I told him how Mom had decided that she didn't need talk therapy because her healers, and all the work she was doing on her own, were enough help. And that Pam, her reflexologist, was now her hyphen-therapist.

"My whole life is cancer. This is all I do," he said. I could hear it in his voice: Dr. Stotland was getting worked up. He sounded agitated. "There's a good chance she'll do nothing. And then it might be hard on you."

I was struck by how this normally self-controlled doctor was displaying so much emotion and distress. It was both heartening and tremendously disconcerting. Although it was comforting to hear him validate my position, I knew what his grave concern implied: Mom was in serious trouble.

"It's not easy watching someone go through something if you think there could've been a better solution," he said with resignation in his voice. "If it were my family, it would be killing me."

I choked back my tears. It was.

12

INTERVENTION WITH A SIDE OF LOX

"Are you sure you're up for your trip to Brazil?" I asked Mom. She admitted that she was feeling very weak in the days after our family visit to Dr. Stotland.

"Oh, I've decided not to go," she said casually, as if it were old news.

"Really?" I squealed. "Why not?"

"I felt that I didn't believe in it enough. It only works if you believe in it. I looked into it. John of God . . . he doesn't charge for his ten seconds, which has helped *lots* of people, but you pay a lot for the herbs and the crystal baths and the—"

"It's okay, Mom. You don't have to explain," I said, breathing a rare sigh of relief. "Just let me have this moment."

I was encouraged by Mom's new—and even somewhat rational—perspective on things. Maybe she was about to finally come around? Our intervention brunch at Teddy's could not have been better timed. On the menu: bagels, lox, stop Mom from killing herself.

As we sat around the dining room table and began assembling our bagels, I laid out the ground rules. "Mom promised that she'll listen to us. We are allowed to be critical for this one hour."

"Can we be critical about other things too?" Josh joked.

"No, there's not enough time," Mom replied, laughing. "Focus your critiques. I decided I wanted to listen without always preparing rebuttals."

"That way we can be free to be honest without you getting mad," I clarified.

"How's the egg salad?" Teddy asked Mom.

"You take charge, Rachel," she said.

I turned to Mom and, like the lawyer I never became, began my opening arguments.

"I hope you can get in touch with the part of yourself that doubts what you've been doing. The same part of you that questioned whether John of God was the way to go. The same part of you that's scared when the doctors are talking. I hope you can listen to that part of you." Mom listened attentively while picking at her scoop of egg salad.

"Four years ago, you were given a ninety percent chance of being cured. You gambled that away with the hope that you could heal yourself naturally. And no signs have pointed to any success with whatever you've been doing. All signs have shown that your cancer is growing, just as the doctors thought it would, just as science said it would. Now you're at advanced Stage 3 cancer. Please, cut your losses. This is your last chance to live. If you gamble this away, you have nothing else."

"Can I have the cream cheese please?" Teddy asked.

I kept going. "The most important thing is that you remove the cancerous lump from your body."

"Can I have some more lox please?" asked Josh.

"Your herbs might be helping, but they aren't going to do the trick. I don't understand how, if you're really, really honest with yourself, you can believe that you can get rid of your cancer by doing herbs and juice, or anything other than surgically removing it from your body."

"I'm listening," Mom said.

Teddy was up next. He turned to face her. "It may be that logic isn't the process that will appeal to you in these circumstances. But all my intelligence, logic, knowledge of life, and hearing what doctors have said have persuaded me right from the start that there's no other sensible way of addressing your illness without undergoing surgery. I thought that four years ago, and I think it even more today. And I think you're fortunate that, despite not having done it four years ago, there's still a chance it can be done. My view is that if it's available, you should grab the opportunity. I would grab it, I would go running for it, I would do it as quickly as possible. Because you may have many more years of life that way. I don't think any of the alternatives you've been pursuing will hold out any reasonable hope of any improvement to your condition. I think they're all a waste of time. Just stop doing that! Quit looking for a miracle cure that's going to come to your rescue. Have the surgery and get on with your life."

I spoke again. "You don't have any more time to try it your way. You tried it your way and it has not worked. It just has not worked. The tumour has grown. I don't understand how you don't think you will die in a year or two."

Teddy jumped in again. "Are you willing to bet your life that Dr. Stotland is wrong? As a matter of reason, you would have to conclude that he's wrong and the other four or five doctors are all wrong, and that despite their views you're going to lick it. If you think they're all wrong, and you're right, you have to re-examine your thought process."

"There are other ways of looking at it," Mom said defiantly.

Teddy looked over at Josh. "Anything you want to add?"

"I was thinking about if I did. I don't know if I do," Josh said.

"You don't want her to do one thing or another?" I challenged.

"I don't know if that's important. It's her life. I've adjusted to the fact that Mom has a deeply held belief system regarding this, and at the end of the day, whether she lives a year or two, or a few years, I want her to feel completely loved and supported, and that every moment is a positive experience."

"That's *not* what I'm asking you," I said, annoyed by his Kumbaya mentality. "First of all, we're talking about the difference between her dying in a year or two and her living for another fifteen to twenty years. And I'm not asking if you want to fight with her. I'm asking you—while we have the opportunity now to be honest—what do you want her to do?"

"In fairness, she's heard far more than I have about what she's facing, what her options are, what her choices are," Josh said.

I pushed him further. "What would you do if you were her?"

"I'm not. I don't know. If I were exactly her, I would do exactly what she's doing."

"So you're just choosing to stay out of it?"

"That's not what I'm saying."

"What if she asked you for advice?"

"She hasn't. She's never asked me for my opinion on what she should do, and I've never told her."

Teddy looked directly at Josh. "I don't think you're responding to the issue."

"I'm not here to be cross-examined," Josh protested. "There's no onus on me to respond in any way other than how I am. I wasn't even planning on saying anything."

"This meeting is explicitly for the purpose of us being able to share our points of view," I reminded him.

Teddy agreed. "We've been invited to state our views for the last time. If I really thought there was no way of reaching her, I wouldn't have agreed to this. But I thought that, so long as there still is an option, people do change their minds. So I wanted to say my piece. After this day, I will never try to persuade her or give her medical advice again."

Josh spoke thoughtfully. "It makes sense to me to get the CT scan. I intuitively think I would get the surgery. But again, I'm not in her situation. I'm also resolute about respecting what she wants to do."

"We want to respect her too," I said. "But what if Little Molly joined some Manson cult one day? We wouldn't just respect that. If you see someone you love in denial, you need to make a plea."

"I get that. I'm just at a point where I accept that Mom has deeply held convictions. This isn't helpful. No matter how much time Mom has, or any of us have for that matter, I want us to love each other well. Do I really think it's helpful for us to sit around and give speeches about why she's wrong and illogical? No!"

Mom piped up: "No one's talking to me anymore! I'm the guest of honour!"

I turned to her. "Are you open to getting the CT scan?"

"I want to talk to my doctor, who really listens to me. I trust her," Mom said.

I tried to refocus, to speak her language: "If you do get surgery, and remove the polyp, you'll be giving your immune system a leg up. Give your immune system a fighting chance!"

"I understand what you're saying," Mom said. "I appreciate all your input and love. I know you all care about me. You all want to save me. It's not as if I'm not scared. I just have to weigh what I can do. I know which way I'm leaning."

"I suggest you also take statistics into consideration," I said. "Anecdotal evidence and scientific evidence don't weigh the same."

"The medical system uses rubber stats," Mom said. She looked at me. "How would you feel if I do what you want me to do only because

I'm worn down and scared enough, and then I get an infection and things go wrong? They cut a nerve by accident. How would you feel if I'm depressed, in misery, and then I die? I think you'd feel guilty for the rest of your life."

Nice try! Mom was doing her best "guilt-tripping Jewish mother" performance, but I wasn't falling for it. (She raised me to be immune to this kind of passive-aggressive manipulation.) Playing the guilt card was clearly an act of desperation—one that revealed more about her fears than mine. If anything, I'd feel guilty for the rest of my life if I *didn't* try to get her to seek medical help.

I shook my head. "If you did surgery and something bad happened, I'd think *At least we gave it a shot.*"

Mom took a second. "I feel that I have a really good shot."

I was trying not to lose my shit. "When I look to the future, I see you dying in two or three years . . . maybe only having another six months of feeling okay before you're in serious trouble."

"The party's over!" Mom announced abruptly. The hour was up, and Mom had to run off to a writing-coach gig. "I do appreciate your honesty. I'm this much open," she said, holding her hands an inch apart. "Gotta go! Thanks for the egg salad, Teddy. Bye Rachie, bye Joshy."

And then she was gone. Teddy, Josh, and I got up from the table and moved to the living room.

Josh spoke first. "I know you think I'm being passive. But it's not true. I'm deeply concerned about the situation. I ask her questions, I talk to her, but her arms are already crossed. I'm submitting to you that telling her how wrong she is will not help achieve what you want. I just believe it's better for her happiness and health for us to support her."

"Denial might be better for her happiness, but it's *not* better for her health," I argued.

Teddy turned to Josh. "When you say there's no point in telling her to have surgery, it's probably true. I recognize it. However, I think that after visiting Dr. Stotland and the conversation today, the chance has gone from zero to two percent."

"I think Dr. Stotland was a great move," Josh said. "I'm glad I was there. I'm just not convinced that you guys telling her what to do helps. It breaks my heart when I think of her not seeing Molly grow up—"

"That's what I want you to tell her!" I said loudly. "It's hard, but the truth is the only thing that ever pierces her bubble of denial. Like when she got the results of her MRI and she said she felt 'gobsmacked.' Or when she said she was 'flattened' after our visit with Dr. Stotland. Sometimes it's important to tell people straight up that what they're doing is wrong. Today was my opportunity to say my piece. Teddy and I took the opportunity. If you don't want to say anything, you don't have to. But don't criticize me for speaking my truth."

"I'm not convinced that an intervention is effective," said Josh.

I tried to calm down and extend an olive branch. "Perhaps what we need is different strategies—to come at her from different fronts. I can be the harsh one. You can be the supportive one. Bad cop, good cop."

"You're right. Maybe different strategies will help," Josh said. "But still, I'm concerned about your relationship."

My relationship—or yours? I thought Josh was projecting. He was the one too scared to rock the boat.

"I think it's important that she know your opinion," I said. "Sometimes she needs to be pushed. If I hadn't pushed her we'd never have gone to see Dr. Stotland."

"I want you to know that I do question her," Josh responded. "But I don't do it in a way that will have her listen to me less."

"I appreciate that," I said. "As long as you know that the herbs are not going to cure her."

"I hope they do."

"But you know they won't—right?"

"I hope we're wrong. I hope she'll live for another twenty years."

I was honestly confused. Did Josh really believe that Mom had a chance of curing herself? Did he just not understand the facts of Mom's situation, or did he actually think she was magical?

"I hear you, I do. But I've got to go," Josh said, looking down at his watch.

Then it was just me and Teddy sitting next to each other on the couch.

"I'm glad you organized this today," he said. "No matter what happens, I think we'll all feel better that it took place."

"I want to at least feel like I've done everything I could do," I said.

"You have."

"It would feel worse to be passive. When people say they just want to be supportive, I don't buy it. I don't believe in neutrality. Sometimes I think you just have to call a spade a spade and say 'NO! This is fucked up!'"

"That's our approach. It's not his," said Teddy. "Josh doesn't like confrontation. That's why he's such a good conciliator. He's good at getting opposing factions to agree on things."

"Yeah, but he can stand up to Ford! Just not to Mom." I sank further into the couch. "The most important thing is that we continue to talk about it. What's most dangerous is when we stop talking. The past two, three years we haven't been talking about it, and the situation has only gotten worse."

"It's an awful situation. I just hope she doesn't come around to wanting surgery and it's too late. I'm concerned that she won't even be a candidate."

"Yeah, that would break my heart too."

"I can't believe how thin she is. She's a pencil. And she talks about it as if it's the result of worms," said Teddy. "When you went through the possible timeline, I think things are worse than that."

"Yeah, it's scary."

I hadn't felt this close to Teddy since we were kids at Disney World riding Space Mountain together. We'd always had a strong bond, but over the past few years Teddy had become a steady emotional anchor. We talked on the phone a lot more than usual. He was always there to listen to me when I was anxious or upset about Mom. He was the only other person in my life who saw Mom's situation the way I did. I might've gone crazy if I didn't have him.

WITH MOM'S VISIT to her new GP looming, I decided to write Dr. Brunt another covert email. I said that Mom may have been misinterpreting things she'd been saying. For example, Mom often reiterated that Dr. Brunt had told her she "must be doing something right"—as if her alternative treatments had indeed been slowing down her growing cancer. I found it hard to believe Dr. Brunt would think that was the case. I closed with "She's not going to listen to me, but maybe she'll listen to you."

The day after the appointment, I went over to Mom's place. "Did you come to any conclusions?" I asked.

"I did. And she did too. And they're not the same."

She told me how Dr. Brunt had suggested she give chemo a try. Mom agreed to get an ultrasound but she still wanted to do her own thing. There were a number of other avenues she wanted to explore.

Other avenues? I clenched my teeth. I was upset, but I wasn't going to bite the hook. Instead of reacting as usual, I would go meta. I spoke slowly and precisely, carefully selecting my words, as if I were questioning a witness: "If denial is a spectrum, have there been times when you have indulged in the protectiveness of denial?"

"Yes," Mom replied without any hesitation. "I've also read that it's a very useful thing for cancer patients to do." She broke into laughter. "It keeps them not crazy!"

"Seriously, when?" I wasn't laughing.

Mom thought about it for a few seconds before letting out a deep sigh.

"When both Feinberg and Stotland said that it was either second stage or none, I went with none. That was denial. But they also didn't know what they were doing."

News to me! I'd never heard the doctors say she might not have cancer at all. Mom's denial was like a Russian doll.

"Any other times?" I pressed.

"When I had all these symptoms from August to December and I didn't think it was rectal cancer, that was denial," Mom said. "It wasn't *conscious* denial," she clarified. "I just didn't get it. My symptoms only happened after I ate sushi at a new place. I was feeling wonderful before then. I was going to hike the Camino again!"

Mom went on, blaming her worsening cancer on her fall in Barcelona. A traumatic fall can shut off the immune system, she said, insisting that if she hadn't broken her elbow she'd still be doing just fine. "I felt better than anyone I knew of my age. I had no joint pain. I could dance. I never felt tired. I felt gloriously healthy except for a touch of cancer."

"Do you ever think that in the future you'll look back and think, 'That was me in denial too'?"

"No," she said. "I've never been sorry that I chose the route I have."

13

ONLY THE GOOD DIE YOUNG

One morning in mid-March, I was on my way to get coffee with Molly when Teddy called. "Have you heard from your mother?" I could tell he was anxious. I hadn't. He said that Dr. Brunt had just called Mom to ask her to come in that afternoon. My heart sank. It's never good news when the doctor asks to see you right away.

As soon as I got off the phone with Teddy I called Mom. I wanted to go with her, I said, and promised I wouldn't say anything—I'd be there just for support. She agreed with a sombre "Okay." I could hear the fear in her voice. She could hear the desperation in mine. We both knew this had nothing to do with bad sushi.

When Molly and I arrived at the café I slumped down into a chair. In chess, it had always seemed to me that the real moment of defeat isn't when you're actually checkmated; rather it's the second you can see your death on the horizon—the dawning of its inevitability. You're already down a piece or more and you know that in a couple of moves you'll be finished. There's nothing much you can do. Your fighting spirit subsides, and you exhale a quiet sigh.

I'd known this moment could—and most likely would—come, but that didn't make it any less of a shock. I poured milk into my Americano, going through the motions, but I'd drifted into a fog.

"Are you okay, babe?" Molly looked at me with tender, sympathetic eyes. She wanted to cancel her plans to head out of town that day for a weekend with friends. "I don't want to leave you like this," she said. I insisted she go. I didn't want her to stop her life for me.

"I'll be fine," I said. But I knew I was about to receive the worst news of my life. And I knew Molly would want to be there for me. And, well, I knew I'd prefer to handle things myself.

THAT AFTERNOON, as Mom and I sat down in her office, Dr. Brunt immediately struck me as personable, someone who exuded positive energy. I could see why Mom liked her so much.

Dr. Brunt started off with some casual small talk. It turned out that her sportswriter brother and I had worked together at *Q*, prompting her to make a few disparaging remarks about Jian. *Seriously, was there no part of my life he hadn't contaminated?* It might've been comical if the sheer mention of his name hadn't ramped up my already high anxiety.

Dr. Brunt opened Mom's latest scans on her computer and finally got to the point. She explained that there were cancerous lesions all over Mom's liver.

"Is this what they call 'mets'?" I asked. I distinctly remembered Dr. Stotland mentioning liver "mets"—metastases—three years earlier as an indicator of having only six months left to live. (It had stuck with me because, up till then, I'd associated the word only with the baseball team.) Dr. Brunt answered affirmatively.

So there it was. Checkmate.

Dr. Brunt kindly yet matter-of-factly made clear to Mom that her cancer was terminal, but that she could perhaps live for another year or two if she did palliative chemotherapy. She said she could make a referral to an oncologist at Princess Margaret Hospital if Mom wanted to explore that. Mom had the recognizable deer-in-headlights look on her face. She nodded slowly and said she'd think about it.

We left the doctor's office in a daze. For once in our lives Mom and I were silent as we took the elevator down to the ground floor. It seemed trite to ask her if she was okay, even though I wanted to make some sort of emotional connection. I didn't know what to do. I didn't even feel like I was in my own body. It was as if I were looking down on us from the security camera in the corner. As if we were playing out a horrible scene that had already been written.

I was at once heartbroken for Mom and supremely angry that she'd let things get to this point. Yelling "I told you so" had been so enjoyable when I was a kid, but now there was no satisfaction in being right. Just a well of pain and anger—and underneath that a vast expanse of sadness I was only beginning to know. But it was strange: on the surface I hardly felt a thing.

We walked out of the building and found ourselves squinting in the midday sun. Mom finally broke the ice. She said she knew of a great Italian restaurant on the next block. She barely had an appetite anymore, but we decided to go for lunch. What else were we supposed to do?

As we walked slowly, arm in arm, down the sidewalk to Nove Trattoria, I was reminded of when I used to walk with my ninety-year-old grandma. For someone who'd always appeared "ageless," Mom was now aging rapidly. Over the last three months it seemed as though she'd lost fifteen pounds and gained fifteen years. She was frail and less steady on her feet. And I'm sure the shock of what she'd just heard wasn't helping. As we strolled along, my resentment melted. I wanted her to be able to lean on me.

We sat down for lunch and Mom ordered a glass of expensive white wine. She didn't care for alcohol anymore, but she would have a sip. "It's for the gesture," she said. When it arrived, Mom raised her glass in resignation and looked me squarely in the eyes. "Only the good die young," she cracked. My eyebrows shot up. It might've been the saddest joke I'd ever heard.

THAT EVENING I went to a friend's birthday dinner. I was still in a daze, floating outside my body, watching myself carrying on like normal. It hadn't even occurred to me to stay home and, I dunno, cry?

When I walked into our neighbourhood wine bar I saw a sea of familiar faces. I took an open chair next to Steph, an ex-girlfriend, and tried to engage in regular conversation. I didn't want to upstage the celebration, but I was distracted by the scrolling news ticker in my head. *My mom's going to die. My mom's going to die.*

Steph picked up on my energy. I might've been able to fool the others, but not her. She asked me how my mom was doing. We'd dated in the early years of Mom's diagnosis and Steph really cared about her, so I was compelled to be honest. "Well, we actually just found out that her cancer has spread," I heard myself saying, amazed that the words were coming out of my mouth. "It's terminal." As I spoke, it was as if I were delivering the news to myself, too. Saying it out loud, even in a hushed, dissociative tone, suddenly made it more real.

I was grateful that it was Steph sitting next to me that night. There was still an easiness between us, and so it was comforting to have her by my side, both of us quiet and deflated, digesting the impossible news. We sat there silently for a bit, conscious of the bizarre juxtaposition: wine was flowing, people were laughing, and Mom was going to die.

Later that night I wrote an email to my bosses at *Q*, letting them know that my mom had terminal cancer and that I'd be needing some time off in the near future. "How it makes me long for the innocent days of last fall," I joked.

It didn't take long before the shock wore off and I could feel the excruciating pain of what was happening. It was now a sure thing: the person I loved most in the world was going to die.

Over the next few days I'd wake up in the middle of the night in a cold sweat, jolted into consciousness by the reality of Mom's diagnosis. The sheer intensity of the panic I felt was new every time. It was a real-life nightmare. I'd never had such an urge to turn back time. My mind kept searching for all the things I could've done differently to convince her to get surgery. What if I'd talked her into seeing a *real* therapist? Maybe I could have physically dragged her into the operating room? What if I hadn't given up so fast?

Once again I was levelled by the difference between kind of knowing and *really* knowing. The warm bath of denial had drained. Familiar feelings of regret and helplessness were rushing back with a vengeance. I'd already been dealing with the blow wrought by Jian; now I was suffering the cumulative effects of these two life tsunamis. I felt heartsick on top of being heartsick, anxious on top of being anxious, depressed on top of being depressed. And once more I had to reckon with the worst part of the bubble bursting—confronting my own self-alienation, the naked fact that I'd been so disconnected from my own voice for so long. *How had I allowed myself to get pulled into the vortex of Mom's magical thinking? How had I let myself get bullied into Jian's reality distortion field?*

Mostly I was back to fixating on why Mom had refused medical help in the first place. She had rejected a *ninety percent* chance of being cured. *Who does that? Why did she make such an irrational decision? Why had she turned away from reality?* I felt strongly that her rejection of conventional medicine went beyond any rational embrace of alternative healing. There was something more powerful driving her actions. *What was she so afraid of?* I couldn't exactly put my finger on it. But all I kept thinking was *It didn't have to come to this.*

STAGE 4

14

PHOENIX TEARS

While I was turning over every conversation, every single thing I could've done differently to steer Mom down a different path, she was staying the course. "They don't know what I know," she continued to say. She decided to make one last-ditch attempt to cure herself and began looking into alternative cancer clinics in Europe—places where they practised unconventional methods like hyperthermia, photodynamic laser therapy, and small doses of chemo in the middle of the night. Mom spent time researching her various options. "This one has a saltwater pool and lovely food," she said, as if she were picking out a spa vacation.

Finally she set her sights on a "biological medicine" clinic near the Swiss Alps. I googled it. It looked nice—and expensive—but it seemed more like a place for people with treatable health conditions, not for those who were *actively dying*. I questioned how legit it was. I mean, they offered ear candling (and even hippies don't believe in ear candling anymore).

I wasn't surprised when Mom asked me to go with her. She could barely drive now, never mind fly overseas on her own. I worried about her going by herself, and I didn't want to miss out on any time I had left with her, so I said yes. I thought it was absurd for her to spend so much money on magnetic-field therapy and mistletoe injections, but if going to one of these last-resort health resorts would make her happy, then why not? She'd get her spa treatments, and I'd lounge by the pool. I warmed to the idea of us going on one last European vacation together.

But I knew the Magic Mountain fantasy was just that—a fantasy. It was clear that Mom was in no shape to go anywhere. She was getting skinnier and skinnier, except for her legs, which were swelling up from edema. It was difficult for her to walk up the two flights of stairs to her apartment. I was afraid that even if we made it to Europe she'd become too sick to travel home. Or worse, she'd die there, and I'd be stuck in the Alps with my mother's corpse. *No. Freaking. Way.*

I tried to dissuade her, but Mom wouldn't budge; her heart was set on it. Even Josh and Aunt Barbara stepped in to try to talk her out of it. Although I still resented them for not having challenged her a lot earlier, I was happy to have their support now. I suppose they were finally willing to risk Mom being angry at them.

I was at work when Mom called to talk about booking our plane tickets. I took my phone out into the hallway overlooking the CBC's atrium and gathered the nerve to put my foot down. I knew she wasn't going to be happy, but I told her that it was just too irresponsible for us to go. "Please," she begged. "This is my last chance." She started to cry. I couldn't bear it. She sounded like she was drowning. "Okay, okay, I'll go with you," I said. She immediately calmed down. I told her I would be there for her, which was true, even if I had no intention of getting on that plane.

I hung up and tried to focus on the script I was writing for an interview with Joan Armatrading. I felt sorry for Mom—I knew she needed the idea of the trip more than the trip itself—but she was driving me bananas. If it wasn't stressful enough to have a dying mother, now I had to deal with a dying mom *on the lam*. By that point I wouldn't have put it past her to fly off without me. I had no idea where she drew the line at "reasonable" anymore. She knew she was too weak to travel, but I knew that her letting go of the dream amounted to a final surrender. Accepting that she wasn't going to Europe meant accepting that she was going to die.

Eventually, to my immense relief, Mom found a loophole. She'd discovered clinics in Toronto that offered "almost the same services" as the Swiss spa, she announced, so she'd stay home and do them here.

"Sounds like a good idea," I said. *Thank fucking god.*

MOM WAS BECOMING a little less avoidant. Her new approach was essentially "Hope for the best, prepare for the worst." And even if the worst wasn't going to happen for another year or two, she agreed that it would be prudent to start getting her affairs in order.

There's no step-by-step manual for how to help someone wrap up their life, but I was a producer, goddammit, and I was determined to produce the best death possible for Mom. I cut down my work schedule to three days a week. Between the shock and the sadness, there was a lot of shit to get done. When my own doctor asked the reason for my time off, I said "Dying mom," then after a pause blurted out "and Jian!" He'd been stressing me out for months, if not years, leading up to Mom's decline—why not let the record show it?

Mom and I first set out to tackle the administrative tasks. We went to the bank to empty her safety deposit box. We met with her accountant to organize her finances and prepare her tax return (still one of life's two certainties, until the other one got her). Teddy found her a lawyer so that she could update her will. Meanwhile, Mom gave me permission to sign her up with the Community Care Access Centre (CCAC) so that she could receive home care from a personal support worker and palliative care doctor. At first Mom was reluctant to accept the help—she found it hard to let others do things for her—but once her new support worker, Maymouna, started showing up to do laundry and other household chores, Mom was extremely grateful. "Dying is hard work," she'd say.

Then there were the finer details. I asked her to jot down her passwords for her email and social media accounts. "70StillSexy," she wrote on a cue card. Next, we created a list of those she wanted notified "if anything were to happen." We began by going through all her contacts and then, one by one, assessing who should make the cut. It reminded me of when I was a kid and Mom would help me narrow down my list of birthday party invitees. Except this was the guest list for her funeral, which we'd started referring to as the After-Party. Mom's Top 100 would be a very exclusive group. She wanted to invite only those people in her life she really wanted there. (It's not as if she'd have to deal with anyone's hurt feelings.)

By April, Mom didn't have the energy to drive anymore, so I kept her car at my place. On the days I drove up to the Hemingway I'd often stop to get her a scoop of artisanal gelato. She wasn't eating much, but she still had an appetite for the finer things. I would gently place her cup of lemon lavender in a cooler bag and then race over as if I were transporting a donor organ on ice.

Being Mom's personal Make-a-Wish Foundation wasn't entirely altruistic. Doing things for her gave me something to focus on—a way to channel my anxiety and feel useful at the same time. There was at least *something* I could do in an otherwise helpless situation. Watching Mom cheerfully devour her gelato with the mini plastic spoon meant everything to me.

WHEN I WASN'T helping Mom prepare to die, I was getting ready for the rebirth of *Q*. Canadian hip hop artist Shad was announced as our new host, and it seemed the storm was finally starting to clear. No more guest hosts, no more intense media speculation about the future of the show. Perhaps there really was a blue sky on the horizon.

Shad wasn't an experienced broadcaster, but what he lacked in interviewing skills he more than made up for in kindness. He was incredibly gracious, humble, and genuine—the anti-Jian. His mere presence was healing. Our first official show with Shad was only three weeks away. We'd all worked so hard to keep the ship afloat, and now we could finally see the shore.

And so, even as the foundation of my life was disintegrating, keeping one foot planted at work gave me a sense of stability and normalcy. Work had always been helpful through tough times. After every breakup, I was glad I had my professional obligations to keep me grounded (and distracted). It would've been too disorienting to leave work altogether. Besides, I still didn't have a real sense of how long Mom had left. Six months? A year? Two? In any case, I needed some time to catch my breath and come to terms with what was happening.

BUT I STILL felt torn when I wasn't with Mom. I hated the feeling that time was running out and I wasn't taking advantage of every minute available to us. On the other hand, it's not as though I could've spent every day with her anyway. Mom was busy. She was still keeping her regular appointments with her herbalist, her reflexologist, and her energy healer. And she was still maintaining her daily routine, which included the Rife machine, the infrared sauna, and meditation. She didn't want me around all the time.

I began to resent her alternative treatments all the more, if that was even possible. Not only had they led to her dying in the first place, but now they were eating up what precious time she had left, time she could be spending with *me*.

Yet I also recognized that her regimen gave her something to focus on. And by that point I was actually fine with her continuing to believe. If she woke up and regretted not having gotten the surgery five years before, it would just be too painful—for both of us. For so long I'd hoped she'd snap out of it and come to her senses, but now it was probably best that she didn't. If a glimmer of hope made her feel positive, that's what was most important.

FOR MOM, HOPE next came in the form of cannabis oil. With hardly any chips left to play, she decided to go all in on weed sap. She learned about the miracle extract from a video called *Run from the Cure* (the cure being Western medicine). "Everyone in the video got better," Mom said. The host, Rick Simpson, had named his oil "Phoenix Tears" after watching a Harry Potter movie.

Mom was determined to score some of these magical Hogwarts tears, and as it happened, Aunt Barbara had a friend who knew a jazz musician who made the proper recipe. This was months before weed dispensaries started popping up around the city, so Mom had to get her drugs the old-fashioned way: by asking her child to take her to her dealer's place.

As we drove up to the old loft building on College Street, it was obvious that it would be too hard for Mom to climb the stairs. I took a deep breath and flashed her an ironic grin. "Thanks, sweetie," she said.

While Mom waited in the car, I hopped up the stairwell to the jazzman's apartment. I handed him Mom's whack of cash, and he put five Phoenix Tears–branded ampules in a brown paper bag. I dashed back down, relieved by the swiftness of the transaction, and saw my friend Nicola standing in the lobby. *Busted.*

"What are you doing here?" she asked.

I held up my bag and smiled. "Just buying some stuff for Mother."

Nicola laughed. She was familiar with Mom's proclivities. They'd connected over their mutual love of literature and woo-woo, exchanging hot tips about astrologers and silent meditation retreats in Oaxaca. She came outside to the car with me. "Hi, Elaine," she said as Mom rolled down her window. It was subtle, but a passing look on Nicola's face told me she was registering just how frail Mom had become. For the first time, I was seeing Mom's state through the eyes of a friend. My heart sank. I forced a laugh about our run-in. As I started the car, Nicola entertained Mom's sales pitch for Phoenix Tears and kindly offered to get her a re-up whenever she needed it.

Mom began a regimen of rubbing a drop of the dark gooey oil on her gums twice a day. When I asked her how it was going a few days later, she reported having felt a little disoriented. "Whatever. It's not like I have executive meetings," she joked.

Mom dialed back the dosage, but meanwhile I was living in my own hazy dream world. I tried to appear normal, and I probably did, but I was sinking deeper into my head. The scrolling ticker was still ever-present and growing louder: *MY MOM IS GOING TO DIE, MY MOM IS GOING TO DIE, MY MOM IS GOING TO DIE.* I was anxious all the time. The air felt thick to breathe. I couldn't relax. I yearned for the days when I could take my mom—her very existence— for granted, knowing that, if I felt like it, she was just a phone call away.

I knew things were about to get dramatically worse, and I wasn't sure how I was going to handle it. When would life ever be okay again? *Would* it ever be okay again? Logically I knew things would have to get irrevocably worse before they could ever creep back toward something better. But I couldn't even imagine "better," because a life without

Mom could never amount to "better." I refused to consider a future without her in it. This was the paradox I wrestled with every night as I lay awake in bed. As someone who relied on the equanimity of logic, I was confronted with a problem that overpowered every cerebral muscle I depended on to make sense of the world. This wasn't something I could think my way out of.

MOLLY'S BIRTHDAY WAS coming up, and I'd planned a weekend get-away for us at a charming country inn with a private cabin that had a fireplace and outdoor hot tub. It was the first birthday of hers we'd be celebrating together since we started dating, and I really wanted to do something special for it. Between my broken leg, work trauma, and dying Mom, Molly was proving to be my rock. She was sticking with me through thick and thicker.

That Saturday I tried my best to give her my full attention, but I was distracted from the moment we hit the road. I wasn't able to enjoy the picturesque scenery or our five-course candlelit dinner. Our "peaceful surroundings" made me feel anything but relaxed. The rushing sound of the cascading waterfalls only increased my agitation. Time was slip-ping away. We were only an hour from the city, but I felt homesick. I'd never considered myself a mama's boy, but now I couldn't deny that Mom was the most important woman in my life. I wished I was able to give more to Molly, to be present for her, but it was next to impossible in the face of Mom's impending death.

In the morning I couldn't wait to get back to the city. Before we got into the car I gave Mom a call and was immediately soothed by the sound of her voice. I told her that I wanted us to spend more time together. She promised we would. We made plans right then to take one last road trip the next weekend to her friend Irene's country house in the Bruce Peninsula. I swung back from child to parent; I kept think-ing, *From now on I'm not gonna let you out of my sight.*

I knew Mom enjoyed my company, but the truth was she needed me too. Although it had always been her rule never to lean on me, she'd become too weak to do many of the things she used to do. She just couldn't continue being so damn fiercely independent. It wasn't easy for her, but she slowly allowed herself to rely on me more and more (beyond end-of-life planning and drug runs). A switch had flipped. Mom had realized that she didn't want to do "this dying thing," as she called it, on her own.

In the weeks following Mom's terminal diagnosis, we tried to carry on somewhat as usual. We celebrated Passover as a family, which we actually hadn't done in years. We threw Teddy a party for his seventy-fifth birthday and retirement from the judiciary. I spoke to an investiga-tive reporter who was writing a book about Jian. (You know, the usual stuff.) I don't remember exactly how I was able to get out of bed every morning and put one foot in front of the other. I guess I didn't really have a choice. Life kept coming. Perhaps sometime in the future I could collapse, but for now the show had to go on.

AFTER MONTHS IN limbo, we relaunched *q* with an eclectic range of guests before a live audience at the CBC. Shad interviewed *WTF* host Marc Maron about his techniques of the trade, and Inuk throat singer Tanya Tagaq put on an electrifying musical performance. The packed theatre cheered. There was a lot of pressure riding on this day, and we appeared to have pulled it off. Afterward we took celebratory photos with our newly branded lowercase *q* tote bags. For management it represented the pinnacle of their Moving On campaign. We were genuinely happy to be going forward with our lovely new host, though for several of us long-time producers, moving on wouldn't be so simple as a new letter case and theme song.

As Canada was welcoming Shad across its radio waves, I was busy customizing Mom's farewell tour. The weather was breaking. Springtime in Toronto always brings with it a palpable sense of relief and optimism. Not this year. Instead of beginnings, it ushered in a series of lasts. We went to see the cherry blossoms in High Park for the last time. We went for "goodbye lobster" at Wah Sing (I ate the fried lobster with ginger and scallions; Mom puked up wonton soup in the bathroom). And we made one last trip to the rooftop of the Park Hyatt.

It was a sunny day at the end of April. We happened to be seated at the same table where, nearly five years earlier, Mom had first told me she might have cancer. I thought back to that time when I still thought she was too full of life to ever die. It's funny how you can trick yourself into believing that certain people are exempt. I remember being dumbfounded by the deaths of Christopher Hitchens, Nora Ephron, and David Rakoff—writers Mom and I had both liked. They were so much a part of the cultural furniture that it was hard to imagine a world without them. When I produced an interview with Nora Ephron more than a year before she died (for what would be her final book, *I Remember Nothing*), I mentioned to her how my mom still made her vinaigrette from the back pages of *Heartburn* (the only salad dressing Mom ever made). Nora laughed. "That's not a bad legacy to have!" She was never publicly out about her illness, but in hindsight, I can see that she already had death on her mind. And if even Nora Ephron couldn't outsmart it, what hope was there?

We ordered fancy cocktails. Mom looked like a skeleton, albeit a very elegant skeleton in her wide-brimmed sun hat and multicoloured knit sweater that hung off her emaciated frame *so well*. We did our best to enjoy the bittersweet moment. Mom had always loved this rooftop bar, and I don't think just because of the spectacular view and drinks. She sometimes brought up how, back in university, a friend of hers named Helen had jumped from a ledge just below the bar and fallen to her death. It obviously still saddened her. As Mom took a few tiny sips of her wild hibiscus flower champagne, it hit me how her conscious choice to savour the small pleasures in life—as she was doing right now—to live *la bonne vie*, had always been a giant fuck-you to death.

ALMOST SIX WEEKS after learning of her liver mets, Mom agreed to see an oncologist at Princess Margaret. Chemotherapy was the last thing left on the menu, but as Dr. Brunt informed us, it could be used only to manage symptoms and give Mom a better quality of life (for what was left of it). Mom was open to hearing what the oncologist had to say. "Maybe something will appeal to me," she said.

Just the energy it took for Mom to go out exhausted her, so once we were shown into the doctor's office, she opted to recline on the examination table while I sat down on a chair next to her. A radiologist entered the room, introduced himself, and asked Mom about her recent medical history. Mom explained how she'd first gone to see Dr. Brunt because she'd been experiencing "all these horrible symptoms"— extreme fatigue, nausea, low appetite—and her liver was jutting out. "I thought, maybe it *is* rectal cancer!"

You think? I braced myself. *Here we go again.*

"Are you taking any medications right now?" the radiologist asked.

"I take very high doses of turmeric," Mom replied.

"Of what?"

"Turmeric."

"Sorry?"

"The spice!" I burst out, looking directly at him. "She's taking a SPICE."

He smiled and nodded politely. I appreciated that, since I could tell he knew something was up. In some way, these doctors' visits were cathartic for me: they were among the few times I had a witness to how totally bonkers Mom could be.

He asked if she was allergic to any medications. She said she might be allergic to latex—that although she'd never had a reaction herself, two of her friends had developed latex allergies later in life. "It doesn't mean *you'll* have a reaction," I said. I was growing more impatient. Here she was, a terminally ill person, worrying about a hypothetical allergy to condoms and medical gloves.

Mom's avoidance was frustrating and painful to watch. She was always worried about everything *except* the cancer that had been slowly but determinedly killing her for the last five years. She worried about catching a cold. She worried about the mercury in her fillings. She worried about toxins in her fish. On one level, I knew this obsession with the small stuff was her attempt to regain some control, to distract her from dealing with the real terror. But it still really pissed me off. Her choosing death over life was painfully impossible to compute. She was choosing death over me.

The radiologist asked Mom if she was interested in chemotherapy. "Probably not," she said. "I don't find chemo sensible." *From the arbiter of reason herself!* Mom explained that she'd read "all of these books" and learned that a "big percentage" of oncologists would never do chemo themselves or advise it for their family members. Mom added that she was maybe willing to do chemo at a clinic in Germany where they give it to you with sugar in a way that "tricks" the cancer. *The irony . . . a Jewish woman trusting only the Germans to administer her poison.*

He asked her point-blank if she understood how serious her situation was. "I get that I'm dying right now—faster than most people," she clarified with a sly grin. "But I haven't given up. I'm trying a whole bunch of stuff."

At this point the radiologist politely excused himself. A couple of minutes later he returned with the oncologist, who'd obviously been brought up to speed. "I understand that you're a bit shy when it comes to regular treatment," he said. Then he paused. "I don't know if that's the correct—?"

Mom and I both laughed. "No, that's very sweet," Mom replied. "I like *shy* better than *pig-headed*!" In those moments, when she at least still had a sense of humour about herself, I felt like we were back on the same side.

The oncologist gently explained that there was a big mass in her liver, and that if they didn't treat it, there would likely be more symptoms: jaundice, bleeding, or a bowel obstruction that could result in emergency surgery. Hopefully chemo would stabilize the mass and stop it from growing. Best-case scenario: it would shrink the tumour, she would have more energy, and live for another year or two.

"Why are they doing lower chemo doses in Europe and here it's higher?" Mom asked. Before the doctor could answer, she offered her take: "I think it's the drug companies wanting to make more money."

The oncologist said he'd be willing to compromise: a lower dose, pill form—whatever she'd accept. He was concerned about how much time she needed to make up her mind.

Mom told him she'd need another week or two to decide. There was one other person she needed to consult.

"Can I ask who?"

"My herbalist."

"Would you consider talking to another oncologist?"

"No."

If she wasn't already going to die, I was going to murder her.

The oncologist was eager to book CT scans and make another appointment. He reminded Mom that chemo could possibly extend her life by a couple of years, but that if she did nothing, she was looking at a few months. "I'm happy to see you whenever," he said. "But please keep in mind there's a time window."

We said our thanks, and both doctors left the room.

I immediately turned to Mom, trying to quash my seething frustration with all the patience and compassion I could muster. "You can try it," I said, "and if you hate it, you can stop."

"I'll definitely think about it," she said. "It's scary. But of course they always try to scare you."

"They're not *trying* to scare you," I said, exasperated. "They're giving you the honest truth—"

"*Their* honest truth."

"But everything they've told you *actually* comes true."

"There's another way of looking at it. I could already be dead, or have gone through hell and been depressed."

"That's what *you* think."

"Please, sweetie. Just let me not talk about it. It makes me feel awful, the constant *push push push*."

"I'm not pushing you. Do whatever you want. You always have!" Thirty-five years of pent-up resentment bubbled over.

"Well, I will," she huffed back. "But I'm also listening to your points. Isn't that enough for you?"

"Sure. Have it your way." I was at the end of my rope.

"Why shouldn't I have the right to do it *my way*, even if I've made mistakes? You may have had four more years of me than you would've had."

"Fine, we'll go by that." My eyes stung with hot tears.

Mom looked confused. She probably hadn't seen me cry since I was a kid. "Are you crying because I won't do what you want?"

"No!" I paused, irked beyond belief. "I'm crying because you're going to die."

It was the first time either of us had said the words out loud to each other. She was going to die. It was a sure thing. It didn't really matter anymore which door she picked.

"I've only ever tried to make suggestions for your own good!" I cried harder. I didn't want to make her feel worse, but I desperately wanted to feel heard.

"I know that's what you think," she said, switching to her wise Yoda self. "But Rachel, you have to respect that the other person has a whole world inside of them, and that they have a right to their decisions. Everybody has a right to be themselves." I didn't want to acknowledge this, even if part of me knew she was back to talking sense.

"It's understandable why somebody who loves somebody so much wouldn't want to have to stand there and watch them destroy themselves," she continued, employing her inimitable logic. "But you have to let them do what they need to do and trust that your point of view isn't the only one in play."

"So I'm supposed to just sit back and watch you make your suicidal decisions?"

"Everyone has to choose their own path. You can't save someone. You can support them, you can love them, you can help them. But you actually can't save anybody from what you see as destruction. Whether they're addicts or whether they're not doing Western medicine."

Technically, of course, she was right. It was all too apparent that I couldn't save her. But if I had to do it all over again, I still would have tried.

Mom took my hand in hers. "Anyway, what you've been giving me the past few weeks has been, like, an elixir. It's part of the reason I'm not depressed. It's been exactly what I've needed." Now *she* started to cry. "I'm really scared, Rachel. It's been *me* going through this."

It was the first time we'd ever cried together. I suppose that, through all my steadfast attempts to rescue her, and her steadfast attempts to pretend everything was just fine, I'd lost sight of the fact that she was simply a person who was terrified. I mean, I'd been experiencing my own worst fears, but Mom was right: it was so much worse for her. It was *she* who was dying.

A sense of surrender came over me. I was so sick and tired of fighting her. I preferred that she try chemo—I wanted more time with her, and I didn't want her to experience any more pain than she had to—but I wasn't going to push. All I could do now was love and support her, and try to enjoy every last drop of time we had left together.

15

GREAT IS BETTER THAN PERFECT

"They tried to make Mommy go to chemo, I said no, no, no . . ."

Mom was singing in all her self-righteous glory to the tune of Amy Winehouse's "Rehab." I had to admit it was pretty funny, if not more than a little ironic considering how things had turned out for Amy. I'd been hoping Mom would consider chemo or at the very least get a CT scan. I'd even bought her a piece of crystallized galena (a type of rock that, according to the package it came in, assists in "countering the ill effects of radiation and electromagnetic pollution"). I was trying to meet Mom on her own wavelength. But I wasn't surprised when her answer was "no, no, no."

"I'm not going to schlep down to the hospital every two weeks to get an IV," Mom said. Also, her homeopath had told her that chemo would interfere with the drops she was giving her. Mom certainly didn't want to mess with *those*.

So that was that. There wouldn't be another year or two. We were looking at months.

For the most part, Mom was facing the fact that she was dying. She was making financial and legal arrangements, reading books on death, and meeting with her palliative care doctor. She was no longer giving herself affirmations, though she still thought there was a slight chance that something she was still doing—the cannabis oil, the herbs, the homeopathy—might miraculously kick in and save her, or at least extend her life in the way chemo might have. "I'm accepting that I'm going to die, and also kinda like, you never know."

Mom decided she wanted a death doula. I'd raised the idea with her after hearing a radio segment about the emerging practitioners who provide end-of-life emotional, spiritual, and practical support. Just as midwives help pregnant people prepare for birth, death doulas help terminally ill people prepare for death. It was definitely Mom's kind of thing.

I wrote to the few I could find in the Toronto area. It would just be a matter of who was the best match. Mom was bound to be as picky with death doulas as she was with men. I felt like I was producing some sort of dating-game reality show. *The Bachelorette: Death Doula Edition.*

"Who will be good enough to hold my mom's hand . . . in death?" I joked in my best Chris Harrison voice.

Mom played along. "I don't want my dying to happen with just *anybody*. It's a very intimate relationship."

For all our morbid jokes, we weren't actually that far off the mark. In what felt like a version of speed dating, Mom interviewed five death doulas by phone. It came down to two contestants: Shirley, an older hippie type who Mom instantly felt she could be good friends with, and Elizabeth, who she pegged as a right-wing Stephen Harper–style conservative.

Elizabeth was a corporate consultant by day; a Google image search revealed her perfectly coiffed hair and penchant for sweater sets. Yet

Mom said she'd felt a strong connection when they spoke. She told me how Elizabeth had listened to her for a long time and then said, "It sounds like you've lived your life the way you've always wanted to, and now you want to die the way you want to." Mom had cried. She'd felt heard. When it came down to it, Mom didn't care whether they had the same politics—as they say, she wasn't here to make friends. Mom was seeking someone who could put their needs and ego aside in order to be fully present for her. And so she offered Elizabeth her final rose.

Mom was getting noticeably weaker and more fatigued with each passing week. She wouldn't be able to climb the stairs to her apartment much longer; we needed to find her a new place to live (or rather, die), *stat*. After scouring the rental listings, I eventually found a furnished condo nearby, on the other side of the ravine, only a couple of blocks away from Teddy's house. It had an elevator, a wheelchair ramp, and a private balcony among the treetops—Mom could still get some fresh air even if she was too tired to go out. It was perfect. It even had an extra bedroom in case I wanted to stay over. Most suitably, it had only a six-month lease. We said we'd take it.

Even though Mom was still kicking, I was already beginning to mourn her. I thought about all the things we'd never do together again: go on a hike, go to the art gallery, go out for a nice meal. She'd never see me get married or have children, and I'd never see her become a kick-ass old lady. I *really* wanted to see that.

One afternoon we were driving past the University of Toronto. Mom was looking out her window at the students walking down the street, talking with friends on their way to class. "I did that," she announced. She was thinking out loud. She explained that even though there was still so much she wanted to do, she felt she'd experienced everything she'd needed to in life. "I wish I could meet you at the Met for coffee when you're fifty," she said, as a random example of what she'd still want to live for. "And there are certainly people I'll miss, or rather they'll miss me," she chuckled. "But I'm seventy-one. And I feel that I've had a very full life."

These moments were becoming more frequent. Mom would speak softly but declaratively, reflecting on the fullness of her time in this world. She meant it, but it was also as though she was reassuring me—and herself in the process—that life had been good to her. "I've had so many wonderful experiences and joys and connections with people. I feel I did valuable work in the world. I've had really good friendships. I think my children are amazing. And I love my ex-husband!" She laughed, and then sat silently for a bit. "I haven't always had an easy life," she said finally, "but I've had a really lucky life."

Once we were home, Mom admitted that it was still difficult for her to let go. "I always wanted the vastest life possible," she told me. "Part of the reason I wrote was to have extra life. I taught myself lucid dreaming so that I could have a night world as well as a day world." She took a deep breath and exhaled. "Now I'm living in a hugely narrowed world."

Somehow, though, in the midst of sober realizations like this, she'd manage to bring it back around and lift both our spirits. I didn't know if she was doing it for me, if she was giving herself a pep talk, or if it was just the cannabis talking, but I appreciated these moments. "I'm not exactly happy, but I'm oddly content," she said. "It's not nearly as bad as it could be. I'm very grateful. And for whatever the reasons, I feel it's some sort of grace."

Mom still had the power to say things that would calm me down in the midst of the ongoing anxiety attack that had become my life. I wasn't as Zen as she was. I was preoccupied on a minute-to-minute basis with precisely everything she would miss, all the things she wouldn't experience. I looked at all the entries in her wall calendar that would never happen. It wasn't as though Mom was joining the 27 Club, but she was too young to die. She still had so much to live for. She wanted to finish her play, teach writing in Italy, and find a truly great relationship. "I have a completely different view of love," she told me. "If I ever am lucky enough to have love again, it will *not* be with a high-achieving, witty, attractive alpha man who's narcissistic. I don't want someone who doesn't care about my feelings. I am *off* that!"

But Mom never felt sorry for herself. "It's not a tragedy at my age that I'm dying," she'd say. I knew she was technically right. People die—and live—in far more horrendous circumstances every day. We were the fortunate of the unfortunate: I could take time away from my job to be with her. We had taxpayer-funded health care and enough money to make the situation a lot easier on us. I was aware of our privilege, yet it still felt like a tragedy to me. My life—albeit small in the grand scheme of things—felt like it was collapsing. I was expecting to have her for at least another twenty years.

PERHAPS IT WAS my radio producer's reflex, but one day I brought home a Marantz audio recorder from work. Inspired by NPR's StoryCorps, I wanted to interview Mom about her life—an exit interview of sorts. The idea was to preserve as many of her stories—as much of her—as I could. I'd been nudging her for weeks to do a recording session with me, but she'd been putting me off. She was always "too busy." Whereas I was constantly unnerved by the *tick, tick, tick* sound in my head, Mom was acting as though there'd always be more time.

But she knew it was important to me, so eventually she acquiesced. I started off with the vitals: family history, her parents, childhood, university years. She told me more about living in Israel in her twenties—how she'd taught English to diplomats and pop stars, edited a book by a former Israeli chess champion, and worked on a border kibbutz where they were shelled every night. Her boyfriend was Shimon Peres's speechwriter, so she attended interesting political parties. It had been an exciting adventure for her.

We got into a routine. Every time I came over we'd do an hour-long session, or until she got too tired. It was a meaningful way to spend time together. What started out as a favour to me turned out to be an enjoyable—and maybe even therapeutic—experience for her. Mom had been doing inventory on her life anyway, but this was an opportunity to really hash things out. It was enjoyable for me, too: I was learning things about Mom I never knew. I'd never just sat and listened to her for hours.

One afternoon we were lounging in the sunroom, savouring our last days before the move, and I was asking Mom about her favourite things. "I love poetry. I've read and memorized tons of it," she told me. She paused. I was learning how to be more patient in these moments when she'd trail off, her mind taking an introverted detour to another place. A wistful look crept across her face. "Can I share a Mary Oliver poem with you?" she asked tentatively. She knew poetry wasn't really my jam.

"Of course," I said.

"Mary Oliver lives in Provincetown, by the way. She's gay!" *As if I needed the sales pitch.*

Mom got up off the couch to look for her Mary Oliver book. This was clearly important to her. A minute later she returned, book in hand. "The poem's called 'The Summer Day,'" she announced as she searched through the pages to find it. Before reading out the first line she looked up at me with a sly smile, acknowledging that yes, we were about to have a poetry reading.

Who made the world?
Who made the swan, and the black bear?

Who made the grasshopper?
This grasshopper, I mean—
the one who has flung herself out of the grass,
the one who is eating sugar out of my hand,
who is moving her jaws back and forth instead of up and down—
who is gazing around with her enormous and complicated eyes.
Now she lifts her pale forearms and thoroughly washes her face.
Now she snaps her wings open, and floats away.
I don't know exactly what a prayer is.

Mom's voice started to crack. Obviously the poem was speaking to her in a way it never had before. She began to cry but kept on going.

I do know how to pay attention, how to fall down
into the grass, how to kneel down in the grass,
how to be idle and blessed, how to stroll through the fields,
which is what I have been doing all day.

Breaking the fourth wall, Mom looked up again. "This is great for me, by the way. It's very cathartic," she laughed through her tears. "And isn't it interesting how everything she says has extra resonance?" She took a big breath and launched into the last lines with zeal.

Tell me, what else should I have done?
Doesn't everything die at last, and too soon?
Tell me, what is it you plan to do
with your one wild and precious life?

Still crying, Mom didn't even pause before reflecting. "Every day since the diagnosis, in the middle of doing my exercises, I would say out loud, 'I am awake to this day of my one wild and precious life.' And I have been. I've lived very richly, darling. Like all my life, but especially in the past few years. I really have." She paused. "I want you to know that. And I want you to think of that too. Think of your one wild and precious life and don't waste any time."

I swallowed the lump in my throat. Even if it was cliché, her dying *was* making me more conscious of how precious life is. In my post-Jian awakening, I was already coming to see how, to a certain extent, I'd been coasting through my days for the past several years, always managing more than truly living. This past year especially, I'd been so utterly consumed with my crazy work situation and Mom's illness that I was just barely getting by. I thought about how, after I'd finished helping Mom die, I would try to live life more fully. Turn up the volume a little. I had a new sense of urgency. I wanted to start actually making the things I'd always hoped for happen. I didn't know exactly what that looked like, but I knew I didn't want to sleepwalk through my life anymore.

ON MOTHER'S DAY I woke up with dread, knowing it would be my last with Mom. Another "last," another part of our life together being ripped away. We never really took Mother's Day that seriously in our family—Mom would often reschedule our family brunch to a more convenient date for her—but this year it felt a little more meaningful.

Josh, Melissa, and Little Molly hosted us at their house. Big Molly came too. It was a warm, sunny spring day and we all sat outside on the back deck. I normally bought Mom quirky jewellery or some artsy ornament on gift-giving occasions, but under the circumstances it seemed silly to get her anything that would outlast her. I guess we'd all had the same thought. Everyone got her flowers; they were as ephemeral as she was.

Mom leaned back on the wicker sectional, making herself comfortable. Her arms looked like pure skin and bones poking out of her grey

AGO T-shirt. Her thick calves bulged from her capri pants. On her feet, too swollen now to fit into shoes, she wore black Velcro sandals.

Considering the subtext, everyone was in a good mood. Mom seemed happy and cheerful. She picked at some fruit while the rest of us scarfed down bagels with lox and cream cheese.

After brunch, I gave Mom a foot rub while Josh got out his guitar to play her some songs. It was very sweet. Josh could be so earnest and sincere sometimes. I often wondered where he got it from. For his grand finale, he stood up and began strumming the theme song to *The Mary Tyler Moore Show*. I think Mary reminded him of 70s-era Mom—her look, her style, the fact that she was an unapologetic feminist on the go. At the first line, Mom and I immediately locked eyes and grinned. We knew what was coming. As Josh belted out the chorus, Mom couldn't resist: *You're gon-na BAKE it after all!* she sang over him, throwing an imaginary beret into the air. I wasn't sure whether she meant her upcoming cremation or her new cannabis oil habit or both, but her ability to laugh and rally in the face of it all filled my heart with even more love and respect for her.

"It's obviously a capitalist made-up holiday, but today was really nice," Mom said when the two of us got back to her place afterward. We were sitting in the sunroom.

"What does it make you think about?" I asked.

Mom began reflecting. "It's not that I'm afraid so much of dying. It's more that I'm afraid you guys will need me and I won't be there."

I nodded. "Yeah, the irony is that *you're* the one I'll need to help me get through the grief of losing you."

"You'll have to sit on the bench," she said. Mom wanted a memorial bench in Cedarvale Ravine so that everyone who knew her could sit and talk to her once she was gone. She'd been a great listener in life and wanted to be one in death, too.

"I'm not going to talk out loud to the ghost of my dead mom on a park bench."

"You might! My friends plan to."

"How about I ask you for some advice now, while you can still, like, answer me?"

Mom happily agreed. I turned on the recorder.

"What should I do when I miss you?"

"Well, I have a lot of diaries, if you want to read them. I'm not going to throw them out," she said, a smirk forming on her lips. "If you want to know about my sex life, you can."

"Mommm." I rolled my eyes.

"But you might want to. Or read pieces of them. It would really bring me back. They're all handwritten. They're pretty raw."

"What else?"

"Another thing you can do is just talk to me. I'm sort of serious. Keep a little jar of my ashes, and just think you're talking to me."

"It's not the same," I lamented. I wanted a more satisfying answer.

"No, it's not the same," Mom quietly agreed.

We both went silent for a few seconds, quietly absorbing the blatant truth of the matter.

Mom then continued. "Or talk to other people. Unfortunately people die. We all die. And the people left behind are the ones who really suffer."

"But what do I do if you're not around for something really big in my life?"

"Oh, cripes." She sighed. "There's nothing you can do. Except, I want to tell you this, and I want you to remember it—I couldn't be any prouder of you than I am today. But I wish I could see that. I do. I wish I could see everything that goes on in your life from now on."

It was comforting to hear Mom say those words. And I knew they were true. She'd always been my biggest champion. I wasn't sure what I'd even be able to achieve without her in my corner anymore.

"I just had a thought," Mom piped up. "If you do have a daughter, will you give her Elaine, even as a middle name?"

"Sure," I said. "*If* I have a daughter."

"Or a dog. I mean, how many dogs are named Elaine?" she said, laughing. "It would be very interesting."

My eyebrows lifted. "Yeah, that wouldn't be weird at all . . . 'Sit, Elaine!'" I held out my index finger like Cesar Millan. "'Roll over, Elaine!'" I kind of liked the fantasy of one day having an Elaine who obeyed my commands.

"But what if I'm jealous of other people who still have their moms?" I asked.

"Well, when you concentrate on gratitude and what you were given, it's hard to feel sorry for yourself. All the good things I've been able to pass on to you, the time and attention I've given you, and support in growing up and having adventures. So I would consciously look for some gratitude in that moment. Like, 'I had a mother who did give me that. I have some of that inside of me now. It's part of me. And I did get some good mothering . . .'" Mom trailed off. "I mean, everybody has issues. It's a complicated relationship. But I think ours has been *great*. And great is better than perfect."

"What do I do if I'm so depressed that I can't get out of bed or go to work?" I asked.

"I would tell you to see a therapist," she said, laughing.

"No, really, what would *you* tell me?"

Mom thought about it for a few seconds. "I would tell you that everyone has a lot of sadness in their life, no matter what they look like on the outside. Everyone suffers. So it's not weird or wrong to be sad."

"But what if the grief is just too much?"

"It won't be easy. Losses are losses. They're really hard. And there's no time limits to grieving, or no way it goes. It can go in waves. You can go for a while where you're not truly suffering and then, *bang!* It hits you again. But also, we're a mother and daughter—uh, son—and so we're very entwined. You'll never forget me."

"So what do *I do*?"

"Well, one thing you can do is just sit with it. That's the Buddhist way. If you're sad, be sad. You just feel the loss and the pain, and it will move. It will move a lot faster than if you try to suppress it or push it away. Sometimes it's just better to say, 'I'm missing my mother right now.'"

I was trying to take in everything she was telling me, but it was still all so hypothetical. I glanced down at the recorder and tried to imagine what I would need to hear in the future.

"Let's role-play this," I said. "Pretend you're dead, and I'm sitting on your bench. I'm really missing you, and I'm feeling down. What would you say to me from the other side?"

Mom took a moment to collect her thoughts. "I'd say, 'I'm sorry you're feeling down. Again, just let yourself feel it.' And then here's what I'm telling you—" She took a deep breath before delivering her posthumous sermon. "You are one of everybody in the world. And, I mean, you can escape it by dying when you're a baby I guess, but you can't escape suffering and pain if you live long enough. Illness, old age. It's part of who we are. It's part of life. And it really sucks, for both of us, that I had to go so soon. But you have in you everything I gave you, including the stuff you may have to talk to a shrink about"—she chuckled—"and you have all your natural, extraordinary qualities, and

I just have *complete faith* that you'll be able to create a good life. A *very good* life. And so you're really, really going to be all right. I just know that for sure."

16

DYING WITH DIGNITY

Mom barely had the energy to leave her apartment anymore, but there was still one outing she was intent on taking. "I'm not afraid of dying," she told me. "But I *am* afraid of being in pain for a long time—that's why I'm going to Dying with Dignity." Mom made an appointment with the end-of-life rights organization so that she could learn how to off herself, if need be. Josh and I both said we'd go with her. It would be a family field trip.

We arrived at the organization's unremarkable offices in a nondescript midtown building, where we were greeted by a counsellor. Nino had a mellow, sensitive vibe. He looked about forty, with a shaved head, intense eyes, and a greying soul patch.

"What drew you to this kind of work?" Mom asked him as he led us into a small meeting room.

"I experienced a deep loss in my life. A person I was close to died," Nino explained. "My regular psychotherapy practice has nothing to do with dying people, but I work here part-time because it's especially meaningful." It was a story I was beginning to hear a lot from those who worked in the death field. Elizabeth, Mom's death doula, had also experienced a profound loss.

The four of us sat down in a circle.

"Do you want to die at home or in a hospice?" Nino asked Mom.

"At home as long as possible. I'm open to a hospice, but I don't want to end up in a hospital," Mom insisted. "I don't want to have to eat their food." She took charge of the conversation. "Whether intentionally or not"—she threw me a glance—"a lot of doctors have scared me. I even had one doctor say to me, 'You will die an excruciating death.' I don't want to spend months in intolerable pain. I *hate* intolerable pain." She rolled her eyes and laughed. "Like, I'm *really* special."

Nino smiled.

"So if I do want to kill myself, how do I do it?" Mom asked. Small talk was over.

Nino spoke slowly, choosing his words carefully. "As you're probably aware, physician-assisted suicide will be legal next year in Canada. But it looks like that option is not something you can wait for. I'm hearing that you may want to do something sooner."

Mom nodded.

"So there are two methods that are supported within the medical community, and you might be a candidate for both—in that the doctors should not have a problem supporting you." Nino proceeded to outline the various methods.

It was the ultimate self-help seminar: How to Kill Yourself in Four Easy Ways!

Option 1: Stop eating and drinking.
Mom didn't like the sound of that. "I don't even like fasting for Yom Kippur," she said.

"Typically, at that point, you're not eating much anyway," Nino explained. Mom looked doubtful. Her one cheese blintz still beckoned every morning.

Option 2: Go to sleep and never wake up.
Terminal sedation involved a medical professional administering a slow and steady dose of pain medication. "Essentially, you lose consciousness and don't come back. It might take a few days," Nino said. "They could do it in a minute, but that could be considered *assisting*, so they need to do it gradually."

"Can't I just get a packet of pills?" Mom blurted out. "Or, I've heard there's some kind of mask you put over your head. Are any of those options offered here?"

Josh's eyes widened. I clenched my teeth. *What was she expecting, a loot bag?*

"So *you're* naming two other methods that are considered reliable." Nino was treading carefully. As he went on to discuss the more legally dubious options Mom had just raised, he spoke in strictly hypothetical terms. It was obvious he didn't want to say anything that could be construed as encouraging us to break the law.

Option 3: Swallow pentobarbital.
The highly lethal barbiturate is the drug of choice for assisted suicide (and capital punishment), though it's most commonly used for euthanizing pets. "But it's illegal in Canada," Nino told Mom. "It literally does not exist here."

"It's okay. I know where to get some," she replied confidently.

"Where?" I asked. This was news to me.

"I'll ask Kay and Richie. Their son is a vet."

Josh and I both snickered. Kay was Mom's oldest friend from Communist Jewish summer camp. She had become devoutly Orthodox and now lived in the suburbs of New York City. There was *no way* Kay was going to be Mom's mule.

Option 4: Inhale pure helium.

"Really? You can die from breathing in helium?" Mom asked.

Nino nodded. "But someone would need to assemble the bag and hose fixture, and that's considered *assisting*," he said, once again warning us. "You could get in trouble."

Josh looked at me. "I'm a politician. *You* do it!"

I smiled at Mom. "We could say I'm making balloon animals to cheer you up?" Keeping the joke in the air, Mom spoke in a high-pitched Alvin and the Chipmunks voice. "Hi, this is my final goodbye," she squeaked. We all laughed.

"When do I have to choose?" Mom asked, as if she had to RSVP her choice of meal for a wedding.

"You should let your palliative care doctor and support team know your intentions as soon as possible, so everyone will know what to do, if or when the time comes," Nino said.

As we stood up to leave, I turned to Mom. "I really don't think you're going to experience any prolonged suffering."

"Maybe," Mom said. "But I'd feel better if I had a safety net."

My eyebrows shot up. "A safety net?" *More like a trap door.* Mom clued in to her choice of metaphor, and we all had another good laugh.

"Thank you, this has been amazingly helpful," she said to Nino as he walked us back to the reception area. "I'm aware that so many people have the exact same illness, but they're in refugee camps or they're homeless or in impossible situations. In the midst of everything, it's nice to have a lot of support."

"It's a complex journey, but the sooner you can name what you want, the better," he said.

I was grateful that we could all talk (and laugh) openly about Mom's end-of-life wishes. For all the things our family avoided, and for all the ways we used humour to deflect, we were also capable of having brutally honest conversations about terrifying subjects—ones that most people would avoid. I'd do whatever I could to help Mom die the way she wanted to, short of killing her.

The next morning I was back at Mom's place. She was sitting in bed, propped up by a triangle meditation cushion, and I was lying at the foot atop her burnt orange duvet cover. It was where we spent most of our time together now, working on crossword puzzles as the spring light shone through the windows. She was telling me about her night. "I woke up and it was the first time I thought, 'I'm *actually* going to die. I won't be here in a little while.' I looked around and started crying." She sighed, then added, "I suppose I don't have to bother getting that root canal now. The silver, uh, mercury lining!"

Mom was happy she'd gone to Dying with Dignity. "He mapped out everything very well. I'm glad there are four options," she said, cracking a smile. "None of them *seriously* attractive." Mom looked down at her skinny frame. "Boy, has my life ever zoomed downhill," she declared, exhaling loudly. She told me how weird it was to see her body in such an unrecognizable state. It was getting harder for her to even get dressed in the morning. She'd asked me to pick up a few thick cotton T-shirts to help hide her ribs and some extra-large underwear that would fit over her protruding abdomen. "It's like my liver has a life of its own. I think I can feel its heartbeat," she joked.

Mom was now approaching death with a sense of inquiry. "Dying is interesting. I'm curious about it as I go along. The main thing I notice is how quickly I seem to adjust to each worse stage, to my surprise. But I do." In a sense, dying was like a new adventure for her, a new dimension of human existence for her to explore.

"My days aren't as horizontal, but they're more vertical," she said at one point, describing how, while the timeline of her life may have contracted, the level of meaning had gone up. "I'm so aware of every hour mattering," she added. "When I'm not lying in bed stoned, that is."

I WAS STILL going over to her place several times a week, and with each visit Mom had some new perspective or revelation to share with me. She spent a lot of time venting about her sister. Barbara had recently come to Toronto to visit Mom and help her out, but everything she did seemed to piss Mom off. She felt that Barbara didn't listen to her and was constantly taking over. When Barbara had suggested she get a walker, Mom bristled. "That's up to *me* to decide!"

Barbara hadn't lived in the city since she went off to university, but she and Mom had remained close. They'd visit each other, go on trips together, and talk on the phone for hours at a time. Barbara was like Mom . . . on speed. Giddy and excitable, she made Mom look like a vision of calm serenity. Still, as chaotic as her energy could be, Barbara had always been a loving, generous, and supportive aunt to me. Mom's relationship with her little sister was, of course, much more complex.

Mom said that her resentment toward Barbara had been brewing for the last few years. She explained to me how, when she was well, she'd been able to handle the parts of her sister's personality—and their dynamic—that drove her crazy. But now she didn't have the strength. "Being weaker than her is an impossibility for me." She was grateful to Barbara for the countless hours she spent listening to her talk about her cancer. And despite her grievances, Mom felt compassion for her. "We were patterned by the same parents," she said. But in the end, Mom was fed up. When Barbara wanted to make plans to come visit again, Mom told her not to. "I want her to *get it* that I'm in a different space," she said.

Mom was being extra vigilant—if not outright cutthroat—about her boundaries. This was *her* time. "I have to put myself first. I've become less overly caring at my own expense. I can't do it anymore," she told me. Mom was dying, but she was no shrinking violet. She had a clear sense of what she did and didn't want. She wasn't gonna die lying down (at least not figuratively).

I made sure to ask about all her preferences, to ensure that everything happened her way. We talked about her wish to be cremated, for her ashes to be spread in the ravine. We talked about the After-Party. Mom didn't want a traditional funeral, but a celebration in which her friends could enjoy fine wine and fancy canapés. "I could get your favourite lemon tarts from Daniel et Daniel!" I almost squealed, starting to get excited about the party planning and all the things I knew brought her joy. Mom smiled; her slightly wet eyes shone with quiet approval. My adrenalin plummeted just as quickly as it had spiked.

Mom wanted the party to be held at a community centre in Chinatown, where we used to take Grandma for High Holiday services after Grandpa died (Mom had chosen the congregation because it was led by a woman rabbi). Every year, Mom and I would laugh when Grandma said, with total sincerity, "It's important not to *gorge* oneself on Yom Kippur." Instead of fasting, we'd just try not to stuff ourselves to the gills during our trips to Lee Garden after the service—that was our version of atonement. But really, putting a synagogue in the middle of Chinatown is just a cruel joke.

Mom said she wanted there to be lots of performances at her party. "Can I tell funny stories about you?"

"Yes, you can." Mom laughed. "I expect to be roasted *after* I'm roasted."

As for speeches, Mom said anyone could say a few words but warned me not to let people go on too long. "You have to cut them off," she insisted. It was in these moments I could see that, despite her easy-breeziness, Mom was still a raging control freak. She even wanted to stage-manage the situation from beyond the grave. At one point, when we started fussing about some minor detail, she broke into song: "It's my party and I'll die if I want to, die if I want to, die if I want to." And then, waving her finger in the air as if she were hitting each word on an invisible cymbal: "You. Would. Die. Too. If It happened to youuuuu . . ."

Through all of this, Mom and I were getting closer—in more ways than one. Sometimes we held hands while we talked. Other than quick hugs, we hadn't been affectionate in that way since I was a kid. (Mom hadn't always been good at hugs—Josh had to teach her how to embrace for more than a nanosecond.) I had even started giving her foot massages. It was something I would normally never have done, but it was a simple gesture that gave her a lot of pleasure in her otherwise miserable state. She'd close her eyes and a blissed-out look would spread across her face. "I'm in heaven," I remember her saying once before opening her eyes wide, like a mummy coming back from the dead. "Not yet!"

Our poetry readings continued. One day, after a recitation of "Spring and Fall" by Gerard Manley Hopkins, Mom broke down into sobs. "I can't help thinking, no matter what my issues are with Western medicine, I should have been tested more often. I'm not beating myself up. I'm just saying, if I regret anything, it's the last year when I started to go off track." It was the first time I'd heard Mom admit any real remorse.

"But you *did* get tested. You just didn't want what they offered." I was confused. "What exactly do you regret?"

"I've never once regretted the original choice I made, but I do wish I would've gotten tested after I started getting symptoms."

"But what would you have done differently?"

"I would've gone to Switzerland. Or gone to Dr. Gonzalez. And I might've had much more of a chance."

"If you had done that earlier, do you mean?"

"Oh yeah," Mom said assuredly, as if it would have made all the difference. I didn't think so. It pained me that she blamed herself for going off her diet, for not being tested enough, as if that was the problem and not a lack of proper medical intervention. But I understood that it would be too hard for her to allow herself to regret not getting surgery, even if maybe a part of her did. It was easier to funnel her regret into not having made it to the Swiss spa earlier. I certainly didn't regret her regret over *that*.

"I've let go of it mostly," she continued. "But I could've had the greatest life as an older woman. I was set to. I really wish I could stick around." Okay, I regretted her regret over *THAT*.

It was easy being with Mom, lounging on her bed, talking about life and death. Sometimes we just hung out in silence. One day I looked up and saw Mom staring at me intently.

"What?"

"I'm remembering you," she said.

I understood what she meant, even though in the end I'd be the only one left doing any remembering. She was taking a picture with her mind. She was trying to bottle the moment—just as I'd been doing with my recorder. The clock was counting down fast, and we were doing our best to capture time—or at least desperately cling to it.

I looked down at her hands. I knew them so well. I could still picture the gold wedding band she used to wear, and the silver snake ring that took its place after the divorce. *Soon they'll be burning in a fire.* It was a morbid thought. But Mom was all I'd ever known. She was right here, right now, right in front of me. How could she just vanish?

"It's just so hard to fathom that *you and me* will never be together again," I said, thinking out loud.

"I know, I think about that too."

I kept staring down at her fingers. "It's just so final."

"I was just thinking the opposite!" Mom's voice perked up. "Like, it's final, but the dialogue doesn't stop. I still sometimes talk to my mother."

"I know," I said, recalling her late-night confabs with Grandma's ghost. "I'm sure I'll still talk to you—just, like, *inside* my head."

"I mean, the person has been, and is, so much a part of you that you can feel them. I used to feel my dad's presence around me quite often. And whatever that meant, it felt like being embraced or held or something."

"Sure, but it's not the same as picking up the phone and talking to you, or meeting up for a drink."

Mom's voice became extra quiet. "Well, we have been extremely lucky, even if luck doesn't seem to be hanging around much lately."

I nodded. We *had* been lucky, and still were, even under the circumstances. I was lucky to have a mom I not only loved but also *really liked.* It made it that much harder to lose her.

BY MID-MAY, I was distraught. The ship was sinking. I couldn't keep one foot at work anymore—all hands, all limbs, were needed on deck.

And so I arranged to go on an indefinite leave. Everyone at work understood and sympathized, yet for me it wasn't so simple. At that point my Stockholm syndrome was only beginning to lift. I knew the show would be fine without me, but I wasn't sure how fine I'd be without the show. For better or worse, I'd been devoted to it for so long. I loved my work, but the situation had an unhealthy grip on me. It was as if I'd been conditioned into a cult for the past six and a half years. And I was a very loyal member. Even when I broke my leg I'd hopped back to work right away. I was afraid to take sick days, never mind take off for an extended period of time.

Looking back, it saddens me to think that it took my mom dying for me to take a step away. I wish I could have found a way out *a lot* earlier, or that my need to be valued and respected would have been enough of a reason to leave. But I can also now see just how intense my attachment was. I needed something as strong, if not stronger, to pull me out of it. I couldn't sacrifice any more of the precious time I had left with Mom.

So, I produced the one last interview I had on my slate. And then, at the end of the day, I tidied up my desk and left the building, not knowing when I'd be back. I knew I was walking into a far worse hell than the one I'd left behind, but I felt so free.

IN A COUPLE of days Mom would be moving to death row, a.k.a. her new apartment. Yet she still hadn't told most of her friends about her terminal diagnosis. Perhaps she was afraid of appearing vulnerable or of admitting defeat, or maybe she was just protecting herself by avoiding their grief and staying in denial a little longer.

I'd offered to write a note to her Top 100 on her behalf, and she finally gave me the go-ahead. I lay in bed that evening with my laptop propped up on my knees, wondering how to begin.

Hello Elaine's dearest friends,

We're sorry to be writing under such sad circumstances, but we wanted to give you a heads-up that our mom now has fourth-stage cancer and most likely only has a few months to live . . .

My fingers froze and my chest tightened. Seeing the words on the screen made the situation all the more real.

I went on to tell Mom's friends that Josh and I were making sure she was as comfortable as possible for whatever time she had left. And following her instructions, I let them know that she preferred notes to visits. With her energy waning, she didn't want to feel obligated to see people, or worse, take care of *their* feelings.

As I pressed send I winced, painfully aware that I was about to break so many hearts with just one fell click.

I lay back on my pillow seized with dread. Suddenly a succession of loud pops and cracks went off outside. *Wonderful.* I rolled my eyes, remembering it was Victoria Day. Every *pop pop pop* felt like an assault on my senses.

Within minutes, the saddest replies began blowing up my inbox, each one punctuated by a chorus of stupid fireworks. *Thanks, Universe. 'Cause I needed this to be an ironic cinematic moment.* Mom's friends expressed their heartbreak and sorrow, but what really threw me was the raw intensity of their shock:

"Rachel, I did not know that your mother was ill. This is devastating news."

"Last I saw her she felt she was 'beating' the cancer through her holistic methods, so this news comes as a real surprise."

"Is this related to her other cancer scare, or is it new?"

"I'm really sad and shocked to hear this news."

"This is devastating news. I truly thought your Mum was doing okay."

I was taken aback by the depth of Mom's deception. What on earth had she been telling everyone? That she'd cured herself? That her cancer had come back? *HER CANCER NEVER LEFT!* I wanted to yell into the screen.

As the soundtrack outside continued, the replies kept landing like missiles. One by one I read her friends' notes of anguish and despair. I felt under siege. I hadn't been prepared for the emotional toll of being The Messenger. It was excruciating. For so long I'd been dealing with this on my own, and now I was being hit by the grief of a whole community of mourners.

Tears flooded my eyes. As well as conveying their love for Mom, her friends also expressed how sorry they were for me and Josh. And for the first time, I let myself feel sorry for me too. I could no longer pretend that my pain wasn't there. This wasn't just about Mom—it was happening to me too. Sitting there in my bed, I went from producer to child. I wanted it all to just go away. I wanted to disappear. But even hiding out under the covers that evening couldn't muffle the mocking *pop pop pop* of my world exploding.

17

A GOOD TIME, NOT A LONG TIME

Mom woke up on moving day and got dressed in all black—a T-shirt, a cardigan (now two sizes too big), and a drawstring skirt that she cinched around her bony hips. It was more an attempt to hide her gaunt frame and bulging liver than a nod to gothic elegance. She fixed her hair and did her makeup in an effort to look like the living, and then made her way down the stairs for the last time. A friend of Mom's was picking her up to take her to her homeopath appointment before dropping her off at the rental condo. Just like that, the Hemingway was in her rear-view mirror.

As Mom later told me, she felt self-conscious as she entered the lobby of her new building. But as far as she could tell, no one pegged her as being on her last legs. She really just looked older. Or rather, for someone who'd always looked ten years younger, she looked her age. She took the elevator up to the fifth floor, where I was already prepping the apartment—unpacking a couple of boxes, putting the few clothes she still wore away in her closet, installing extra safety handles in her bathroom. Sort of like setting up a nursery for a baby's arrival. But the opposite.

Mom was in good spirits as she took inventory of her new digs. The walls in the kitchen and bedroom were sponge-painted in various shades of terracotta. In the living room there was a purple couch, a collection of odd-shaped ceramic vases in various shades of teal, a rococo wall mirror, and a range of Asian-inspired furniture. Mom laughed at the cheetah-print chairs in the dining area. She had fun imagining what the woman who owned the place was like: "I bet she wears leather pants!"

I was surprised that Mom was in such a good mood, considering she'd just left her home of twenty-two years. I suppose she was better at saying goodbye than I was. Mom had told me how, after we moved houses when I was five, I cried "I want to go home!" every night. And when Teddy sold the house when I was fourteen, I was more distraught than I'd been about the divorce. I went through about ten rolls of film, photographing every room, every nook and cranny, so that I'd never forget it.

"How do you feel?" I asked Mom as we lay down on her new bed.

"So far I'm pretty thrilled," she said, looking out the window. "I see beautiful trees, all these different shades of green." She paused thoughtfully, and then turned to look me in the eyes. "And I'm so grateful I never have to walk up all those damn stairs again." We hung out on her bed and watched a documentary about Iris Apfel on my laptop. The ninety-three-year-old style maven was a witty, age-defying, eccentric woman—exactly how I imagined Mom would've been in her nineties.

"Are you planning to stay over tonight, sweetie?" Mom asked casually, so as not to put any pressure on me. I wasn't. I'd figured the spare bedroom would come in handy, just later on. But I could tell she wanted me to stay, even though she'd never ask outright. I was touched.

"Yeah, I'd like to."

Mom smiled. I didn't know it then, but I'd just moved in. I would stay with her day and night until the very end. We were there for a good time, not a long time.

ON ONE OF our first evenings together, I crawled into Mom's bed beside her. I don't remember exactly how it happened, but I had an urge to cuddle with her. I felt vulnerable and a little shy as I turned and put my arm across her chest. To my relief, Mom didn't flinch at all. "It feels so nice to be held," she said. We just lay there, silently staring up at the ceiling. I was pretty sure we were both thinking the same thing: *How the hell did we get here?* We were now in the home stretch, holding onto each other like two Scooby-Doo characters anticipating the monster closing in.

Mom and I were setting forth on one last adventure together, though I was the only one with a return ticket. But would I ever *really* come back from this? Tears trickled down my face, dampening the pillow beneath my cheek. Mom was dying, and it felt like a part of me was dying too. The person I was when I was with her would die when she did.

The next morning, when I entered Mom's room, she was sitting up in bed. She'd already been awake for a while, reading letters from friends on her iPhone. "The press release you sent out is getting a big response," she said cheerfully. In the days since I'd delivered the bad news Mom had received dozens of lengthy, heartfelt notes from those who loved her, telling her what a gift she'd been in their lives. She let me read some of them. They were all so specific and detailed. I recognized so many of the things people cherished about her. Her "quick-wittedness," "radiant energy," "zest for life," "adventurous spirit," "infinite generosity," "enthusiasm for teaching," and, of course, "relentless insistence on living life on her own terms."

It was hardly the first time I'd heard people sing her praises. In the alternative high school community, Mom had been a living legend. I couldn't count the number of times we'd be out together and a former student would run up to her—"Elaine!" they'd yell excitedly—and tell her how she'd been their favourite teacher, how she'd changed their life.

Mom had also been an inspiration to so many women of her generation, especially those in her writing group. "As our mentor, you embodied the rarest and most transformative type of leadership," wrote Bonnie. Many of them credited her with making them become more authentic. "Because of our friendship, and the many hours we spent laughing about our own foibles, I am more real as a person," wrote Lola. Mom saw and encouraged people's special qualities. "Whenever I'm with you I feel really good about myself in a way that doesn't happen with anyone else. I think it's a kind of love you emanate," wrote Irene.

It was clear that Mom was going to be missed. *Like, really fucking missed.*

"These letters mean so much." I could hear her choking back the tears. "I knew I'd inspired people, but I don't think I realized the extent of the impact."

It was a good reminder for me. When she wasn't busy shutting me down or defending herself against my criticism of her choices, Mom had represented something else to so many people—a strong, effervescent woman with a reputation for always being open about her self-doubt and insecurities, which gave her peers permission to be honest about themselves in a way they'd never been before. Yet it still baffled me. How could she be so insightful with others and have so many blind spots when it came to herself? Why was she capable of being so present for other people's needs and fears and so delusional when it came to her own?

"I was surprised that so many of your friends were shocked to hear you're dying," I said. I couldn't help calling her on it. "Many of them were under the impression that you'd cured yourself."

"I thought I had! I was feeling wonderful."

My brows furrowed. "You didn't know you could feel wonderful and still be dying?"

"No, I didn't," Mom admitted defensively. "There were lots of indications that what I was doing was working. Anyway, I don't want to talk about it."

As usual, whenever the truth poked its head up, Mom whacked it down. It was *her* story and she was sticking to it.

DURING OUR FIRST week as roommates, Mom and I found ourselves embarking on a marathon of films set in Paris. It started with *Le Weekend* and kept going. If we could never travel there together again, we could at least visit in the movies. *Before Sunset, Le Divorce, Frantic*— it was nice to be reminded of the memories we'd made there, like the time we were invited upstairs for tea at Shakespeare and Company, or when Mom spontaneously got us into a Michelin three-star restaurant.

In the middle of *La Vie en Rose*, she turned to me and said, "I'm sorry I'm not the best company." Mom still felt she had to be the life of the party. She'd always been the one to do the heavy lifting in social situations, keeping the conversational ball in the air, making sure people felt engaged and entertained.

"It doesn't matter. I just want to be with you." I tried to lighten the mood, to reassure her that she didn't have to be anything other than her wonderful dying self. "Whatever. It's not like I'm the best company either. My mom is dying! I'm miserable, so let's be miserable together. And if we happen to laugh while watching movies—"

"All the better!" Mom chimed in.

"MOMMY, YOU'RE ALIVE!" I sang as I entered Mom's room one morning with my arms outstretched.

"Rachie, I'm alive!" she sang back, holding out her arms to embrace me. It was a funny little piece of theatre we'd continue to play out, knowing full well it had a limited run.

We quickly settled into a routine. Every morning I'd open her blinds, make myself coffee, and then sit down on a chair next to her bed. We'd talk for a while, then I'd get out an ampoule of her liquid dope. With a big grin she'd extend her index finger, waiting for her morning fix. I'd squeeze out a sticky drop and then she'd rub the oil onto her gums like a stereotypical dope fiend, bobbing her head up and down in approval. I even prepared her homeopathic potion. I'd count out precisely eight drops into a small glass of water. *God forbid I give her an overdose.*

Mom's appetite was unpredictable. She still mainly wanted to eat one cheese blintz in the morning, but she also started having cravings for things her dad used to make her when she was little. I cooked up fried liver and onions, noodles with cottage cheese and butter. She'd eat only a couple of small bites. Her diet mainly consisted of homemade chicken broth that her friend Arei brought over and a steady stream of kombucha.

Maymouna, Mom's personal support worker, would arrive mid-morning to help her bathe and get dressed. She was now coming over every weekday for a few hours. Maymouna exuded warm, loving energy and intuitively knew how to assist Mom without taking over. She was the third member of our core team.

Mom's new uniform was just a T-shirt and underwear. Even yoga pants felt too uncomfortable over her extended stomach. For the first little while she still made an effort to put on makeup every day; I smiled at the sight of her propped up in bed, looking in her compact mirror, applying blush to her pale cheeks. She glanced up at me and smiled. "This is what *I* call dying with dignity."

When she started having difficulty getting up from bed, the CCAC coordinator suggested that it was time to get a hospital bed. "It's best to be prepared, even before it's needed," she told me on the phone, kindly trying to soften the blow. Getting a hospital bed was a scary step, but the reality was that Mom needed it. I suppose we could have just told ourselves it was a Craftmatic adjustable bed—"Sleep, watch TV, and relax in supreme comfort!"—but we both knew exactly what it would be: her literal deathbed.

Mom agreed to it. In dying, at least, she was a pragmatist. When it arrived, she lay down on it to try it out. She could raise or lower any section of the bed with just a push of a button. Holding the controller in her right hand, she sat back and attempted to reposition herself. "I'm going to put myself down now," she announced before lifting her head to look at me. "I wish!" she added, laughing at her own joke.

ALTHOUGH MOM HAD said she preferred notes, she did write back to a few of her closest friends to let them know she'd be up for a visit. It really mattered to her to say goodbye, but it was also draining. "I have difficulty getting people to understand that I have very little energy. I can fake it for a while when lying on the sofa," she told me. "But I get tired very quickly." Mom wanted to keep her audiences short.

After a few visits, we developed a routine. Mom would lie down on the purple couch. I would put out a selection of French cheeses and artisanal crackers on the glass coffee table next to the Kleenex box. When her guest arrived I'd greet them, offer them a glass of Sancerre, and then show them to the armchair facing Mom. Then I'd excuse myself and head up to the roof to give them alone time. The roof was only two floors up, but it felt like a world away. I'd relax on a deck chair or go for a quick swim in the pool. The cold shock of the water felt good, like a jolt to the system. I might have cried. Who knows—it was all wet.

About twenty minutes later I'd come back down. I'd take a deep breath before opening the door, anticipating the invariable backdraft of emotion. I'd usually catch Mom's friend wiping away their tears. I could feel the sadness in the room like a heavy blanket. The cheese spread was never touched.

My premeditated return would give Mom an opportunity to wrap things up. Sometimes she'd ask me to get out her worn brown leather jewellery box so that she could give away a piece—a parting gift of sorts. It was killing me, day after day, watching one dear friend after another leave with tears in their eyes, the door shutting behind them, always for the last time.

"How do you do it?" I asked Mom one day after a friend had left. "Isn't it torture having to say goodbye to all the people you love?"

Mom's voice became solemn as she delivered the simple truth of the matter: "It's better to be able to say goodbye than not." I agreed.

She continued to make her way through her letters. "Here's David's," she said. "'I will always treasure the intensity of our love and regret that it went astray. Tin Pan Alley wrote a lot of true songs about such stuff. I am emptied at the thought of your spirit being still. I would love to see you.'" Mom started to cry. "I was really fed up with him at the end, but this is *lovely*," she laughed through her tears.

David came over. When I came back down from the roof I sat with them for a bit, happy to see him again. He begged her to get blasted with high doses of chemo (he'd just met someone who'd done so and her tumour shrank). *Where were you five years ago?!* The man who once insisted that herbs worked "just like chemotherapy" was now singing a different tune. The next day Mom called David to give him shit. She still had energy for what mattered.

As Mom's executive producer, every morning I'd go over the day's agenda with her—who was coming to visit, what supplies we needed, an update on the business of her death. (Teddy had agreed to be the executor of her estate and was going to arrange her cremation. Josh was in charge of her memorial bench.) There was a revolving door of visitors. Teddy, Josh, Melissa, and Little Molly visited every few days. Plus there were personal support workers, the palliative care doctor, Pam the reflexologist, Elizabeth the death doula, Arei with chicken broth, and still more friends coming over to say goodbye.

When Mom's friends emailed me asking what they could do, I told them to send flowers—peonies, lilacs, snapdragons—bouquets that looked "more wild than cutesy," as per Mom's instructions. She was not a fan of sunflowers, daisies, or carnations. Mom's dying world was continually stocked with fresh flowers. We always had a minimum of five vases going at a time. And then there was the friend who brought flowers from her organic garden—or rather, just the green buds. ("Some people bring me chicken soup, others bring marijuana!")

Between the many visitors and the flower deliveries, we were constantly buzzing people up. The concierge was getting a workout downstairs. I wondered what she must have thought was going on. Mom was one very popular new mystery tenant.

I was no longer part of the living; I was in Mom's dying world. I'd become something of a hermit since everything went down with Jian, but this was next-level. I wasn't going to work. I wasn't seeing friends. I wasn't going to shows. I put my weekly chess match on hold. I put my whole life—even my relationship with Molly—on hold. Being with Mom was the only place I wanted to be. If I went too far out of range, the *tick tick tick* of my anxiety would go off.

During the day I'd only ever leave the building to run errands: pharmacy, bank, Whole Foods to replenish the kombucha stock. Driving around Forest Hill in Mom's silver Chevy, I started connecting to Top 40 pop songs like never before. Ed Sheeran, who normally made me gag, was suddenly giving me all the feels. I wasn't going to cry on the job, but alone in the car I could loosen the faucet a little. Mostly I managed to keep my emotions down by keeping busy, but even just stopping at a red light could allow my sadness to surface. My tears were now jumping like lemmings, and I wasn't even trying to hold them back anymore.

Mom got into the habit of reading the obituaries on her phone first thing in the morning. "It's really interesting," she said. "You get a personal story with each one." They were also *short* stories—Mom didn't have the energy to read for that long anymore.

Before she started to slow down, Mom would plow through several books a week. Now she'd been plodding through the same Ram Dass book for a month. The American spiritual teacher formerly known as Dr. Richard Alpert had been a psychology professor at Harvard in the 1960s, where he'd experimented with LSD with Timothy Leary before taking off to India in search of enlightenment. After returning with a new vision (and a new name), Ram Dass became an icon for a generation of hippies with his 1971 bestselling book *Be Here Now*. Mom was reading the more recent *Still Here: Embracing Aging, Changing, and Dying*, about Dass's struggle to accept his physical limitations and altered life after suffering a stroke in his sixties. It gave him a new perspective, a new humility, that was resonating with Mom. "It's about learning to accept dependence," she explained. "It's useful for me."

Mom was still constantly reminding me that "it's the dying person who takes the lead." But her newfound vulnerability was enabling us to connect in ways we hadn't before. We were letting our respective guards down and inching closer to each other than we'd ever been. The caretaker–dying person dynamic really wasn't an issue. We were really just two people who loved each other, hanging out.

"I don't think I could do this dying thing without you," she told me. It was sweet of her to say, but the truth was I needed her as much as she needed me. Mom had always been the person I turned to in hard times, and this was without a doubt the hardest. She was the only one who could help me through it.

"I don't want you to ever feel like you're alone," I said. "I'm going to be with you until the end." I'd never spoken in so many corny clichés before. As someone whose mother tongue was sarcasm, it was hard to reconcile all the sincere things I heard myself saying. But they were true. In that moment, they didn't sound overly sentimental or melodramatic. They were the only things *to* say. I suppose there's nothing all that original about death.

While I was learning to accept interdependence with Mom, I was taking two steps back with Molly. She wanted to come over to the condo, but I asked her not to at first. Mom's dying world wasn't exactly the most romantic setting for a budding relationship. I also wanted to be fully present for Mom. She was my priority. I needed time to figure out my new life with her before I could think about bringing Molly into it.

But the truth was that I was also afraid of being overwhelmed by Molly's feelings. She'd cry for me—*more* than me. So it wasn't conscious, but I was keeping her at bay. Although, two or three times a week, after I'd completed my evening routine—packing and charging Mom's vape, putting her to bed—we'd go out for dinner. Aside from my regular errands, those dates were my only contact with the outside world. I felt like an interloper sitting at Terroni on Queen West. How strange it was to see people normally going about their lives. *That used to be me.*

Elizabeth the death doula continued to come to the condo for regular visits. She knew exactly what to say to put Mom at ease. "The only agenda that matters is yours," Elizabeth would tell her, speaking precisely Mom's language.

One afternoon I joined them in the living room after their session. Mom still didn't know that much about Elizabeth. Their focus, naturally, was on Mom. But she couldn't hold back her curiosity any longer. "Do you mind if I ask you what your politics are?" she asked.

Elizabeth smiled and looked toward the ceiling. "I'd probably say Green Party, but I'm actually more left-leaning than that."

Mom's jaw dropped, and I burst out laughing. Elizabeth looked puzzled. "Mom was convinced you were a Conservative," I said, filling her in.

Now Elizabeth laughed. "I have my disguise," she said, looking down at her crisp blue button-up. "But my Birkenstocks are by the door. I'm passionate about environmental sustainability, and I'm a vegan," she added. By now Mom was practically levitating off the couch.

And for the kicker, Elizabeth shared how she was trying to be a good ally for her teenager. "They recently came out as gender-fluid," she said. Mom nodded along furiously, pointing her finger at me as if to say, "Me too! Look! I have a genderqueer child too!"

MOM WAS SITTING up in bed writing notes for us to open after she was gone—plain white cue cards in lavender envelopes. She wrote Little Molly a card for her sixteenth birthday and then dropped a favourite necklace of hers—a delicate gold chain with little pink pearls that her father had given her on her own sixteenth birthday—into the envelope. "It's really neat to think of her opening it," Mom said, getting a faraway look on her face.

"Do you want to hear what I wrote for Teddy?" she asked.

"Sure," I said, more curious than fully comfortable with the prospect of reading Mom's final words to my dad. How would she say goodbye to him?

The front of the envelope read "When all was said and done . . ." I was anxious to see whether the rejoinder would be serious or funny—or both. I opened it: "You were the love of my life." I was surprised. I knew she'd loved him, but the certitude of the declaration—and the vulnerability of the admission—overturned my expectations. It was big. Bigger than I'd ever imagined. I smiled at the thought of her flirting with him from beyond.

Mom could sense my surprise. "For years I would say I'd be devastated if anything ever happened to Ted. Of all the men in my life, I would've been hardest hit if he died. And I think he feels the same about me. I really love him. It's been a good bond, even if it wasn't a good marriage."

I understood. For a long time after the divorce, I'd hoped they'd get back together. But once I saw that they'd formed an even better friendship, I didn't care anymore. They had one of the best relationships of any parents I knew, including the married ones. It was a hundred percent voluntary. There was no legally binding contract that required them to go on bike rides or sing off-key together in the car. They truly loved each other's company.

"Anyway, I thought it would make him happy." Mom smiled, imagining him opening her love note. "And he won't have to worry about commitment!"

Then she began thinking out loud. "Maybe I wasn't meant to be a partner for life, except for Teddy, in our own way. Maybe I was meant to have affairs that were meaningful."

I grinned at her. "You've had it all."

"That's true," she laughed. "At times I've been ashamed of my record, this trail of bloody male bodies behind me. It wasn't on purpose—I tried to be as fair as I could be. But since I've been sick I've been reflecting on everything, and I'm so glad I mostly just did what I've wanted to in the last many years."

Last many years? As long as I'd known her, Mom had always done what she wanted. I started thinking about her boyfriends, her retreats, the choices she made when I was younger.

"There were times I was upset with you when you spent so much time away," I said, surprising myself. "But it made me realize that you were a person with your own needs."

"Not a martyr," Mom jumped in. "With my mother, the big wish I had was that she'd have a self of her own. My mother didn't give me role modelling for how to be a strong woman. It makes a huge difference."

I nodded.

"I remember thinking that I didn't want you to see a miserable housewife, baking cookies and wishing she could be doing things that were more interesting to her. I wanted you to see a mother *with a self.*"

"You were a strong role model," I reassured her. "Even though I really missed you when you'd go away, I think it did a lot of good for me."

"I never felt that you and Josh were calling out or begging me to stay," Mom said. "Teddy did. And I had my own ambivalence. A lot of people told me I was crazy for leaving. But sometimes you have to stop thinking about everyone else. I mean, it's your life!"

Even when you're a parent? I wonder that now.

It's true that Mom had shown me it was okay to live your life, to write your own script, to do things differently. So much of my strength comes from her, and I'm grateful for that. But if I'm being completely honest, Mom's drive to live her own life had also had some negative consequences for me, her child. Her need for romantic love and spiritual growth happened at a time when I really needed her.

Looking back now, it's striking to me that during this exchange

I couldn't express my sadness without just as quickly justifying her choices. I was undoing what I was saying as fast as I was saying it. What was wrong with me? Who was I protecting? Why was it so hard to be honest about how I'd felt abandoned? It's fascinating how I couldn't stand to be with my emotions for even a complete sentence.

It's not that I blame Mom for having left town just when I was becoming a teenager. She felt trapped in her marriage. She wanted to find passion, to find herself. It was complicated. And she definitely became much more present over the years. But why hadn't I allowed myself any space to feel upset about her hands-off approach to mothering when I was little? Just how funny were my childhood stories really? Only recently, in reflecting on this exchange, would the irony hit me: I wasn't in touch with the truth for the same reason Mom wasn't—reality can be pretty fucking painful.

In short, at the time of that conversation, I didn't question her. (Apparently I too was unaware of the resentment in my field.) I had only a hugely idealized version of Mom—the hugely idealized version she had of herself. I was a mirror for her. I had to be. Mom wasn't going to change her view of the world for anything. Either I was with her or I wasn't.

It was then, with my mommy-myopia, that I decided to write her a goodbye letter. I wanted to tell Mom how much she meant to me while she was still alive so that she could appreciate it. Eulogies are almost always glorified—and I meant everything I said—but it reveals just how on board I was with her idealized narrative. I stayed up late writing in bed on my laptop, thinking about all the good times we'd had.

Dear Mom,

Why do most people wait until after a person dies to deliver their eulogy? I figure it's more useful for you to read this *before* you die.

The art gallery and Wah Sing lobster, prosciutto in the car, McDonald's hot cakes, watercolour painting in the Adirondacks, the Russian Tea Room on my sixteenth birthday, the three-star restaurant in Paris, martinis on the roof of the Park Hyatt—we've had so many good times (and great food).

Thirty-five years with you isn't enough time. Although you're going too soon, I'm still the luckiest boy-girl in the world to have had you as my mother. I'm one of the rare fortunate ones who absolutely *loves* and *likes* their mother. You've been my mom and a true friend.

You've been my go-to person for advice, always making me feel better when I'm sad or broken-hearted. I'll miss your voice (recognizable from across the room), winning laugh, huge, shimmering smile, the way you talk with your hands and tell non-linear stories like a tree branch.

I've always been so proud that you're my mom. You lived by example, showing me that it's important to be true to yourself and live authentically. You've lived life to the fullest and, even in dying, have been a role model for how to say goodbye with such grace and Buddhist-y acceptance.

Speaking of being authentic, you are perfectly "inappropriate." Shall we talk about furries? You're hilarious. Never boring, that's for sure! We have laughed so much together (no one laughs harder at my twisted humour than you). The amount of material you've given me will surely fill up a comedy act, maybe even a book.

Thanks for naturally delivering all ten pounds and two ounces of me, letting me wear ripped jeans to synagogue when I was five, being extra proud of my aggressive hockey playing, showing me how to cross the street (and then letting me go off on my own), supporting me in quitting high school to be a travelling hippie, and always being a phone call away.

And thanks for not being "that kind of mom"—of course I much prefer you. You're right, you have been way more fun!

You are an extraordinary, larger-than-life person who's touched so many people's lives. You've filled such a space—life will be less without you.

But I'm going to be okay because of you.

I love you so much and will think about you every day.

As Grandma would say, roses in your pillow . . .

Rachel

18

THE TIP OF THE EMOTIONAL ICEBERG

The next morning I felt shy as I entered Mom's room. When Mom didn't say anything, I asked her if she'd gotten my letter.

"I did," she said in a quiet voice. "I read it and I cried all the way through."

That was all I needed to know. I didn't care to talk about it. I'd just wanted her to understand how I felt about her, and it was easier for me to say it in a letter.

"How are you feeling today?" I asked, quick to change the subject.

"I wake up, and every day I'm not in pain, I think I'm so lucky." Mom was feeling crummy a lot of the time, but the pain wasn't too sharp. She was lucky that her cancer hadn't caused any blockages or spread to her bones.

"All three of the surgeons said I'd have the most terrible, anguishing, painful death *for sure.*"

"Do you want to go back and complain?" I joked. "'You *promised me* a painful death!'"

"I was hoping I could go back to them in five years and say 'ha ha ha.'" Mom's voice softened. "I hoped to escape it." The wished-for future she'd written for herself hadn't come true. As I saw it, the only thing she'd escaped was reality.

And yet, despite this, Mom had a Buddhist perspective on dying. "Death is a part of life," she'd said at one point, "and impermanence and change are a part of life. Two things we know for sure are that we're going to die and that we don't know when. I'll suffer less if I go along with it rather than fight it."

I admired her live-and-let-die serenity—it certainly made her dying easier on both of us. But I wasn't as accepting as she was. Sure, death is a natural part of life, but Mom's dying didn't feel natural to me. As human life forms, we have *some* cards in the game. I think I would've been a little more at peace if I'd felt she'd done everything she could to save herself. Mom had tried a lot of stuff, but it was all just incense smoke and mirrors. By the end, her terminal cancer diagnosis was a scapegoat for her own bad choices. How could I ever accept them?

WE SOON RAN out of Paris movies. I thought a whole season of a TV show might be a little too ambitious, so we started in on some mini-series—*The Honourable Woman, Top of the Lake*. Mom, who'd been going to sleep at 7:00 every night, was suddenly staying up until 10:00 or 11:00 p.m. "One more!" she'd demand. "Let's keep going." She was high as a kite. Forget cannabis—binge-watching was Mom's dope.

It didn't take long before we made it through all three seasons of *The Americans*. Politics, espionage, relationships—thrilling TV was bringing Mom back to life. We eventually settled into *Borgen*, a gripping political drama about a woman prime minister in Denmark. We were engrossed. What would happen to Birgitte next? We *needed* to know. As long as there was another episode of *Borgen*, Mom had a reason to live.

Mom had never watched so much TV in her life. But it made sense. She was too tired to read anymore, and TV provided an escape. The characters were easy to be with and didn't demand anything from her. She could just lie back and be transported to another world where her dying wasn't the main plot.

"What did I do with my final days?" Mom joked aloud to an imaginary audience. "Did I spend my time with my family and friends, who I adore?" She laughed. "No. I spent it with Birgitte."

From her perch on the purple couch, Mom turned to me. "In the middle of all this shit, we have such a wonderful connection." It was true. We'd put aside our bickering and were being kind to and appreciative of each other like never before. Smiling back at her, I was overcome with regret. It sucked that it took her dying for us to have a weeks-long pyjama party. We were only just beginning to hit our stride in our adult relationship, and I wished we had a future together where we could always be this way.

JOSH, MELISSA, AND Little Molly had been coming over once or twice a week to visit. Teddy too. He'd always bring a big bouquet of flowers for Mom, but he never stayed long—he was clearly restless and needed to keep moving. I think it was too painful for him to see Mom this way. She wasn't able to do much, so we mostly just sat around talking.

One afternoon, Mom and I were sitting with Josh and Teddy in the living room. At one point they were both deeply absorbed in their phones. Mom and I smiled and rolled our eyes at each other. I knew exactly what she was thinking: *I'm about to die and these guys can't tear themselves away from their phones?* Mom and I got each other without saying a word. Just then, a wave of sadness came over me. Who would be there to make fun of Teddy and Josh with me when she was gone? Mom was my ally within our family unit. I suddenly became aware of how our dynamic was about to change forever. I loved Teddy and Josh with all my heart, but I was worried about being left alone with them. It hadn't worked out so well the last time.

One morning Mom had a craving for palatschinke, a type of Hungarian crêpe with cheese and jam filling, so we decided to have a family pancake breakfast. Josh was going to pick up the palatschinke from a Hungarian restaurant in the Annex on his way over. As we waited for the others to arrive, Mom reflected on our family get-togethers. "I hope they'll continue after I'm gone."

"You're leaving the party too soon," I said. "And I'll be stuck at the party that won't be as good without you."

Mom looked at me. "I don't want to leave!" She burst into tears. I saw pure anguish in her watery hazel eyes as she said those words—as though all her grief, terror, and regret were being expressed through them. As accepting as Mom was, even the most enlightened Buddhists don't want to die.

I felt helpless, paralyzed. *It's too late.* She was drowning in front of me and I couldn't do anything but watch her sink. It was torturous not to be able to help her. I knew she wasn't my responsibility—I was *her* child, after all—but I couldn't shake the feeling that I'd failed her, just as how I imagined a parent must feel after losing their teenage addict to a fatal overdose. It had always been my job to bring her back down to earth. I was the realist, the level-headed one. She was the dreamer, the magical thinker.

I set the table for our pancake party, unable to shake the image of that pleading, regretful look in her eyes. There'd been many sad moments up until then, but I didn't think it could get any more painful than that.

On another afternoon, Josh, Melissa, and Little Molly came over to watch home movies. I'd found some of my grandpa's old silent 8 mm films from the 50s and 60s and had them transferred to DVD. I heated up some chicken broth for Mom, with one matzo ball and one carrot, just how she liked it. Josh gave her a foot rub on the purple couch as we settled into the living room for our screening.

Mom must've been the one holding the camera most of the time, because we mainly saw her parents, always immaculately dressed, and her little sister. We caught Mom's instantly recognizable smile from time to time, but only in quick flashes.

"There's you, Mom!" I said excitedly, spotting her in a family party scene. She looked radiant in a sleeveless polka dot dress.

"Your mother is fixing your hair," Melissa commented, noticing Grandma tucking back a few wandering strands.

"She always told me how to wear my hair, until the day she died. She always wanted to control how I looked," Mom said, sighing. "Eventually I developed a sense of humour about it."

In another scene, Mom, probably in her late teens, is dancing for the camera. She has a long-stem rose between her teeth and is twirling around outside on the grass, looking free and happy.

"Good moves, Mom," I said. "You're gorgeous."

"You are so beautiful," Josh added.

"Too bad I didn't think so," Mom said, her voice heavy with regret. I looked over at her, wondering what exactly was going through her mind as she watched her younger self. Mom was obviously processing something internally that we didn't quite understand.

JOSH AND I made plans to go out for dinner together. We hadn't had any one-on-one time in a while. Before heading out to meet him, I opened Mom's door to say goodnight. She was sitting in bed reading the *Shambhala Sun*, her favourite Buddhist magazine. The new issue was all about "The Dharma of Death."

"I'm reading about killing myself," Mom announced nonchalantly.

I gave her a long look from the doorway.

"Don't worry, I haven't started yet," she said.

I met Josh at a neighbourhood Italian restaurant. Over matching bowls of seafood linguine, we talked about what life might be like after Mom was gone.

"I know that Mom is your person, just like Melissa is mine," Josh said. "She's the one you talk to when you're sad and need compassion and understanding, and she's the first person you call when you have something to celebrate." He put down his fork and leaned in closer. "I want you to know that you'll always have me. I adore you. I can never be what Mom is for you, but I want you to know that you're never alone in life."

As uncomfortable as Josh's earnestness made me feel, his words were a balm. He looked me in the eyes and smiled. "You are my gift."

I smiled back. I knew exactly what he was referring to. Mom had told us how, when I was born, she'd told Josh that I was a present for *him*. As the story goes, Josh was less than thrilled—I'm pretty sure he inquired about the return policy.

I'd built up a grudge toward Josh, feeling like I'd fought for Mom on my own. But in that moment I started to let it go. Josh was a good brother. I was lucky to have him. As people go, he and Teddy were pretty great ones to be stuck with.

That night, Josh and I decided to sell Mom's apartment. It seemed crazy that in the midst of everything we were adding real estate into the mix, but her place was just sitting there. And, honestly, I couldn't bear the thought of having to deal with it after she was gone. I figured it would be easier to say goodbye to the Hemingway while I at least still had Mom. Besides, I was afraid that if I ran out of things to do, I'd fall apart.

I began going over to the Hemingway in the evenings after Mom went to sleep to get the staging in order: packing, painting, organizing her belongings. One night Molly, Nicola, and Anya came over to help me pack Mom's many pieces of art in bubble wrap and sort her books and other sentimental possessions into boxes. (Josh was charged with carrying the boxes down to the storage room and disassembling the infrared sauna.) We sifted through Mom's clothes, saving signature pieces for friends who might want them and gathering the rest for Goodwill. But as I sat down on the carpet in front of her closet, I hesitated. *What if she recovers and all her stuff has been given away?* It was a strange thought that took me by surprise. She wasn't going to get better. Why would I even consider she would? As much as I intellectually understood she was going to die, it was still hard to believe. I guess I had some magical thinking going on too.

I told myself that if Mom pulled through we'd be so overjoyed that the lost clothes wouldn't matter. She'd buy a whole new wardrobe! We could go shopping together! It was a nice fantasy to indulge in for a few seconds, before the closet shelves came back into focus. I grabbed Mom's blue silk pyjamas and, wincing, threw them into a black garbage bag. I felt like I was killing her before she was even dead.

I WAS DOING my best not to think about Mom's past choices and just be in the present. One of her favourite sayings was "You can be right, or you can be happy." So I was trying to be happy with her. But I was perplexed by how she could approach death with such conscious awareness yet still be unaware of what an unreliable witness she'd been—*and still was.*

She'd say something like, "I wish I had the type of cancer where you can still walk around and do things."

I'd raise my eyebrows. "What do you call the past five years?"

One morning I overheard her talking to a new naturopath over the phone. She was telling the same old story about her diagnosis, including how she'd be stuck with a colostomy bag for the rest of her life. I hated this part of her—this thing that had led to her dying. How could she continue to be so disconnected from reality? *THE JIG IS UP, goddammit.*

It gnawed at me for a couple of days. I tried to let it slide, but I had a compulsive need to correct her. Was it the journalist in me wanting to keep her honest? Was it my own need to set reality straight? Or was it perhaps a desire to minimize the distance between us, to bring our perspectives to bear on the same truth so that we could finally come together on the same story? We were close in so many ways, and yet our lack of shared reality would always be a wedge.

And so I had a relapse. "This isn't to get into a fight or anything, but I still get frustrated and confused when I overhear you telling the naturopath, for example, that it was 'a hundred percent for sure' that you'd end up with a sac. You *know* that's not true."

"Well maybe there was a three percent chance I wouldn't have," Mom replied. "I remember Feinberg went over to his desk and pulled out pictures of pretty women with sacs, one in a bathing suit and one in a prom dress, and said, 'See, you can still live a fabulous life! You can wear a sexy dress!'"

I remembered that. I was there when he presented her with the fashion spread; it had been interesting to see all the clothing options. But I also remember—and had it documented in my notes—that Feinberg had said there was only a five percent chance she'd end up with a permanent bag. "I think he was just trying to reassure you that even the worst-case scenario wouldn't be so bad."

"I don't know. I just believed it," Mom said grudgingly.

It was the first time she'd admitted that what she *believed* may not line up with the facts. And now she had that scared-deer look again—a look I'd come to know intimately. Her own words had gotten to her.

"So that's it. That's the end of the comments," Mom said, abruptly ending the conversation.

One afternoon after she'd finished her session with Mom, Elizabeth the death doula knocked on my bedroom door to see how I was doing. "My job is to tend to the dying person, but also what's around that person," she explained. Elizabeth said she was moved by how Mom and I related to each other so easily. "It's really beautiful. I see that you're doing everything possible for your mom. You're at her beck and call, wanting to get every moment in with her," she said.

I liked and trusted Elizabeth, so I decided to fill her in on the *E! True Hollywood* story. She wasn't surprised to hear there was a larger dynamic at play. "You have a tremendous connection. I see the depth of love you have for each other. So in the midst of all that love it seems inevitable that a pile of questions come to mind. How can you clearly love someone who means so much and also be so angry at them for their decisions? What do you do with that anger? How can someone who loves you so much make decisions that would hurt you so much?"

Elizabeth was concerned about me getting the professional support I needed to tackle those questions. "The thing is that anger and grief can be a pretty toxic combination that creates a lot of extra agony down the road," she said.

"I'm not angry at Mom. I'm angry at *the situation*," I insisted. (That was *my* story, and I was sticking to it.) "I'm angry at the circumstances that allowed her to end up here." I could be mad at her so-called healers, at whatever had compelled Mom to reject medical help. But I couldn't allow myself to be mad at *her*. In her final days, I needed to preserve our good relationship.

LIVING WITH MOM, each week folded into the next. In her dying world, there was no difference between the days of the week. The usual markers—*Mad Men* on Sunday, hockey on Monday, chess on the weekend—no longer applied. Now the passing of time was marked by other things: another worse stage of Mom's illness, new flowers in season (tulips were done; we'd moved on to peonies), how many friends were still owed a goodbye, how many pieces remained in her jewellery box. She was deteriorating faster than any of us had expected. At the rate she was going she wouldn't make it to the end of the lease, maybe not even to the end of summer.

Meanwhile I kept busy, tackling one task after another. Pulling off a good death for Mom was the most important thing I'd ever do in my life. I may have been hanging out with her on the edge of death, but with such a clear sense of purpose, I'd never felt more alive.

Teddy praised me for how well I was taking care of Mom. And Mom's friends all remarked on what a "good daughter" I was. Their acknowledgments were nice to hear, even though the description made me cringe. (If anything, I identified more as a dutiful son.) I knew I was doing a good thing, but it certainly wasn't out of obligation. It's not as though I have a caretaker personality—I can barely keep my plants alive—and Mom never guilted me. She trusted that I didn't do things I didn't want to do. In fact, I think that's why she allowed me to help her in the first place. (That, and I just kept showing up with gelato.)

Josh too was grateful, since he could continue working and being a present father and husband. And yet he told me he felt pushed away—that he wanted to visit more often, but Mom didn't want him over more than twice a week. In retrospect, I think she didn't know how to be in his company without feeling she had to take care of him. In contrast, Mom saw me as self-sufficient. It had taken me months, if not my whole life, to prove I required nothing of her. I was safe; everyone else was a threat.

In the evenings I'd go through my usual routine getting Mom ready for bed: close her blinds, plug in her phone, and place a bottle of cold vanilla Ensure in a frozen drink sleeve on her bedside table. It would keep it cool, how she liked it, for a few more hours. Then I'd clean out her vape and repack it with a couple pinches of weed from her jar.

One night she offered me some. *Why not?* I might as well try to relax a bit. I sat down next to Mom as she clicked on her vape. Once it was heated up, she took a pull and then plugged her nose to hold the vapour in her lungs. It was adorable, like a kid in the swimming pool. We chatted for a bit, passing the vape back and forth, and then I got up to give her a hug.

"Goodbye," she whispered in my ear.

"No, Mom," I said, laughing. "It's just goodnight, not goodbye."

"Oh, right." She laughed. "Goodnight, darling."

As I lay in bed stoned, staring up at the ceiling, images from the past few weeks floated through my mind. I was starting to see some patterns, connecting some puzzle pieces. Suddenly it was so obvious. The biggest piece of the puzzle—had I been staring at it the whole time? Mom spoke openly about so many personal things: her insecurities, her anxieties, her dating life. But there was one thing she never talked about. With anyone. Her best friends didn't even know. I didn't find out about it until I was a teenager. And even then I'd never really understood why it was such a big deal.

But I knew it was a big deal to her. So although it wouldn't be easy, I resolved to ask her about it. As I drifted into a weed-induced fog, I told myself not to forget.

The next morning, my revelation passed the sobriety test. I was nervous as I broached the subject over our coffee and kombucha. With time running out, all topics were on the table. And my recorder gave me added permission.

"I have another question," I said. "I've been noticing a bit of a theme: the times we've been looking at old photos of you, the old family movies. We comment on how gorgeous you were when you were young, and every time you say you wished *you'd known* how pretty you were." I had to spit it out. "I get the sense that the nose job was a huge trauma for you."

"It was," Mom said without hesitation. "It was like a rape. I felt mutilated. I didn't want it."

I'd never heard her talk about it like that, in those words. When Mom was sixteen, her parents sent her to get a nose job. As far as they were concerned, it was just what Jewish girls with Jewish noses did back then. Her mother felt happier and more confident after she'd had one. Her dad told her he'd started putting away money when she was born so that he could give her the gift of this operation. It wasn't a discussion. They thought they were doing her a favour.

I could sense from the few times she'd talked about it in hushed whispers that it had caused her a lot of grief. She hated her new Gentile-looking nose. She ended up getting two or three more surgeries over the years to try to make it better. (There was a small indent that no one else would have noticed, but it bothered her.)

"I think it was about confidence. I think I was beautiful rather than pretty, but I just felt like there was this little thing in the middle of my face. And it did feel like a rape. And on top of that, they sent me to a school without my closest friends. It's like I was completely unmoored."

"I don't know if you've thought about it, but how much did that inform your decision not to get the surgery for your cancer?" I asked.

"It probably did. I've thought of it. I was really scared. I haven't had good experiences in hospitals. I was kind of brutalized when I had Josh, too. And then there's my elbow. It wasn't conscious mostly, although I certainly thought of it—but yeah, I'm sure it did."

Mom was being honest with me and herself. In times like this, I felt closer to her.

"Yeah, I think it goes beyond being conscious," I said. "Just like if somebody, as you said, took away your body, like being raped, and did something that left you feeling mutilated and traumatized—"

"—in the middle of the face!" Mom interjected loudly.

"You might think, 'Never again am I going to hand over my body to somebody to do something that I don't want.'"

"I'm sure I did. I didn't think those exact sentences, but I'm sure I did. Because I did think things like, 'Once they get you, they'll keep doing stuff to you.' You know, 'They'll give me chemo when I don't want it.' I have very little trust."

I was beginning to understand just how deep Mom's distrust and need for agency went. And although I still couldn't exactly articulate it, I was sensing that the injury went further back than her bad medical experiences, that the operation was just the tip of the emotional iceberg.

"My dad never told me I was pretty when I was growing up, and my mother would say, 'You're so beautiful, if *only* you would do this, or do that.' That's more crucial than the nose job. There are people who have way worse nose jobs than me who are very confident. A lot of it has to do with your self-image as you're growing up. Barbara was the cute one because she had a smaller nose. I wasn't."

I felt a burst of compassion in place of my usual frustration. I was starting to understand just how traumatizing the nose job had been for her, and more than that, the underlying message her parents had sent her—that she wasn't okay the way she was, that she was defective, that she didn't have inherent value just for being the intelligent and beautiful Jewish girl she was. Perhaps that's why she always felt she had to sing for her supper. They'd removed only a bit of cartilage, but took away so much of her self-assurance in the process (Mom had mentioned how she lost herself in adolescence). I could see how it had taken her decades to build herself back up from the shame her parents had dumped on her.

Even if the picture was becoming clearer, I knew this was a bigger puzzle than one late-night marijuana epiphany could solve. "I think it was a perfect storm of different things," I said.

"Of course," Mom said. "Including my original GP saying that I didn't have to get a colonoscopy five years before I got one. I wasn't pushing for it because they *do* puncture about ten percent of them, so it was easy for me to think that will happen to me."

Ah, there they were: the false facts and fatalistic attitude I'd come to know so well. Mom had a streak of throwing in the towel before she'd even played the game. It was as if she couldn't stand to be disappointed, so she didn't even try.

"You always think things won't go your way," I said. "When they first caught your cancer, and the doctors said there was a seventy to ninety percent chance you'd be cured, you never thought 'I'm going to be in that majority.' It seems you always assume you'll get the short end of the stick."

"Not in my whole life," Mom said in her defence. "I know you have this thing about me and parking spots. But given my circumstances, and my age, and what women were like, I've accomplished quite a lot, and I've been brave in a lot of situations." She paused. "But this one, you're right. It's a conglomeration of a whole bunch of stuff that came together."

"I wouldn't say that about you in general," I clarified. "But for some reason, when it comes to parking spots and getting medical help, you assume the worst."

"I do. So that's the way it is, and that's why I'm here."

We were both silent for a few seconds before she once again stepped away from the truth and turned things around for herself.

"But I could have been dead four years ago. Nobody knows for sure. You had me for a nice five years . . . even though you were nervous all the time," she added with a chuckle.

Mom was still justifying her decision, but at least she'd somewhat acknowledged that it had affected me. And, for the most part, we did have a nice five years. Except that while Mom was off gallivanting, I was taking one for the team. Maybe I faced reality so she didn't have to.

19

TEMPURA-GATE

"How much time do you think I have left?" Mom asked her palliative care doctor when he was over one day for a checkup. We were in the living room. Mom was sitting back on her new La-Z-Boy powerlift recliner we'd rented. She didn't have the strength to get up from a chair on her own anymore.

He could see how little energy she had. "I'd say you're looking at weeks now," he replied.

"Wow, okay." Mom nodded, taking it all in.

It was now June. "It feels more and more real," Mom said. She agreed that it was time to put her on the list for hospice care—although there was only one place she was interested in. Kensington Hospice was located in an old converted church hall on a beautiful tree-lined street in the Annex. It had stained-glass windows, exposed brick, and iPhone docks in all the rooms. It was like a five-star boutique hotel for dying people—the place to go if you wanted to *go* in style.

Kensington had only ten rooms, so someone would have to dearly depart for Mom to get a spot. It was going to be as difficult as getting a toddler into a prestigious daycare. Josh and I made an appointment to look at the place. It wasn't the kind of sibling outing we'd expected so soon in our lives, and we were grateful we had each other.

We met with the head nurse, who gave us a tour. As Josh and I followed her up the stairs, I turned to him and whispered, "Let's see who's paying their bill." We made eyes at each other as we walked around, peering into open doors to see who looked like they were ready to check out (spoiler: everyone). We'd entered into a kind of earthly purgatory, somewhere between life and death, where even our jokes couldn't shield us from the palpable sense of gravitas in the air. People were there to die. It wasn't a sad place per se, but I had an immense feeling of gratitude and lightness being able to walk out of there.

Josh and I gave Mom a full report when we got back. We were impressed with the caring and attentive staff we met. And the place itself was charming, cozy, and modern, just as in the brochure. There was even a grand piano in the communal area. Mom raised her finger in the air and declared, "I'll be disappointed if I die anywhere *but* Kensington!"

AS MOM'S CONDITION changed, so did our routine. There was a constant recalibration. Mom now divided her days between her bed and the purple couch in the living room. The only time she got up anymore was for her morning commute to the living room, bathroom breaks, and shuffling back to bed. She was too weak and tired to get up to shower, so Maymouna gave her sponge baths in bed. As much as I wanted to take care of Mom, I was never going to help her in the bathroom or change her diaper. That's where I drew the line. Mom always taught me it was important to have *boundaries*.

Mom was still into cannabis because it made her feel good—oil in the morning, bud in her vape at night—but she was no longer bothering with Michael's herbs or homeopathy. She now preferred Percocet, which I'd place in her mouth before bed. ("Okay, Baby Bird, time for your pill," I'd sing, playing out some twisted game of "Who's the Mommy?")

One night I was awakened by Mom calling out for me. There was panic in her voice. I hopped out of bed and ran to her room. When I opened the door and switched on the light, I saw Mom lying face down on the floor with blood on her face. In a pained voice, she explained that she'd been trying to make her way to the bathroom when she took a nosedive. She couldn't get up.

I jumped into action, squatting over her and getting a good grip under her armpits. And then—using an improvisational wrestling move of sorts—I flipped us both over so that she was sitting between my legs. It didn't take that much strength, but my heart was beating fast. Mom was breathing rapidly, too. I was pretty sure we were both thinking the same thing: *Holy shit holy shit holy shit.* We just sat there for a few seconds, terrified. I had a flashback to Barcelona, the shock of seeing Mom so helpless and vulnerable. But this was a hundred times harder. With her broken elbow, the threat to her mortality was still abstract. But now she was fully in the process of dying. It was impossible for me to repress that fact anymore. There would be no cast to wrap her in, no stabilizing the situation.

I got around in front of her and pulled her up onto her feet. She was very heavy and wobbly. It clicked what the palliative care doctor meant when he'd said that her body was like "liquid cement." I helped her back into bed and gently wiped the blood off her face with a wash-cloth. We didn't talk. We were putting up a good front, but both of us were shaken. There was a lot of joking, easiness, and even fun during Mom's dying. But there were also instances like this when we came face to face with how awful it truly was.

It wasn't safe for Mom to move around on her own anymore. She needed a spotter when getting in and out of bed, up from the couch, or walking to the bathroom. She'd place her hands on my shoulders and I'd walk backward with my hands on her hips—like an awkward junior high slow dance. I had to wake up two or three times during the night to take her to the bathroom or get her a cold Ensure from the fridge. "Rachel!" she'd holler, and I'd hop to my feet. The interrupted sleep was making me loopy.

By this time Molly had started staying over two or three nights a week. She'd even been giving Mom foot massages. And so one night, desperate, I asked her to get Mom to the bathroom. Molly was happy to help. But neither of us was exactly thrilled about having to get out of bed in the middle of the night. "Your turn!" we'd say to each other in groggy voices. It wasn't even a year into our relationship and it was as if we were sleep-deprived parents of a newborn. After a couple weeks of this routine, we reached a breaking point. It was clear that Mom needed round-the-clock care.

BY THE THIRD week of June Mom was sleeping away most of the day. She described being in another world, where she was half gone. "I think about everyone, but I just don't have the energy anymore to really be in the world with them," she told me. I was lucky if I got a few minutes with her every day. When I'd check on her, sometimes she'd wake up for a bit or just give me a wave. Other times I'd sit next to her and read while she slept.

On one occasion I asked, "Is there *any* silver lining to this?"

As I ran my hands through my hair like a nervous wreck, Mom looked at me with her big glassy eyes. She barely had the energy to talk anymore. There would be no more sermons. Mom got straight to the point.

"No."

Her truth bomb hit me right in the chest. I don't know what I was hoping for. That there was wisdom to be gained? That I'd become a better person? I wanted to hear that this hell wasn't all for nothing. But Mom was right. It just deeply, horribly, resoundingly sucked.

Day by day I was losing her more and more to the other world. I was extremely anxious. *What do I do when I have a broken heart again? What kind of French cheese do I buy?*

"I don't know how I'll live without you," I cried.

Mom kept my gaze as she summoned the energy to speak. Slowly. "You . . . will . . . grieve."

As death approached, Mom was prescribed morphine to help ease her discomfort. I never would've imagined I'd be injecting morphine into my mom's abdomen. A palliative care nurse prepared a bunch of syringes and showed me how to flick the air bubbles out and then squeeze the drug into Mom's stomach. No more cannabis oil. No more vaporizer. It was Percocet and morphine from here on in.

We started developing our own language. Or rather, I was learning Mom's new language. She now spoke mostly in winces, scrunched-up faces, and the slightest of nods. By late June she couldn't stand up at all. She was officially bedridden, and miserable.

The last few days of June brought a torrent of rain and dark, dramatic clouds. Thunder crashed and lightning lit up the sky. *I get it, I get it!* I wanted to say to the Universe. One afternoon I watched Mom wake up and slowly summon the energy to speak. "I want a Perc . . . and a *Borgen*." I laughed. She hadn't been up for watching TV in at least a week. I thought our *Borgen* days were over, but Mom was back! I held a Percocet above her mouth.

"Baby Bird," she whispered before opening wide. I pulled up a chair beside her, placed my laptop in front of us on her rolling tray table, and turned on the show. I tried to savour the completely ordinary yet entirely blissful moment. I knew this would be the last time Mom and I would ever watch TV together. We lasted for about ten minutes before she fell back asleep.

That evening for dinner, I ordered takeout from the Japanese restaurant down the street. I had fond memories of Mom taking me to Edo for my favourite shrimp tempura after the divorce. It was my comfort food. I went out to pick it up, and when I returned, I discovered to my dismay that they'd forgotten to include the tempura dipping sauce. All I saw at the bottom of the plastic bag were two soy sauce packets.

It was the dipping sauce that broke the camel's back. I was enraged. *SOY SAUCE DOES NOT GO WITH TEMPURA! HOW AM I SUPPOSED TO EAT MY TEMPURA WITHOUT ITS RIGHTFUL SAUCE?* If it wasn't bad enough that my mom was about to die, now I had to eat dry tempura. The indignity! I called the restaurant and was brushed off by the manager with a simple sorry. I didn't want an apology. I wanted my dipping sauce! I wanted my mom not to die! I wrote to the owner, and then complained to him over the phone that night. In short: I was a crazy person.

ON THE FIRST day of July I received a call from the head nurse at Kensington. A bed had opened up. *Finally!* I didn't know how much longer I could keep managing Mom's palliative care unit on my own. We made plans for the nurse to come over at the end of the week for an assessment.

When I woke up that Friday morning Maymouna had already arrived, so I figured I'd take the opportunity to get outside for a few minutes. I went into Mom's room: "I'm going out to get a coffee, Mom. I'll be back soon." When I leaned in to give her a hug, she whispered in my ear, "Get two."

"You want a coffee?" I asked, grinning. I was puzzled. She hadn't drunk coffee in months. She was barely able to drink water anymore. She nodded.

"Okay, Mom. I'll get you a coffee." I assumed she was confused, but what the heck.

When I returned from Starbucks I poured some of my Grande Americano into a mug and then dug into the cardboard box of dental sponges that had been sitting in the corner of her room. I unwrapped one of the grey foam lollipops, dipped it in the mug, and put it in Mom's mouth. She perked up immediately, going to town on it like a hamster on a bottle feeder.

"This is delicious," she muttered under her breath. "It's been so long."

My heart burst with joy. It was a far cry from our cappuccinos in France, our café con leches in Spain, and all the mornings we'd spent chatting over coffee in her sunroom, but being able to have one last coffee with Mom made me somehow deliriously happy. I dipped the sponge back in and Mom kept going.

When the nurse from Kensington arrived we sat down on either side of Mom, who was in bed, seemingly asleep. I told the nurse that I honestly didn't know if it was best for Mom to move to the hospice at this point. She was on the brink of death. I wasn't sure if it was worth schlepping her down there, even though, selfishly, I was afraid of handling her death on my own.

"I think it would be better," Mom whispered, barely awake. I was surprised she'd been following the conversation.

"To stay? Or go?" I asked her. I wasn't sure which she'd meant.

Mom breathed the words out. "To go."

The nurse nodded. I was relieved that Mom still wanted it, and that I didn't have to make the decision for her. If Mom was still alive on

Monday, an ambulance would arrive first thing in the morning to take her to the hospice.

FOLLOWING TEMPURA-GATE, MY anger was still sizzling away. I had to channel it somewhere, and this time my target wasn't quite so oblique:

Dear Michael,

My mother is now nearly dead and there are a few things I want to say to you. All things considered, my mother was very lucky to have been diagnosed five years ago with Stage 1 rectal cancer. She was given a 70–90% survival rate. However, she rejected the recommended medical treatment in favour of taking your herbs.

I'm not sure if it's your ego, misguided belief in the ultimate power of herbs, or genuine wish to help—I assume a combination —but it was astonishingly irresponsible of you to tell my mom that your herbs could help her. There is NO evidence to suggest that herbs can cure rectal cancer. My mom said that you were "surprised" to hear a few months back that her cancer had progressed to Stage 3. Were you actually surprised??? Did you really believe your herbs would cure her???

Furthermore, as you suggested in your previous email, "absolute faith" may be important, but evidently it's not a cure on its own. My mom needed to have her cancerous tumour removed—that's NOT just my "personal belief"—but instead she followed your precarious guidance. My family should sue you for practising medicine without a licence.

Ultimately, I know it was my mom's choice to go down the alternative path instead of the one the doctors recommended. But I do hold you responsible for enabling her lethal decision, even profiting off of it. (I can't believe you have the nerve to offer to sell her more herbs while she's on her deathbed!)

Since being diagnosed five years ago, my mom has been extremely vulnerable. Due to a combination of fear, trauma, and a general mistrust for conventional medicine, she wasn't acting rationally and was clearly not grasping what the doctors were telling her. However, as someone who supposedly works in the field of health care, it's your job to look out for patients not acting in their best interests. You should have pointed her in the direction that was best for her health, or at the very least, clearly stated to her the limitations of what your herbs could offer, rather than enabling her to kill herself.

Rachel

MOM AND I made it through to Sunday; now we just had to make it through one more night. I placed a few of her things in a box: a couple T-shirts, her hairbrush, a favourite blanket. It wasn't going to be a long stay. A little after 11:00 p.m. I went into Mom's room to say goodnight. She was still breathing, but she looked like a corpse. Her face was pale and skeletal and her mouth hung open.

Somehow I managed to squeeze myself into the single hospital bed next to her. I rested my head against her bony shoulder, put my arm around her chest, and held her tightly. I could feel she was still there. The last time we'd been in a hospital bed together was thirty-five years before, when I was born. And now our time was almost up.

I'd read somewhere that it's important to give a dying loved one permission to die. Apparently people sometimes hang on too long and continue to suffer because they don't feel they can let go. I thought I'd perform my due diligence.

"If you want to go, you can go," I said, my eyes welling up with tears.

Mom suddenly shifted. "What?" she muttered, semi-conscious and confused.

Well, this is awkward. I hadn't thought she could hear me.

"I mean, I prefer you don't," I said, backpedalling. "Stay as long as you want."

20

COLD STORAGE

The alarm went off at 6:30 a.m. *Is she still alive?* Mom's impending death felt like a morbid game of Hot Potato. When would the music stop? Who'd end up holding the potato? I really wanted to be there when Mom took her final breath, but I was terrified of discovering her already dead. I hopped out of bed and peeked into her room. She was still breathing. *I guess we really are moving.*

I got dressed and finished packing my bag. As I tossed my toiletries into my knapsack, I caught a glimpse of myself in the bathroom mirror. I stopped to take a closer look—it had been a while. I appeared swollen, dishevelled, totally worn out. I stared into my own eyes: *Today is the day my mom is going to die.* I said a silent goodbye to the me who had a mom.

It was dark out and eerily quiet in the condo. That stillness, like waiting for an early morning taxi to the airport. Our bags were packed and we were ready to go. *Was anyone really coming?*

At precisely 7:00 a.m. there was a loud knock at the door. I opened it to see two medics standing in the hallway with a stretcher, ready for action. I showed them to Mom's room and watched as they each held two corners of her bottom sheet and, on the count of three, swooped her frail body from her bed onto the stretcher. *Genius!*

I put on my knapsack, picked up Mom's box, grabbed a couple of morphine syringes for the road, and followed them out of the building. As we passed through the lobby I said a chipper "Good morning!" to the concierge as if nothing were out of the ordinary. (Maybe if I acted as if everything was normal she wouldn't notice my nearly dead mother being wheeled out on a stretcher?)

I jumped into the back of the ambulance and sat by Mom's side. She winced at every bump in the road. Fearful she might die en route, I talked to her the whole way, offering a play-by-play of the landmarks we were driving past: Casa Loma, the Annex, the University of Toronto. The streets where she'd lived her life. The Free Times Cafe on College Street, one of her favourite spots, disappeared in my peripheral vision as we took a right on Major Street, arriving at Kensington Hospice. I was relieved. This is what she wanted. Our death plan was working out.

Mom was wheeled through the front door and taken up to her new room on the second floor. I put on some classical music (baroque, her favourite) and collapsed onto the recliner next to her bed.

Josh called. He had important city council business that week and said he'd come as soon as his meeting was over.

I hesitated, looking at Mom. "I don't know . . . if she'll . . . make it until the evening."

There was a pause before he spoke. "Should I come right now?"

My instinct was to tell him it was fine to come later, that he shouldn't miss important voting. But I couldn't deny what I was seeing before me. Mom was actually dying. I took a deep breath and made an executive decision: "Yes."

Mom's room was freezing. She hated to be cold, so I asked a staff person about turning down the a/c. Apparently it was stuck; maintenance had to be called in to fix it. I covered Mom with extra blankets and gave her one last foot massage. Then I wedged myself in next to her on the hospital bed and stroked her hair. A hospice volunteer brought me a grilled cheese sandwich. It felt nice to be taken care of. For the past many weeks I'd been Mom's producer, her caretaker, her nurse. Now, for whatever time she had left, I could just be her child.

JOSH AND TEDDY arrived mid-morning. The original four, together for one last hurrah. One of the nurses told us that she could tell from the stiffness of Mom's feet that she didn't have much longer. "Maybe a few more hours."

Josh and I razzed Teddy into admitting to Mom that she was right, about everything. She gave a slight nod, and we all laughed.

"I have a craving for a blueberry bun," Josh announced. Mom used to buy them for us from Harbord Bakery when we were little. I told him that if Mom could talk she'd say, "They aren't as good as they used to be." Mom gave another slight nod.

Teddy's phone rang. Josh and I exchanged a look as he answered it. *Are you kidding me?* Josh shooed him away to take the call in the hall. When he returned, we asked him what was so important. "It was the auto shop," he said. "I had to take it."

"Oh, of course!" We laughed. "We mistakenly thought it was some trivial business you didn't need to take care of by Mom's deathbed," Josh joked.

The hot July sun was shining in through the window, but it was still freezing in Mom's room. We inquired again about when maintenance would be coming. "Either the a/c goes or she does," I said, knowing Mom would appreciate my play on Oscar Wilde's last words.

Mom began to wince, squeezing her eyes. It was similar to how she looked when she was in pain, but not quite.

"Are you in pain? Do you need morphine?" I asked. She kept her gaze straight ahead. "Are you sad?" She kept her gaze still. She continued blinking hard. It looked as if she was crying, but there were no tears. "Are you happy, Mom?" I asked. "Are you happy we're all here?"

She gave a slight nod. *Incredible.* I could hardly believe her focus on gratitude in the midst of losing everything. She might've been the most enlightened tragic hero there ever was.

I stayed in bed next to Mom all day long, getting up only to use the bathroom. In the afternoon, Teddy and Josh went out to get some food. Melissa came to say goodbye on her way to pick up Little Molly from preschool. Molly left work early to do the same.

By evening Teddy couldn't handle just sitting in the room, so he went out to the common area. I was still in Mom's bed. Josh sat on the recliner on the other side. There was nothing to do except just be there with her. Mom's breathing got louder and deeper. Josh and I stared into space. The only noise was a rhythmic gurgling, which a nurse explained was the result of no longer having the strength to clear saliva from her throat. (I was getting a real education—you never hear dying people gurgle in the movies.)

I suddenly detected a slight variation in her breathing.

"Josh!" I yelped, whipping my head around to meet his eyes. We didn't say anything. We both knew: This Was It.

We sat on either side of her and each took one of her hands. "I love you, Mom. I love you," we both said, over and over, as the gurgling quieted and long silences stretched between breaths. Breaths turned to gasps, then to gasping in slow motion, like a fish out of water. She took one last inhalation and then slowly exhaled, her head lowering gradually with every bit of air released, before coming to a full and complete stop. Her large hazel eyes went blank. I was shocked by how totally empty they were. Josh glanced up at the clock on her bedside table. "7:23 p.m.," he pronounced.

I kept staring into Mom's hollow eyes with disbelief. "Where did you go?! Where did you go?!" I cried. I slid my hands under her limp torso and hugged her tightly. I didn't ever want to let her go. My mind was flooded with one thought on repeat: *I want my mom, I want my mom.* I must have uttered it out loud because I heard Josh say, "You have me."

"I know," I said, thankful he was there with me, "but I really want my mom right now." It had been so abrupt. In a split second she was gone.

I stood up and took a step back, keeping my gaze fixed on her. "I can't believe you just went and died, Mom! I can't believe it! YOU JUST DIED!" What I was processing with my eyes was so baffling; her lifeless corpse was so strange, eerie, freakish. "You've done some pretty weird things, Mom. But this is definitely the weirdest."

"I'm not so sure about that," I heard Josh say behind me. We burst into laughter.

Josh went down the hallway to let Teddy know. I sat with Mom—what used to be Mom—for another minute. She was already stiffening, and her face had gone chalky pale. Mom had left the building.

I texted Molly: "Mom is dead. Please don't text back for now." (I know, I'm a weirdo, but I couldn't handle my own feelings in that moment, never mind Molly's bundle of emotions.)

When nurses came in to clean Mom's body, I joined Josh and Teddy in the common area. Josh told me that Teddy had just cried in his arms. I'd never seen Teddy cry before. I realized that underneath all his restlessness, he was really suffering. The love of *his* life had just died.

I sank down into the couch. I'd been dedicated to Mom for so long, and now, suddenly, there was nothing for me to do. Teddy came over and sat beside me. "There's nothing like losing a parent to make you feel like an adult," he said. He was trying to comfort me in the best way he knew how, but in that moment I felt like the furthest thing from an adult. I felt like Bambi.

BEFORE LEAVING, TEDDY called the funeral home. Josh and I walked back to Mom's room. From the doorway we could see that she'd been positioned with her hands clasped above her stomach. The odd sight made us laugh. We'd never seen her look so proper before.

Over by the window, two maintenance workers were finally fixing the air conditioning unit. One man was on a stepladder and the other was passing him tools. I felt like we were in the middle of an absurdist "better late than never" skit. They were clearly not clued in to the fact that the woman on the bed was dead (and no longer gave a damn about the temperature). We stared, speechless, at the bizarre scene for a few more seconds before Josh finally asked if they could come back another time. The workers looked over at Mom's corpse, then at each other, and then bolted out of the room.

The funeral director soon arrived, pushing a stretcher with a red velvet body bag on top of it. The red velvet struck me as dated, and maybe a little sensual for the occasion, but definitely nicer than the black heavy-duty plastic body bags on *CSI*. Mom was wearing a lavender T-shirt and a diaper when the funeral director and one of the nurses placed her inside the bag. They stood to the side as I leaned over Mom's head and ran my fingers through her hair one last time. Tears blurred my eyes. A suffocating sadness began to rise in my chest.

"Goodbye Mom," I whimpered, letting out a single involuntary chest-heave cry. I'd been keeping it together for so long, and now I was afraid I'd come undone. I forced my sadness down and took a step back. And then, just like that, Mom was zipped up.

The head nurse placed a special procession quilt over Mom's body. A few more hospice staff joined our train while we followed Mom out.

I walked behind the stretcher and kept my hand on her head through the velvet as we took the elevator down to the first floor and then down the hallway. When we got to the lobby, everyone stopped. The head nurse lit a candle and said a few nice words about Mom, an especially kind gesture considering she really hadn't had much time to get to know her. Mom was then wheeled out through the front door—the same door she'd come in earlier that day.

Out front, Mom was lifted into the back of a black hearse. I was surprised by its modern, angular design—hardly the old-school *Harold and Maude* car I was expecting.

"Where are you taking her?" I asked the funeral director.

She hesitated before answering matter-of-factly: "Cold storage."

Ouch! It's not like I was expecting her to say "Heaven," but I wasn't exactly prepared for the icy truth. I had to appreciate her honesty, though. Why sugar-coat death? It never goes down easy anyway.

Josh and I watched the hearse drive off up the street. I had my knapsack on and Josh carried Mom's box of things—we'd never even had a chance to unpack. It was dark outside, with a warm breeze. The world already felt different: foreign, strange. Shell-shocked, I took the first few steps in my new life without Mom. We walked to College Street, where Josh gave me a big hug and put me in a cab. I was confused. *Where should I go? Where's home?*

I decided to go back to the rental condo, the home Mom and I had created. Molly met me there, and I poured us some wine. Then I sat on the purple couch and wrote an email to Mom's friends, letting them know she'd died and to "save the date" for her After-Party.

Our amazing mom passed away peacefully this evening at Kensington Hospice. We were with her until her last breath, telling her how much we love her. We believe it was, as they say, a "good death."

I stepped into Mom's abandoned room. Her hospital bed was in the flat position, the mattress stripped bare, just as she'd left it that morning. I grabbed her vape and my newly inherited Mason jar of organic weed. Back in my room, I took a few pulls from the glass mouthpiece, hoping it would help me fall asleep. I was exhausted, shaky, in shock. I said goodnight to Molly, grateful she was by my side even if I felt a world away. It was all so surreal—I was lying in bed on a warm summer night and Mom was lying on a gurney in a freezer.

THE NEXT MORNING I woke up to my strange new world. Teddy, Josh, and I texted each other right away. It was obvious that none of us wanted to be alone. We didn't know what to do with ourselves, so we made plans to have brunch at Teddy's. Lox and bagels would provide the stability we needed.

Molly and I took the elevator down to the lobby. "How's your mom doing?" the concierge asked. I panicked. "She's . . . she's had better days," I replied. I wasn't ready to say the words. (And it *was* true.)

It was comforting to be with Teddy, Josh, Melissa, and the Mollys that morning. And in the evening Mom's friend Lola hosted dinner for us at her home, where everyone shared their fondest memories of Mom. ("Grandma changed my diaper!" Little Molly fondly recalled.) It never dawned on us to have a traditional shiva—even though I understood its value, it wasn't Mom's style.

The next day Molly and I went to book the venue for the After-Party and apply for a liquor licence. As long as I had things to do—arranging a weekend getaway to wine country for my one-year anniversary with Molly, organizing the closing of Mom's apartment, planning another hiking trip in Europe—I wouldn't fall apart.

The city seemed incredibly quiet, a post-apocalyptic ghost town. I knew this place. But it didn't feel like the place I knew. The colour had drained from the world. I felt so raw and exposed, as though I had no skin. I was surprised that strangers couldn't detect my grief. If I felt like this on the inside, how could people not see it on the outside?

I spent the next few days cleaning up the rental condo, putting everything back the way we'd found it, throwing out bouquets of dead flowers. The CCAC took back the hospital bed and medical equipment.

While clearing out Mom's room I spotted her little amber bottle of Michael's herbs in its suede pouch. Anger rose in my chest. I *hated* these herbs. And now I could exact my revenge. Five years of pent-up rage surged through me as I chucked the bottle into the garbage bag. Next I headed for the ampoules of Phoenix Tears in the fridge. I considered they could still be of use to some stoner, but they made me mad —I tossed them in the garbage bag, too.

Then I opened the cupboard doors above the kitchen counter. Suddenly, my rage dropped. There must've been about seventy bottles of vitamins and supplements in there. *This was a woman who really did want to live*, I thought. She wouldn't stop reaching for a cure, even if she was just grasping at straws. It was such a goddamn shame. My rage rose back up and, one by one, I whipped the bottles into the garbage bag.

"I'M GOING TO pick Mom up," Josh told me over the phone. It had been a few days since she'd died, and her cremated remains were now at the funeral home.

I'd been browsing online for cremation jewellery, a vial I could put a bit of Mom in and wear around my neck. Thinking I'd sport a Billy Bob–Angelina look for the After-Party, I'd ordered a simple, tasteful silver chamber on a chain.

When it arrived I went over to Josh's house to pinch some of Mom's ashes. Teddy, who happened to be visiting, looked uncomfortable when

Josh brought out the wooden box containing Mom and placed it on the living room coffee table for me.

"Can you take it into another room?" Teddy asked, shuddering.

I picked up the box and carried it away, along with a small jar, scissors, and a roll of duct tape. Little Molly looked up at me. "What you doing, Wachie?"

"I'm going to put a bit of Grandma in the jar so I can keep her at home with me," I replied. As I headed for the dining room, I could hear Josh behind me explaining: "Grandpa doesn't want to watch Rachie pour Grandma into the jar."

At the dining room table I opened the wooden box. Inside was a thick, clear plastic bag of ashes—probably a couple of litres worth. The bag was twisted tightly at the top and secured with a metal tie and ID tag. A black-and-white label read "Elaine Ruth Mitchell 61409." It was surreal to see Mom distilled into a bag of dust (never mind the disconcerting association of Jews, ashes, and assigned numbers). I made a small slit near the top and poured roughly half a cup of ashes into my glass jar.

It wasn't until later that day, when I was filling up my pendant at home, that I noticed something dark among the light grey powder and white bone fragments. I dug my fingers into the jar and fished around for it, like a kid digging for a toy at the bottom of a cereal box. Then I pulled out a smooth round granite stone, the same size and shape as a sweet tart. It looked like some sort of runestone inscribed with two identical stick figures, side by side, their hands up in the air.

What the actual fuck?

I'd never seen it before and was pretty sure it didn't belong to Mom. So I called the funeral home and explained my unusual situation. They were as dumbfounded as I was. They did admit that even though the chamber is cleaned between incinerations, it was conceivable that the stone had been lodged in the cremation furnace or processing machine prior to Mom going in, and that it came loose during her turn. But there was no way to know for sure. I tried to keep a sense of humour about it. After all, Mom probably would have found it funny.

FOR THE NEXT three weeks I put all my time and energy into planning the After-Party, coordinating the venue, the catering, the programming. Molly helped me create photo boards of Mom throughout the ages. I asked David to pick out the wine. The community centre felt more like a school gymnasium than a fancy hall, but that was Mom's style: she was all about the affordable small luxuries, not the showy stuff. We didn't need pomp and circumstance; we had tasty hors d'oeuvres and mini lemon tarts from Daniel et Daniel. At one point while we were setting up, Molly tried to put her arm around me. I shooed her off. I didn't want to be consoled. I had a show to put on. I was in producer mode—even if I was running on autopilot.

More than a hundred people showed up: friends, family, colleagues, former students, ex-boyfriends (I'm not sure who had more exes there, me or Mom). Michael and plant-spirit-medicine Monika showed up, too. I was on my best Buddhist behaviour, knowing it was what Mom would've wanted. I even shook Michael's hand. He looked nervous, as if he thought I might punch him, but I'd already thrown all my punches in my email. Aunt Barbara, whom I hadn't seen since Mom cut her off months earlier, appeared on edge. A friend from the women's writing group broke down when she saw Mom's Silver Fox jacket hung next to an enlarged photo of her mounted on an easel.

Standing onstage next to Josh, my co-emcee, I opened the ceremonies with my hand on my heart. "Mom is in here," I said to the crowd. I waited a beat before holding up the pendant dangling over my chest. "It's true! Her ashes are inside this necklace I got from EverlastingMemories.com."

As long as I was telling jokes—my defence mechanism of choice—there'd be no crying on the job.

There were songs and dances—both inspiring impromptu audience participation—and many, many speeches. Even the husband of the woman who did Mom's nails stood up and gave a speech. David said some nice words: "Elaine was a special woman. A force of nature. A woman who could, and did, magically create the person she wanted to be, in the world she wanted to inhabit. Elaine believed in the power of stories. Anecdotes trumped statistics for her, nearly every time." *Did they ever.*

Teddy stood up and gave an off-the-cuff speech about the evolution of their relationship, from their early infatuation to the unorthodox post-divorce close friendship they'd developed. "After sorting out some silliness, Elaine and I became friends. And although we dated others, there was some force between us that tied us together." He pointed to the audience. "Even while she was horsing around with some of the guys in this room, she was going to the movies with *me.*"

By the end of the speech he was visibly choked up. "I love her. I loved her," he corrected himself. "I don't think I'll ever meet anyone like Elaine."

Josh thanked me in front of everyone for taking such good care of Mom. I brought some levity with tales of our ayahuasca trip and my adventures in buying pot for Mom. "She always said, 'Well, you can put THAT in your act!' So, here I am, with an abundance of material, and . . . an act." I also read the eulogy I'd written for her before she died, managing to stay composed until the end, when I had to choke back tears. "Life will be less without you. But I'm going to be okay because of you." I couldn't break down.

Soon it was time for me to announce the evening's special guest. I'd edited together a short audio piece from the recordings I'd done with

Mom. "Elaine would be delighted to welcome you to her after-death party," we heard Mom say over the loud speaker.

"Everybody who's in this room has touched my life and meant something to me, so to all of you I say thank you for the pleasure, the good company . . ." She trailed off as Leonard Cohen's "Anthem" played underneath. She talked about her bench in the Cedarvale Ravine: "I thought everyone who cares about me can come and sit there and talk to me." The piece ended with her singing, "It's my party, and I'll die if I want to." Everyone laughed and cried all the way through the five-minute piece. You could feel the collective surge of love for her in the room.

For the final performance of the evening, Lola sat down at the piano and Josh took the microphone. Lyric sheets were passed out. Josh crooned the opening lines to Frank Sinatra's "My Way." Could there have been a more fitting theme song for Mom's life? Everyone sang along with smiles and teary eyes, a communal celebration of Mom's determination and defiance. I sang through gritted teeth. Why did she *always* have to do things Her Way? Let the record show, her decisions affected me. *I took the blows!*

At one point, Little Molly ran up to Molly and me. "Where's Grandma?" she asked. Molly and I looked at each other, our eyebrows turned up and lips turned down. How would we explain to a two-year-old that her grandma was dead? "There she is!" Little Molly announced excitedly, running toward the poster-board photo of Mom at the side of the stage—she'd been playing with it earlier and had misplaced it. Molly and I laughed with relief.

We invited guests to write in a memory book that I'd one day give to Little Molly, and to take home a photo of Mom from the display. And since Josh and I had inherited a few hundred copies of *Silver Fox* we had no idea what to do with, we gave them out as party favours. "Read at your own risk," I warned Mom's men in the audience.

At the end of the evening, just when the last of us were walking out to the front steps, a dazzling fireworks display began going off in the distance, as if on cue. We all stopped, tilted our heads back, and watched the colourful bursts of light explode in the night sky. I'd done everything I could to pull off a good party for Mom, and now the Universe appeared to be finishing the job. I finally surrendered my producer duties, and for a few minutes just enjoyed the show.

THE NEXT MORNING I got right back to work. The closing of the Hemingway was only ten days away, and so was my trip to Europe. There was still much to do.

I thought it would be nice to bring some of Mom's ashes with me on my trip. She loved hiking and mountains; I could spread a bit of her in the Alps. I stared at my little jar of ashes. Mom had told me I could talk to it if I wanted, but this wasn't my mom; this was a shitty consolation prize. I shook the jar around like a snow globe. *What the?* There was another identical mystery stone! And another!

Okay, that's too many flies in my soup! I drove right over to Josh's house and poured the entire bag of Mom's ashes, little by little, into an extra-large Tupperware container—picking out even more stones as I went. After sifting through its entire contents, my pile of prizes included two tooth caps, two small screws, and a tiny piece of metal from Mom's elbow surgery (reassuring me that these were indeed her ashes)—along with several more mysterious stones, some cracked in half. In total, there were twelve. It was a literal, if not true, baker's dozen.

I called the funeral home again. "Might someone have brought them in last minute to add to someone's coffin, and by mistake they were added to my mom's?" I asked.

"Not possible. No one would have had access—we make sure of

that. My wife put your mother in her casket then took her directly to the crematorium."

Later, he called me back. He said he'd talked to every person who'd had any contact, and no one had any idea what the stones were or where they came from. He added that Mom had been the only one cremated at the facility that day, with two people cremated the day before and one the day after. I joked about the possibility of him reaching out to those families, imagining what he might say: "We wanted to check in to see how you're doing. By the way, do you happen to be *missing anything?*"

There could be only two possible explanations: the stones were inside her when she died or someone at the crematorium tossed them in there. I felt certain it was the latter, but many of my friends believed it was the former. Everyone had a theory.

"Do you think she swallowed them?" was the most common question.

Mom wouldn't have swallowed rocks! She was afraid of pain. Even if she'd somehow believed they were magical healing stones, the prospect would have caused her way too much anxiety. Besides, I was aware of every belonging brought into the rental condo, not to mention everything she'd ingested in the last seven and a half weeks of her life.

My friends delicately pointed out that the stones were not unlike something she would've owned. True, she might have had some reiki healing crystals at some point, but I'd never seen these particular lucky charms. I'd also sent a photo of them to a few of Mom's "healers," including Monika, and none of them recognized the stones either.

Was Mom having the last laugh? Was she messing with my logical brain from beyond? Was she testing my faith in Newton? Had she manifested the stones via the quantum plane? ("It's all energy!" she'd say.) Did the symbol represent us, with our hands up in surrender? A truce? It was certainly tempting to read greater meaning into it all.

And I had to admit that there was something so *Elaine* about it. In the end, I suppose it's not about the truth; it's about what we think is possible. She was so persuasive that she could get you to consider any possibility—even that she was magical. My takeaway? There was nothing mundane about Mom. Even her ashes were extraordinary.

POST-MORTEM

21

THE HAPPY SIDE OF THE POOL

After the After-Party, I kept on going. I hosted an open house for Mom's friends at the Hemingway so that they could look through her remaining possessions and take whatever they wanted. A sort of going-out-of-business sale. Everything must go! I wanted her clothes, books, and art to go to those who loved her.

The day after the closing of Mom's apartment, Molly and I took off to hike the Tour du Mont Blanc. Over ten days we traversed roughly 170 kilometres—circling the highest mountain in the Alps and passing through parts of Switzerland, Italy, and France. I literally would not stop. (This time I wore boots with extra ankle support.)

I was happy on the trail, eating fondue and playing chess with new friends, but almost every night I had nightmares. In them, Mom was refusing treatment and I was freaking out, crying to Teddy over the phone, "Mom is killing herself!" I didn't need a dream dictionary to crack this code. I'd wake up exhausted and shaking, my chest pinned to my dorm-room bunk bed. I was still having the occasional Jian nightmare too, just to mix up the nighttime programming.

On our last day, I decided to spread Mom's ashes. "She took the easy way," I joked. Molly and I sat down on a rocky slope overlooking the Chamonix Valley, where I pulled the baggie from my backpack. Molly wanted to have some sort of ceremony, maybe say a few words. But I wasn't feeling it. I just emptied out the ashes into the wind and got up to go for lunch.

For the most part Molly and I had been getting along well, but I could sense her growing frustration. She wanted to connect more deeply with me, to cry together. I just wanted to relax and eat pasta with truffle sauce.

Before heading home, we spent a few days in rural Tuscany. I splurged and booked us a room at a boutique country inn, a centuries-old converted farmhouse that looked out over rolling green hills and the medieval towers of San Gimignano in the distance. Molly and I were in the swimming pool, an oasis of calm surrounded by olive trees, when she finally pulled the plug on my avoidance.

"Why aren't we talking about your mom?"

"I don't want to," I said. "I just want to be happy." I splashed around. It was a beautiful day, and truly, all I wanted to do was bask in the hot Tuscan sunshine.

Molly pouted. "Well, I'm sad!"

I was annoyed. I thought I should get to take the lead on grieving my own mother's death. I drew a line in the water between us. "This is the happy side of the pool," I said, pointing to my side. "If you want to come over here, you have to be happy."

BY THE TIME we returned from Europe I'd developed lockjaw from clenching my teeth at night. My jaw felt bruised; I could barely eat any solid food. I had to sleep with a mouth guard for my newly diagnosed TMJ.

Suddenly there was nothing for me to do. I finally stopped—and crashed. Hard.

I was in the shower when the snaps finally came off my inner compression sack and I broke down. That suffocating sadness came to the surface and I cried harder than I'd ever cried in my whole life. It was guttural and involuntary, and it hurt like hell. "WHAT DID YOU DO?" I cried, flooded with regret over how Mom had so royally fucked up. But more than anything, the thought that I'd never see her again was too much to bear.

At first I tried to pretend that Mom was just off on one of her silent retreats (and actually following the rules this time). But soon, when I wasn't wandering around in a fog, I was staying in bed for days at a time. It took all the energy I had to go outside, to even make a phone call.

Molly would visit me in the evenings, and we'd watch TV. I wasn't the best company. I mostly lived in my head, obsessively ruminating about everything that had happened, wondering how I was ever going to move forward.

To comfort myself I'd pick up takeout from Pusateri's (Mom's "home-cooking") and revisit my recordings of her. The sound of her voice soothed me, and her words started to take on new meaning. I now understood what she meant by "There's no time limits to grieving, or no way it goes." And I finally opened the lavender envelope she'd given me before she died. The note was short and her handwriting was messy—Mom had put off writing mine till near the very end.

Dear Rachel,

I have always loved and respected and admired you. But mostly just loved you. And you've been so easy to love.

I have been so blessed that you want to help me as much as I want to be helped—your competence, great love, and company have been seeing me through what could have been much harder.

My advice. Take advice. Then be yourself. Your extraordinary self.

Much love, e/mom

It was short and sweet, but it was all I needed to hear. For all my worrying about how I'd be able to survive without my biggest support, my adviser, my *person*, Mom was confident that I'd make it through if I just stayed true to myself.

IN SEPTEMBER, AS per Mom's advice, I started seeing a therapist. Pat was in her early fifties, a stylish lesbian with a short blond bob and a calm, confident presence. She had a dead mom, too. I liked her immediately. She was compassionate, but not too warm or bubbly, and she appreciated my dark humour. Her office was cozy, decorated with lots of plants and drawings of trees, lakes, bees, and whales. She had a few tasteful therapy posters (no "Hang in There!" kittens), including a print bearing the word "Repetition" over and over—an ode to Gertrude Stein.

During my first few visits I was disoriented and overwhelmed. *WTF just happened?* I was still doubting myself and trying to get a grip on reality. What was true? What had the doctors said? *Maybe I've got it wrong, maybe it's my fault, I should have done more.* People kept telling me there was nothing I could have done to change Mom's mind. I'd nod along, but secretly I still believed there was. I was experiencing, as they say, *complicated* grief.

"That's really tough what you went through," Pat said.

Was it? I wasn't sure. I knew it was shocking, and that I was deeply affected, but I wasn't able to open up to how damaging it had been for me. So when it came to talking about grief, and Mom, we never stayed on the topic long.

Instead, conflict with Molly became my distraction (er, focus)—it took up most of the space in our sessions. Molly and I weren't communicating well. She felt she didn't know what was going on in my head, and that I couldn't talk to her about my feelings.

But how could she possibly understand? As usual, I was shutting her out. It was easier for me to talk to friends or even strangers—other members of the Dead Parents Club— than it was to cry on her shoulder. We'd barely had a chance to build a foundation in the first place, and now it was slowly crumbling.

IN MID-OCTOBER, I had to go back to work. I took a low dose of SSRIs to help me get out of bed (how far I'd come since my teenage days of pharmaceutical abstinence). It was nice to see my friends at *q* again, and getting up every morning helped me cultivate a sense of normalcy. I was grateful to be working on the show with Shad as the host, but a part of me was still haunted by his predecessor.

The following June, almost a year after Mom died, Jian was scheduled to deliver a public apology to one of his complainants, a good friend of mine who used to work at Q. He'd been acquitted of all charges in his first trial involving three other women—a verdict that left many people profoundly angry with the flawed justice system and led to calls for sexual assault case reform. With mounting evidence, including an eyewitness account, it would prove harder for him to get out of this final count of sexual assault.

I rode up to the courthouse on my scooter at the precise moment his limo pulled up on the other side of the street. I glared into his tinted window and slowly shook my head, though I'll never know if he saw me. I sat in a pew while he read his apology, struck by the dullness with which he delivered his words. This was a guy who had lifted words off the page and made them sing, someone so skilled at inhabiting other voices. Now he was talking in a monotone, with hardly any affect—likely a protest on his part. His voice had been in my head for so many years, but I'd had no idea who he actually was.

In the fall of that year, I finally left *q* for good. It was time to move on.

Molly and I went on a hiking trip to Everest Base Camp, and the following January she left to help the refugees in Greece for a few months—a welcome reprieve from our increasingly tense relationship.

In the summer after she returned, we finally called it quits. I'd been dealing with my grief and depression for so long that I didn't have anything left for her. I couldn't absorb her grief over the sad state of the world, all her big feelings, and Molly was tired of being patient with me. Her anger and irritability had only expanded. She wanted me back—the playful, energetic, sturdy me she'd gotten to know in our first couple of months together. But I wasn't sure I'd ever be that "me" again.

22

NO STONE LEFT UNTURNED

I t had been two and a half years since Mom died, and almost as long since I'd been seeing Pat in therapy. Over that time we'd spoken of many things, usually whatever was coming up for me in the day to day. But through it all Pat would find ways to circle back to Mom, and as the months passed she was able to keep me on the subject for longer stretches, to question me further on how I was coping—or not—with her loss.

And so, eventually, I found myself ready to finally dig in to the question that still vexed me. I had my half-baked theory about the nose job, but I still didn't really have a deeper understanding of what had guided Mom's decisions. I'd continued to use my rational mind to figure out the irrational.

"Why did she do it?"

I was sitting on Pat's couch. "I don't understand," I kept saying, over and over.

Pat was concerned about colluding with the part of me that intellectualized everything—"You tend to think instead of feel," she'd pointed out on more than one occasion. But she knew that's how I processed, so she indulged me.

"I didn't know your mother, so I have to be careful," she made clear. "I'm talking about her through proxy—through you." She went on to explain how it's common for children of narcissistic parents to become self-reliant. They fear dependency because their emotional needs were never met. Their parents' needs were prioritized over their own.

This made sense to me. Mom had told me how her father hadn't acknowledged her feelings growing up, and how her mother called her a "cold potato" if she didn't attend to *her* needs.

In my search for answers, I finally read *Silver Fox* (making sure to skim over the part where she dresses up in a sexy maid outfit). In it, Mom described herself as "a psychological parent" to her "needy parents." *Huh.* She was affirming our theory in her own words. "Unremittingly sweet to the rest of the world, my mother used me as a repository for her unowned depression and anger," she wrote. "When I was a child I felt like an orphan, I thought I had to take care of myself."

Check.

Check.

Check.

It was safe to say that Pat and I were on to something.

For the next few months I saw her every week. With the benefit of time, and Pat's psychological insight, I could make sense of what had happened with greater perspective. I'd had no idea just how deep Mom's fear of dependency went—before the nose job, before the bad hospital experiences. Like all roads, it led back to her parents, particularly her mother. Mom experienced dependency as a horrible thing that brought only disappointment. She couldn't drop her defences for fear she'd be obliterated by her mother's overbearing needs. She learned to depend on herself—and to defend herself—at all costs.

I'd known that Mom felt she'd had to mother her own mother—it was why she'd been so adamant about never leaning on her children—but it dawned on me that she never actually leaned on *anyone*. I'd always thought she questioned authority simply because of the problems with, well, authority. But now I could also see that she needed to *be* the authority. She was comfortable only when she was being the leader, the teacher, the mentor, the advice giver. She didn't follow anyone (not even Thich Nhat Hanh).

Having been assigned the role of helper early on, Mom had learned to deny her feelings and cater to others. "I had decided at the age of five to be independent, charming, outgoing, and funny," she wrote. "I had decided never to cry." I was starting to see that she felt like she wasn't valued for being herself, but rather for how she could satisfy others' needs.

"To be vulnerable would be a crisis of self-worth," Pat commented. "There was no way she was going to let the doctors take control of her treatment."

I thought about how hard it was to maintain autonomy within the medical system. Surgery is one of the most powerless and vulnerable situations we can put ourselves in. We're forced to place absolute trust in the person at the other end of the scalpel.

"Perhaps to lose control would be to lose herself, to be subjected to things she didn't want. It was just too scary for her," Pat said.

Ding ding ding! Mom had worried that the doctors would "get" her and "keep doing things" to her. "They'll give me chemo when I don't want it," she'd said.

"What exactly was she so afraid of?" I asked.

Pat thought about it for a few seconds. "I think your mother was afraid of being devoured."

Devoured. I'd heard Mom use that word before. I flashed back to Mom reading me her play: "You want to devour me—just like my mother, just like my lovers, adore me and devour me." I hadn't understood what she'd meant at the time, but now it made more sense. Mom was afraid that she'd be subsumed by the medical system—just as she'd been subsumed by her mother. Mom had told me several times, "I don't want to fall into the clutches of the system."

"I never understood the extent to which Mom felt suffocated by her mother," I said.

"There was no way she was going back," Pat replied. "Even at the expense of her own life."

I came to understand that Mom was afraid of self-annihilation, of her autonomy being taken away. She'd been obsessed with self-preservation from a young age and was intent on creating a separate person from her mother. "Be True To Self," she'd underlined in her diary. Mom's whole life had been devoted to honouring, building up, and reclaiming her authentic self. After decades of working on personal growth, she'd finally come into her own as a confident, "ageless" woman. And then, suddenly, that self was being threatened.

"I know I'll get well as long as I don't abandon myself," she'd told me. At the time, I didn't get what she meant by that either. I hadn't understood what was at stake for her emotionally. I realized now that Mom hadn't chosen death over me—she *had* fought for herself. I think we just had different definitions of what that meant: I'd meant a fight for her physical self, whereas she was fixated on preserving her *sense of self*—the fully realized woman she'd worked so hard to become.

Reading *Silver Fox*, I got a fuller picture of who Mom was—notably, how difficult reciprocity was for her. For her, "we" was a trap. When it came to relationships, there wasn't much middle ground. Everything was extreme. She felt either free or trapped, independent or contained, in control or devoured. Yet despite this, Mom was always on a search for love: love that wouldn't devour her, love that made room for her needs, love that didn't take, take, take. "Perhaps love will trump my extreme need for freedom, my deep fear of being trapped," she'd mused in her book. As a wife, mother, girlfriend, friend, she was afraid of losing herself. "I'm scared to be diminished into a wife, scared to be loved for my use, not for me."

With Mom, it was always a Battle of Needs: hers versus others'. "For years, I put others' needs first. I didn't want anyone to be angry at me. I believed I had to see all the people in my life at regular intervals. I would put aside my writing schedule, or my wish for alone time." Mom was done with reducing herself in order to, as she put it, "fit into someone else's agenda."

Mom had clung to this story since she was a child, but the story never seemed to change, even when the conditions of her life did. "Your mom couldn't write her way past her core belief that there was no room for her needs—and that others' needs would engulf her," Pat said. "No matter how much she put herself first, the child in her could never be sated." Mom believed everyone was a threat. And the medical system was the biggest threat of all.

At my coming-out winter solstice party, Mom had chanted, "Freedom comes from not hanging on, you gotta let go, let go-oh-oh." But she struggled to follow her own mantra. "The choice to trust is like choosing to let go of a trapeze in order to grab the next rung," she wrote in her book; "you need to tolerate the uncomfortable gap."

"But there were times when she *did* jump," I said to Pat. "Mom did tolerate the uncomfortable gap when she travelled overseas in her twenties, when she left her marriage, when she took that job in Switzerland."

"But she only ever let go when it meant relying on *herself*," Pat noted. "She couldn't jump when it meant relying on others to catch her. She had no tolerance for the uncertainty of the situation—it caused her too much anxiety."

"Take the faraway parking spot she could control rather than a chance at the spot right in front!" I joked.

"Every time something that looked like a tiger came near her, she took off," Pat explained. When faced with the terror of cancer—the thought of her life being limited, of losing control—flight was a familiar defence mechanism. "If someone has a flight defence, you're going to see it recurring over time. It comes in early," Pat said. I thought back to how Mom was always trying to escape her mother's clutches. "I was a runaway before I was five," she wrote in *Silver Fox*. "In the late forties in Toronto, I followed the iceman and their horses, followed parades, chased a cute little white dog. When I got the tricycle I longed for, the one I slept with my arms around in my fourth year, I knew I could go farther. Wheels!"

There was also her intellectual flight—always in a book—and her imagination sprees as a child, disappearing into her rich fantasy world. Mom had a pattern of turning away from reality. Reading *Silver Fox*, it was all right there in front of me. At the top of page 25: "Always fearful of being trapped, I've looked for alternative worlds." *YEP.* As Mom got older, tricycle wheels turned into cars and planes, Buddhist retreats, Paris. And her fantasy life continued in her writing, her lucid dreaming, her visualizations. Even talking to her cancer cells.

When faced with the fear of cancer, she retreated into magical thinking—an old favourite. I think fantasy allowed Mom to control the unknowableness of cancer, to write the outcome. It was easier to create a narrative she could direct, even if it was just a fantasy. She chose to believe that the doctors were giving her minimal hope; it was a way to justify taking control. She convinced herself that she was the holder of the knowledge.

"She had an aggrandized belief in her own autonomy," Pat said. "The tragic irony is that autonomy is an illusion. We live in a web of relationships. No one gets by on their own."

After staring at the Magic Eye puzzle for so long, I could finally see the 3D image hidden within. It had been there the whole time. Now there was no unseeing it: Mom was a minefield of defence mechanisms and contradictions. She'd used the genuine benefits of natural medicine, legitimate critiques of conventional medicine, liberal feminism, and anti-authoritarianism as a screen so that no one would detect what was really going on. She was in camouflage, masquerading as her true self—her intellectual knowledge was a cover for her emotional avoidance.

Mom played a very clever shell game. She distorted reality and constantly confused the situation. She was able to get her audience to focus on one thing in order to distract their attention from another, successfully reframing their perception of the situation. (As any magician will tell you, misdirection is key.)

Mom had a way of turning everything on its head. I thought back to how she could even co-opt something as innocent as the Buddhist practice of "staying in the present" to justify her avoidance. (If she stayed in the literal present, she wouldn't have to look to the future and consider the deadly prognosis awaiting her.) Mom had an answer for everything. There was no way she could lose. I'm sure it wasn't conscious, but it was pretty freakin' genius.

"Why didn't I understand that back then?" I asked Pat, thinking about how I'd been constantly arguing with her, desperately trying to appeal to her with logic and facts.

"You didn't understand how much of a false self you were constantly in contact with," Pat said. "You were caught in a power struggle with her defences. You thought you were speaking to the mistress of the house when really you were talking to her armoured guard, who was doing a brilliant job of not allowing any new information past the gate."

"I guess I didn't understand how afraid she was."

"You didn't understand how much your mom was afraid of *being afraid*," Pat clarified. "She shut the door. Her story was locked tight. No one needs that much control unless what they're feeling would overwhelm them. Her system would not budge. Her control was absolute." Pat's gaze turned to the floor. "But not really . . . because she died."

A long pause followed.

"There was really nothing I could have done?" I asked.

"No," Pat replied, without hesitation. "You were outmanoeuvred."

I sat back. My shoulders lowered a centimetre. I finally got it.

Mom had been operating from an emotional place where reason was suspended in the face of fear. I had underestimated *her* truth, her emotional reality. My logical arguments were no match for her slippery sleight of hand. There was no way I could've won. Mom was a better illusionist than I was a chess player. Surrender came over me, and I tipped my king.

I LEFT PAT'S office that day feeling lighter than I had in a long time (maybe not since the opiates). For once I actually agreed with what everyone had been telling me. I could finally accept that Mom was the only one who could have saved herself.

And yet a part of me still didn't get it. Mom had been aware of her issues. She'd written about how "chronic worrying leads to unnecessary control" and how "the less free-floating anxiety we have, the less we try to impose control."

And so, at our next session, I put it to Pat: "Why couldn't she follow her own advice?"

"She had the intellectual knowledge, but healing oneself is an emotional accomplishment," Pat explained. "Was she really ever pulling up the memory and sitting with it? Did she feel it in her body? Did she ever process the emotion?"

I'd always thought the reason Mom bounced from one self-help fix to another was that she was curious, always seeking, always discerning. But now I could see how jumping from one remedy to the next was also a distraction from feeling her fears. Mom went for breadth, not depth. She pursued one shiny crystal after another, never sticking with anything long enough for doubt to arise.

With cancer, Mom looked for a quick fix. A shortcut through the acute discomfort of fear. "You can't process your emotional life without being uncomfortable," Pat pointed out. "You need to be able to tolerate pain."

But Mom didn't like to do anything too uncomfortable. She didn't really ever follow strict alternative protocols. She didn't like to be cold. She didn't even like to sit cross-legged while meditating. "Sounds like sitting with herself was going to be difficult," Pat said.

THERE WERE A lot of lessons here for me, too. "To do emotional work is to surrender," Pat told me. To surrender to the fact that I couldn't have controlled the situation. To surrender to my own childhood feelings—or the fact that I even had any.

Mom believed that by loving me less intensely and less intrusively she was breaking a pattern of what she called "overinvolved mothers and their weakened children." There are ways in which her laissez-faire mothering style had served me well in life. She'd helped me become strong, confident, independent. Yet in overcompensating for her mother's neediness, Mom reproduced some of the same consequences. The pendulum swung too far. It was awesome getting to eat all the ice cream I could stomach and not having anyone tell me what to do, but it was also lonely at times. Mom taught me to have a self, but she also taught me to be self-reliant—too self-reliant. Like her, I'd learned to be wary of dependence. I dismissed my emotions. (I, too, had decided never to cry.) Like Teddy, I processed everything through logic.

"You lived in a household where feelings were intellectualized rather than felt," Pat said. I imagined that if we had a family boat, its name would be *Avoidance*.

"It's ironic that your mom wanted to see you as a separate person—because she actually gave you what *her* inner child needed, not what you needed," Pat noted. "You needed her to be more involved when you were young."

I realized that when I was a kid there'd been an unspoken deal: Mom didn't have expectations of me, and I shouldn't have expectations of her. She needed a lot of alone time, and in turn she never made me feel guilty for doing my own thing. We all acted like islands. But we weren't.

Beyond our shared interest in art galleries and raw French cheese, I never understood just how similar Mom and I were. We were both fiercely independent. We both wrote our own life scripts. We were both storytellers. Not to mention that we both minimized our pain and had difficulty depending on others. And like Mom, I was capable of my own denial. What stories did I tell myself to cover the pain? (Pat didn't think my childhood anecdotes were all that funny.)

For most of my life I'd been unable to see Mom as anything other than an amazing mother. I needed that story. *Her* story. To admit otherwise would have been to admit the sadness that came along with the part of her, albeit small, that hadn't always met my needs. Sitting in Pat's office and revisiting these stories and memories forced me to sit with my emotions—for more than a complete sentence, if not a whole book. I had to open up to my anger, my confusion, and my own guilt. I had to go to much more uncomfortable places than I'd ever expected and experience deeply uncomfortable emotions. Coming to understand Mom's issues meant I had to look at my own. *Not so fun.*

"We often pick partners who embody our disowned self or unlived life," Pat remarked during one of our sessions, steering the conversation back to me. There was no mystery with Molly. She would mirror my pain and multiply it by a hundred. Molly had embodied my unfelt emotions, so I'd held her at bay. All those times when I'd *literally* told her not to react, or to just be happy, I'd been terrified of my own feelings. Molly wanted me to cry with her. She wanted to be my person, to support me, but she didn't know how. And, well, I never really gave her a chance.

"I THINK YOUR mother had a form of *psychic* cancer," Pat hypothesized one day. "The defences that were supposed to protect her turned against her and kept her from getting the help she needed." The same was true for me. My defences—logical thinking, self-reliance, emotional avoidance—failed me too. They kept me safe, but they stopped me from growing.

"Am I slow? I asked Pat. "How did I not get all this before?"

"In the past four months you've advanced at lightning speed," Pat replied, smiling. "It's as if you've made fifteen years of progress overnight."

I laughed. "That's what they say about ayahuasca!"

Maybe Josh was right after all about Mom having always been this way. Not just in the sense that she was alternative, but in her extreme need for autonomy and her propensity for magical thinking. It took extreme stakes to reveal how extreme her need for control was.

Josh had his own defences, just as I did. He was aware that Mom had threatened to cut me off, so in turn he accommodated her. Once I realized this, I could fully make peace with him. We began spending more time together, talking on the phone more often, channelling Mom to give each other life advice. He started joining me for lobster at Wah Sing. We even went on a couple of trips together, including a hike up Crane Mountain in the Adirondacks, where Mom and I had gone when I was thirteen.

In the spring of 2018, almost three years after she died, we went on a weekend trip to Zion National Park, in Utah. At the airport in Toronto, waiting in line to check our hiking poles, I told Josh some of the things I'd been working out in therapy. "I never realized just how much Mom flew into fantasy," I said.

Josh erupted with laughter. "Fantasy is where Mom lived! It was her *default position*. Once in a while she flew into reality!"

I'M OFTEN AT a loss when people ask me how my mom died. Although the quick answer is "cancer," it doesn't exactly feel accurate. After a quick intake of breath and a tightening in my chest, I usually add, "It's complicated."

There was the cancerous polyp. There was the nose job, which Pat agreed was pivotal. ("It was the moment the medical system became devalued. When it got lumped in with her parents. The emotions she felt toward her mother and father—feeling devoured, betrayed, the lack of trust, their not looking after her best interests—that all got transferred onto the doctors.") Then there was, as Pat would put it, Mom's "overactive defence system that operated way past its best-before date," along with the other factors that supported her defences: the lack of a straightforward diagnosis in the beginning and the second-wave feminism that supported her self-reliance.

Mom was aware how lucky she was to have been born in her time and place. A white, middle-class, heterosexual woman in North America. She and her friends were part of a generation of women who

straddled the feminist movement of the 1970s and 80s. What independence they achieved in their lives wasn't taken for granted. Mom
saw how her mother had to ask her father for money. That was never
going to be her. Mom had to fight to become a liberated woman, not
only from her overbearing mother, but from a sexist society. She was
intent on being the protagonist of her own life—a fully autonomous
person in the world. It made sense that, when faced with a threat to her
liberty, it would be that much harder for her to relinquish any agency,
and that her feminist friends wouldn't dare challenge her right to make
her own decisions.

If I had to distill what killed Mom (using my new therapy lingo), it
was her fear of dependency and an inability to tolerate her fear in order
to face reality. I think the tragic, simple truth is this: she killed herself.
(Not intentionally, but still . . .)

And yet, despite all my theories, the question is ultimately unan-
swerable. Like the mystery stones, Mom's psyche would be a riddle for
the ages. I'll never know for sure what led her to make the choices she
did. What I do know is that the doctors gave her hope, and she chose
to turn away. Something was so threatening that she needed to believe
something else. Pat explained the paradox of trauma: "In order to heal,
you need to remember. But in order to survive, you need to forget."
I saw this tension play out in Mom—the way she vacillated between
facing reality and denying it.

I WANTED TO share my new revelations with Mom's friends. I was
still in touch with a couple of the women in her writing group, who
were very surprised to hear my version of the story. They hadn't had
all the information. And even if they had, they didn't know what they
could've done. As Lola confirmed to me, "I knew I couldn't challenge
her and keep our friendship."

Nearly three years after Mom died, my aunt Barbara was back in town. We'd seen each other a few times since, but we hadn't really talked about what had happened at the end. I'd sensed her distress when Mom cut her off, and I hadn't wanted to get drawn into their dynamic. For a long time, I'd remained Team Mom all the way.

But when Barbara and I met for lunch, I decided to bring up my theories. She nodded along fervently.

"It was *so crazy* what she did," Barbara blurted out.

"Yes, it was!" Her declaration was validating, but I was confused. I took a deep breath. "Then why, when I called you back then, did you tell me that 'belief is the most important thing'?"

"I could only see things through her eyes," Barbara confessed. "I couldn't question her. I knew she would cut me off. And she *did*!" She shared with me how hurt she'd been and how she'd been working on forgiveness. She told me how she'd even sought out a friendship with Kim Phúc (a.k.a. "the Napalm Girl"). "I thought she could teach me how to forgive," she said.

After Barbara, I met with David at a barbecue joint. I smiled at the sight of him entering the restaurant in a T-shirt that read LIFE'S TOO SHORT TO DRINK BAD WINE. As soon as we sat down with our trays bearing ribs and smoked chicken, he got out a familiar-looking amber glass bottle. *Michael's herbs!* It was like the Twilight Zone. I watched him put the dropper to his mouth, just as Mom used to do. *Those fucking herbs.*

Once we'd caught up a bit, I finally asked about his perspective on what had happened. David insisted that he never actually believed Mom's herbs would cure her, but he also didn't think it was his place to tell her what to do.

"I felt it was my job to support her," he said.

But, he admitted, in the end it was too much. "I couldn't keep doing mental gymnastics to keep up with her. I felt like I was losing myself."

I was taken aback. Mom had complained of the same thing. I'm sure she'd had legitimate issues with David, but it was ironic how, in her steadfast need not to lose herself, she'd forced others to compromise their own selves.

"Your mother was a force of will," David declared, still in awe of her. "She willed reality to conform to her narrative." Then he added, "I still wonder what I could've done to make our relationship work."

I understood his pain. Until recently, I'd suffered a similar plague. I tried to tell him that there was nothing he could have done; Mom was never going to release her grip and surrender. David seemed lost in thought, a distant look in his eyes. "She was a woman like no other," he said. A smile spread across his face. "She sparkled."

I LET GO of being upset with everyone for not having done more. They'd had their reasons. No one could have changed Mom's mind anyway.

In her book, I was surprised to find, of all things, a eulogy Mom had written for herself back in February 1992. The goal of the writing exercise was to "praise yourself for the life you're living, the life you intend to live."

Elaine was so extraordinarily filled with life that it's hard to believe she's dead. She always had an idea on the go, laughed a lot, loved to be with people, do things, go places, and share what she had with her friends and family. She was fun and generous and caring. She was a good mother who was able to break some of the patterns from her own childhood to really come through for her children.

Elaine was very brave and dared to do what she needed to do in spite of her many fears. She became a role model for her bravery, her sharing, her insistence on a fair life for herself and others, and her vitality. She was creative and enriched others' lives with her creativity.

She will be missed. Often someone will think, "If only I could talk to Elaine."

I had to admit, it was pretty bang on. Mom had eulogized her ideal self—the person she wanted to be—into being. She'd pulled it off. She *was* a force of will. I think that's partly why she was so surprised when the cancer got her in the end: it might've been the only time she failed to make reality comply with her story. But it's also why so many people went along with her. She was magical. Persuasive. *She sparkled.* And just as Mom had self-eulogized, she was brave—yet there were significant fears she didn't face. Her idea of bravery was more of the conquering kind, not the vulnerable kind. In order to protect myself, I too had a romanticized view of who she was. I was naive; I took Mom at face value. But she was indeed human—wonderful, but with her own shit.

Perhaps, like Mom and her mother, our relationship has gotten better since her death. In shedding my idealism about her, I've been able to get to know her as she really was, imperfections included. I'm able to appreciate the truly amazing person she was and have compassion for the early suffering she experienced, and at the same time to hold space for my anger and disappointment. "Our love deepens when we face the truth about a person and still stay connected to them," Pat told me. I think I'm learning to love my mother *better*.

I have no doubt that I loved her and that she loved me. The last five years with her were difficult, but we had a whole lifetime of great memories, including at the end. We laughed. We were connected. Our bond will never be broken. I'm not motherless; I have a dead mom. There's a difference.

It's true what she said: I have everything she gave me (including the stuff I talk to my shrink about). The love and support, the time and attention, the lessons in joie de vivre, the way her eyes lit up every time she saw me—it's all a part of me.

Let the record show: Mom did not bake muffins like some sort of June Cleaver. But she gave me so much more than muffins. And whatever her flaws, she gave me so much more than her own mother had given her. "Who you are is not okay" was the message she'd received. But the message she always gave me was that I was *more* than okay. I felt immensely loved and *liked* by her.

"There was this incredible closeness between you. She couldn't be with her mother when she was dying. But you *wanted* to be with your mom," Pat noted. "*She* accomplished that." It was true. As I've mentioned, Mom could drive me nuts, but there was pretty much no one in my life I'd rather spend time with.

"And in the end," Pat continued, "she did the thing that was most difficult for her. She put herself in your hands." I thought about that. Perhaps it was only in dying that Mom learned to be truly vulnerable. (She really didn't have a choice.) In facing her demise, she was forced to be brave—*internally*. I thought back to her Ram Dass book, when she was reading about learning to accept dependence. Mom never fully let go—maybe only truly in her last breath—but she did allow herself to lean on me. And I allowed myself to be more vulnerable with her.

Pat smiled with glistening eyes. "It's a love story."

OUR FAMILY STILL gets together regularly—Teddy and his partner Barbara, Josh, Melissa, Little Molly, and me. Our gatherings are admittedly quieter and far less amusing without Mom, but we're carrying on. Little Molly and I call each other "Monkey," and she thinks it's cool that I'm "half boy, half girl." At age five, Molly reminds me a lot of Mom: smart, funny, feisty. She's even taken over as the family bandleader. And whenever she sees a Monarch butterfly, she calls out, "Grandma Elaine!"

I'm walking through the world with more ease. I like to think I'm on my way to creating the "good life" Mom envisioned for me. The grief has faded, but sometimes it still really hurts. I'm learning to live with the shrapnel. One of Mom's Missoni outfits hangs in my closet like a colourful shroud. I still have her number in my phone. I wish I could talk to her about all this. But mostly I just wish we could sit in the sunroom with a glass of wine and chat about nothing in particular.

EPILOGUE

It's been exactly three years since Mom died. I'm at her memorial bench in the Cedarvale Ravine. It's a sunny day with a few passing clouds; birds are chirping, joggers are running by, people are walking their dogs. The bench is beside a gravel path, a couple of stone throws from the Hemingway up at the top of the hill. Mom and I used to take a shortcut down to the ravine from the back of her building; we'd surface onto the path right here. It's where we spread the majority of her ashes.

A small silver plaque on the bench reads, "In memory of the vivacious Elaine Ruth Mitchell (1943–2015). She lived life to the fullest and touched many lives." The plate has her picture on it, just like she wanted.

If I'm being honest, I wish this monument brought me more comfort. But, like my jar of ashes, it's mostly a sad reminder of all that's not here. I'm heartbroken. I'm pissed off. I want my mom, not a dumb bench. I take a deep breath (I'm trying not to be so phobic of my emotions). It's what Mom told me to do, even if she didn't always do it herself: "Just sit with it. You just feel the loss and the pain, and it will move. It will move a lot faster than if you try to suppress it or push it away."

I'll never be okay with her decision not to get surgery. I still hold her accountable for not holding her fear long enough to do what was best for her, for me, for us. But if I turn down the volume in my head for a damn minute, and just sit with how I feel . . . *I'm missing my mother right now.*

ACKNOWLEDGMENTS

Writing this book was *way* harder than I ever imagined. There's no way I could've done it without a lot of help from a lot of wonderful people.

I'd like to thank my magnificent editor, David Ross, for seeing the potential, for not running away at the sight of my "vomit draft," and for tirelessly polishing my words until they sparkled. Thanks as well to my eagle-eyed copy editor, Karen Alliston, and to the rest of the team at Penguin Canada: Nicole Winstanley, Beth Cockeram, Claire Pokorchak, and Ann Jansen.

Thanks to my literary agent, Samantha Haywood at Transatlantic Agency, for your terrific guidance and boundless positivity.

I'm especially grateful to my friend Nicola Spunt for encouraging me to write this book in the first place. Your emotional support and genius editing were invaluable.

Special thanks to my fairy god-sister, Kathryn Borel, for helping me make this project a reality, contributing astute notes, and always having my back.

Many thanks to my brilliant bibliophile friends for taking the time to read an earlier draft of the manuscript and offer their excellent editorial suggestions: Rachel Giese, Julia Gruson-Wood, and Karen Levine.

This book couldn't have happened without the help of my therapist, Pat Durish. Your support and insight were instrumental in helping me figure this shit out. Thank you for shining the light.

I'm grateful to the many people who provided me with support and encouragement along the way: Lola Rasminsky, Arei Bierstock, Barbara Mitchell-Pollock, Linor David, Molly Kraft, David Oved, Irene Grainger, Syd Grainger, Lyndsay Moffat, Elizabeth Lancaster, Joel Graham, Josh Knelman and The Banff Centre, Becky Vogan, Amy Macfarlane, Jane Rabinowicz, Zoe Tennant, Stephanie Markowitz, Talia Schlanger, Zoe Whittall, Thea Lim, Gill Deacon, Sophie Kohn, Samra Habib, Lisa Godfrey, Peter Mitton, Brian Coulton, Sean Foley, and all my friends from *Q*.

Thanks to my family, Teddy Matlow and Barbara McKay Ward, and Josh, Melissa, and Molly Matlow for your love and support and continued laughter.

Not too long before my mom died, she handed me a little ceramic statuette of a rabbit scribe, a favourite talisman of hers. "Here, this is for you," she said. "You're going to write a book one day."

Last but never least, thank you, Mom—for the material, and for always being my champion in life. *You really were amazing.*

© Tanja Tiziana

RACHEL MATLOW (they/them) was a long-time producer on the arts and culture program *Q* on CBC Radio, where they also worked on *Spark* and *The Sunday Edition*. Their audio documentary "Dead Mom Talking" won a 2016 Third Coast Award and a 2017 Gabriel Award. They have written for *The Globe and Mail*, *National Post*, and *The Believer*. They play chess every weekend and are forever planning their next long-distance hike.